Village India

Comparative Studies of Cultures and Civilizations

Editors

ROBERT REDFIELD *and* MILTON SINGER

Studies in Chinese Thought
Edited by ARTHUR F. WRIGHT

Language in Culture
Edited by HARRY HOIJER

The Little Community
ROBERT REDFIELD

Unity and Variety in Muslim Civilization
Edited by GUSTAVE E. VON GRUNEBAUM

Village India
Edited by MCKIM MARRIOTT

Chinese Thought and Institutions
Edited by JOHN K. FAIRBANK

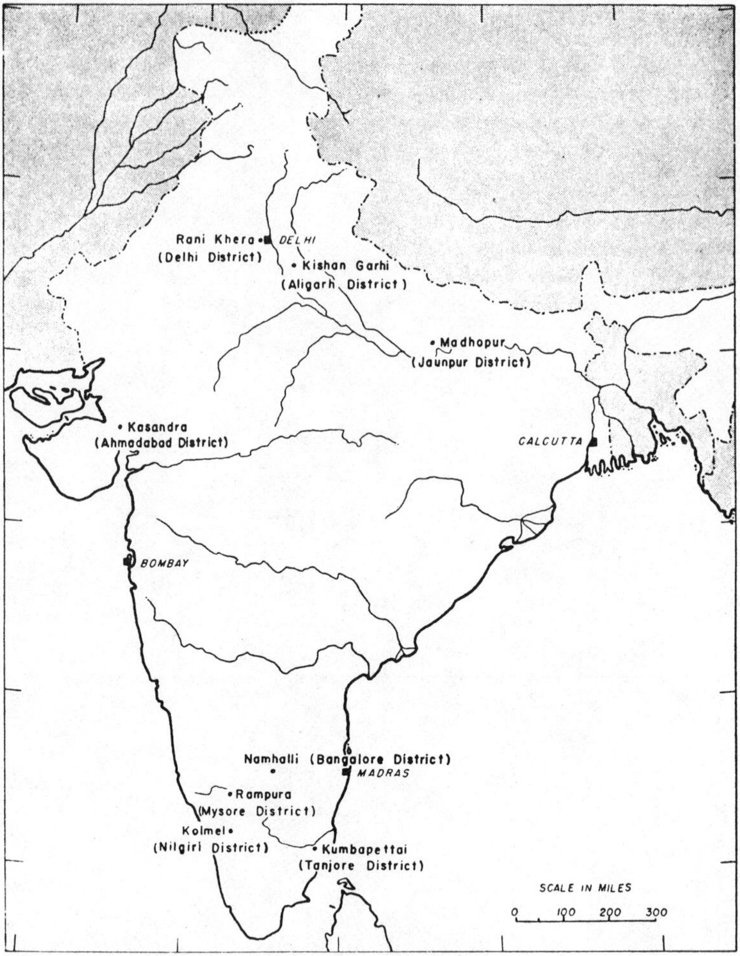

Map of India Showing Locations of Villages Described

VILLAGE INDIA

Studies in the Little Community

By

ALAN R. BEALS

BERNARD S. COHN

E. KATHLEEN GOUGH

OSCAR LEWIS

DAVID G. MANDELBAUM

McKIM MARRIOTT

M. N. SRINIVAS

GITEL P. STEED

Edited by

McKIM MARRIOTT

THE UNIVERSITY OF CHICAGO PRESS

CHICAGO AND LONDON

THE UNIVERSITY OF CHICAGO PRESS, CHICAGO 60637
THE UNIVERSITY OF CHICAGO PRESS, LTD., LONDON

Midway Reprint edition 1986
Printed in the United States of America

International Standard Book Number 0-226-50645-2
Library of Congress Catalog Card Number 55-9326

TABLE OF CONTENTS

FOREWORD

THIS volume is one of a series which explores various ways to the scientific and scholarly understanding of civilizations. The first of the series, *Studies in Chinese Thought*, represents an effort to understand a civilization primarily through its expressions in articulate cultural products—art, literature, philosophy, language. *Studies in Islamic Cultural History* concentrates on the social and cultural processes incident to the development and transformation of a civilization. In *Islam: Essays in the Nature and Growth of a Cultural Tradition* these two emphases are combined: the shapes of a distinctive Islamic pattern are traced in Muslim literature, science, urban structure; and the processes of interaction of Islam with other civilizations. In *Language in Culture* a very special possibility for the understanding of civilizations and primitive cultures alike is examined: the question whether the forms of a language affect the thought and so the culture of those who speak it.

In none of these books does one see a civilization *in vivo*—within the contexts of family, neighbors, work, ceremonies, and other circumstances that make up the round of life of a people. It is this close view of a civilization that is provided by the anthropological study of small communities. This is the view of Indian civilization that is taken in the present volume.

Eight villages are described in the following pages. There are about a half a million villages in India. It would be foolish to claim that what we have here is a representative sample. We have accounts of eight small communities that resemble and differ from one another in ways that cannot now be systematically ordered. Just what about each village is peculiar to it or characteristic of that region or generally true of India remains to be determined. As anthropologists continue to make Indian community studies, they will be more and more required to exercise their scientific strategy in justifying the choices they make of the few villages, out of the many, that it will be possible to report at all fully.

Nevertheless, these eight accounts do communicate to the reader a grass-roots view that is more nearly representative of India today than any single account would be. The book conveys a general impression of great variety within prevailing similarity. To guide him who reads the book for what it has to say about India as a whole,

Professor Mandelbaum has fortunately provided a comparison of the eight villages in the second part of his paper (pp. 239–53). It is proper, in a book by anthropologists, that Mandelbaum's village should be the point of departure for the comparisons he offers. For his small community, of all here represented, comes nearest to realizing the self-contained isolate which has been commonly studied in anthropology. Not long ago these *Kota* were a tribe, notably apart from the main streams of Indian life, and the four kinds of peoples of the Nilgiri Plateau constituted a little separate world of tribal peoples. Now the *Kota* have experienced the double movement that is mentioned again and again in other papers of this volume: Sanskritization, the extension of native Indian civilization to depressed or isolated peoples; and Western-urban influences.

The reader will first find in Mandelbaum's paper an account of some aspects of the way *Kota* look upon things, and especially of the importance that every male *Kota* attaches to the struggle to defend his status, his social self, against the threats of others to exclude or reduce him. A single ritual, the bowing to the relic of the corpse at a funeral as a gesture of respect and alliance to the deceased, is chosen as the element of custom through which we are led to understand this struggle.

Beginning with the third section of the paper, Mandelbaum comments on certain differences and resemblances between *Kota* life and the modes of life reported for the other seven communities. The reader is introduced to village India from one of its least typical corners. Yet the comparisons begin to show some of the things that are widespread: the balance of caste separation and intercaste dependence; the relations of land tenure to social structure; the importance of maintaining status relationships as between castes and as between individuals, and the possibilities of change in status of groups or individuals; the anxieties and quarrels that have to do with status; the influence of ancient codes or ideals—aggressive protection of honor for "warriors," ascetic withdrawal for others. Widespread also are general processes of change: the disintegration of social systems based on group or corporate relations of status; the decline of occupational specialties; increasing use of money; growth of factionalism; changes in the interdependence of castes and a tendency for the depressed to find common cause in economic or political interests; the double process of Sanskritization and Westernization. And Mandelbaum equally calls attention to many differences as between communities reported.

Thinking of India, one is most strongly impressed in reading these papers by the fact of change. In village India the traditional landmarks lose their outlines—caste, joint family, festivals and religious beliefs. The school, the political party, the movie, the community plan, begin to reach even remote villages. The changes, we are here helped to see, are in important degree but not entirely to be explained as a result of Western influence. We need also to consider the ancient culture of India and the processes of maintenance and transformation of culture that went on before Western influence began. It takes more than differences in Western influence to explain why Miss Gough's Tanjore village is so much less "progressive" and "democratic" than the Mysore village Mr. Beals describes, or why the depressed *Camārs* in Madhopur, described by Mr. Cohn, seek to raise their status by adopting some of the practices of orthodox Brahmans. The changes that are taking place in villages may transform India into a "modern" Western-like nation, or may not, but the changes will not be understood without reference to the traditional civilization that is being transformed.

Indeed, the primary interest that brought about this volume is not the effort to understand India and her changes. It is the effort to understand how to seek understanding of any great civilization and its enormously complex changes through anthropological studies of villages. The questions asked in the seminar that gave rise to this book were questions of "method": What forms of thought for understanding a small community are relevant when the community is an Indian village? What changes in ways to which anthropologists are accustomed when they work in isolated tribal communities are demanded when they work in a village that is part of a large society, when they study a local culture that is part and cause and product of an ancient civilization? In the fifth volume of this series, *The Little Community*, a review was offered of some forms of thought for conceiving and communicating a small community more or less as a whole under the assumption that it may be considered as an observational isolate—as a thing, a system, to be analyzed in terms only of what is right there within that village. A band or village of isolated tribal peoples almost justifies that assumption. A village within a civilization, a village of peasants or of rural participants in a national life, of course does not. What then are anthropologists now to consider, to learn to study, to include in their widening responsibilities, when they study a village as it relates to state and to civilization?

These papers may also be read as various attempts to answer these questions. In one way or another they show developments of anthropological interest and procedure as awareness grows of the great society and the great tradition within which the Indian village lies. The following review of the first six papers is guided by this concern with developing viewpoint and procedure. In the following pages it is not asked, "What does this say about India?" but rather, "What does this say about the interests and way of work of the anthropologist who wrote this paper: what did he try to find out and how did he go about it?"

In Professor Srinivas' paper we see a Mysore village almost as if it were an isolate. It is described as a structure of relationships of role and status. Presented first are the relationships of caste to caste. As a ranked order of castes the system is complex and contains ambiguities: no single vertical series can express it; some groups (e.g., the Smiths) are not defined by others as they define themselves; to the core of castes that form the village society other groups—Muslims and itinerant specialists—are plainly peripheral; migratory castes contribute only occasionally to the structure; and alternative canons of status put a man high on one basis and low on another.

The castes, kept apart by endogamy and the rules of commensality, are brought together by institutions and sentiments that unite the whole village: the ceremonies, the village political organization and the court of justice; the common dependence on the dominant peasant caste. Individuals and families of one caste are brought together with those of other castes through a variety of relationships of patron and client, friendships, or party politics. This village is no simple layered structure of functions and statuses. It is rather an intricately woven network of relationships between this man and that, this family and that. The hereditary factors only limit and only partly predetermine who is to be related to whom and how.

Professor Srinivas shows us the workings of competition and personal choice within the structure. People decide to do something they did not do before, or strive to establish a new relationship with somebody. In the course of a dispute a traditional relationship may be broken off. There is struggle for position. One Smith is the rival of his fellow-Smiths and competes with him for customers. The establishment of relationships of master and servant, landowner and tenant, creditor and debtor—all of which may cut across the barriers of caste—bring about changes in the social system as that system appears to the individuals and families affected. "Obligation" is everywhere, but not all obligations are hereditary, and we learn that these villagers regard obligation and claim as something to be managed and improved upon. The social system as it appears in Rampura is a matter of pushing, trying, perpetually rearranging.

The system we are shown persists by the inherited monopoly of useful function, by traditional status and obligation, and by the availability of agriculture to draw off specialists who are supernumerary in the village. It changes, too, relatively rapidly for that man who finds a new patron, more slowly for the caste, and so eventually for the village seen as a body of interrelated corporate groups.

As a persisting social system, the village described by Kathleen Gough used to correspond, very generally, with the village which Srinivas describes as still so persisting. There was, before recent changes, a similar village solidarity, a similar close interdependence of status and useful function, a similar dependence of the lower castes on the economic power and rule of a dominant caste, a counterbalance of village unity and caste unity.

But where Srinivas shows us the internal changes which made it possible for Rampura to persist as a social system and an isolable unit of study, Miss Gough shows us how the social system of Kumbapettai is undergoing radical change and how, in its declining integration and growing dependence on urban or national institutions and a wider economy, this village ceases to be a significant unit of investigation. It is change in the sense of transformation that Miss Gough reports. In one paragraph Professor Srinivas only mentions some of the kinds of events that do effect changes in Rampura; for Miss Gough it is just these events that in Kumbapettai break up the traditional local social structure: the loss of land by Brahmans; independence from the Brahman achieved by lower castes through acquisition of land or by entering business; political organization and agitation. These events lead to breakdown of some of the taboos that keep the castes apart and in hierarchical order. Also they lead to a union of people from different castes in what we recognize as classes —people conscious of common cause in the struggle to improve life chances.

Dr. Cohn's paper also describes transformations in the social structure of a village. In this case the changes are presented in large part from the viewpoint of a depressed caste group (*Camārs*) in their struggles with the upper and landowning caste (*Ṭhākurs*). Again one understands that formerly the relations of economic dependence and those of status between the caste groups made the old-time village a well-integrated local structure. Then the *Ṭhākurs* entered urban employment; both upper- and lower-caste groups came to use British courts; the local and regional political organization lost its effectiveness; as population increased, *Camārs* left the land and found work outside the village. These and other events brought it about that the *Camārs* came into open conflict with the landowning upper-caste group. We see the development of aspiration and the formation of policy in the depressed caste: the *Camārs* organize to achieve new power and status. In their struggle to free themselves from the *Ṭhākurs*' power they fail for the present, but one feels that they will try again.

Along with this struggle for power there comes about a curious change in the customs and religion of the two caste groups. The *Ṭhākurs*, affected by Western models of conduct, become more individuated and secular; they relax traditional caste rules. At the same time the *Camārs* seek to improve their status by tightening the traditional rules of commensality, by giving up despised occupations, and by adopting Sanskritic elements of custom. One might say that the *Camārs* strive to move into a culture and its associated status which the *Ṭhākurs* have vacated. Social change in India is both a movement toward an urban and cosmopolitan mode of life and also a revival and penetration downward of ancient Hindu elements of culture and religion.

By the time we reach Alan Beals's paper the interest has quite shifted from an analysis of the maintaining interactions within the social structure of the village to an analysis of the factors external to the village which account for the transformations that have taken place in it. For Namhalli, a relatively recent settlement, is so near a great city that its history has been in large part determined by events in the economic and political life of the city and state. We barely see the traditional social structure. In this case the multicaste village was organized in economic dependence on a single man, the founder and headman, and decisions on behalf of all were made by a small panchayat. But since 1876 this village "has become more and more an aggregation of small and comparatively noninterdependent families." What interests Beals is to discover the way in which, at succeeding periods, a limited number of factors (six) arising from outside the village interacted in different ways to bring about this great change in the character of this village. Some of these factors flowed from the mere growth of trade, transportation, manufacture, and state-wide government. Others are the growth (and occasional decline) of population and the increasing emphasis on a cash economy. This is a study of urbanization as it appears in a village, not a study of the social structure of a village as an isolate.

Mrs. Steed's paper is concerned with the formation of personality within a social structure, but it is not the typical or modal personality that is accounted for but rather the personality of one particular individual. We are asked to examine biographic and other information about one certain *Rajpūt* as these data help us to understand two things: how this man made adjustments to the expectations arising from the structure of his society while at the same time preserving and developing a private life inconsistent with those expectations; and how it came about, by what accidents of circumstance peculiar to his history, that he developed a personality that deviated from the ideal norm. Once more we see a social structure in which caste unity counterbalances a village unity of interdependent castes. Once more we see a traditional society dominated by a landlord caste of high status. But now it is not only the social structure that is made explicit: we are shown explicitly the ideal virtues, the value orientation, of these *Rajpūts* (pp. 114–15) and the ideal biography (pp. 123–24). This community is in part seen as the inside view of the good life. Further, the dimensions of society, from circles farthest from the individual to those closest to him, are presented in such a way as to focus our attention upon the single *Rajpūt* whose life, outer and inner, is the real subject of the paper. Moreover, social change is here a part of the context of structure and event within which this individual is to be understood. The abolition of the landholding system, threatened at the time of Mrs. Steed's observations, provided a crisis, the possible resolution of which stimulated conduct and comment by the man whose life is under examination here.

In the course of the comparisons which Professor Lewis makes between a village in Delhi District and a village in Morelos, Mexico, we are returned to problems of social structure. But now it is not only the organization of social relations within the village that interests. The interrelations of the village with the national culture and civilization, a matter in earlier papers recognized but not stressed, is brought to the fore by the identification of the two villages as instances of a societal type, peasant villages. This type demands a unit of description and comparison that is much larger than a single village. It is as if we now looked down not upon a village (much less a single human being within a village) but upon the wider rural community that includes more than one village and upon the relations of villages with the institutions of the state. The contrasts Dr. Lewis brings out are contrasts between villages; they are also contrasts between rural-urban social systems. We see a Mexico of "relatively self-contained nuclear groupings or pockets of a small number of villages centrally located within *municipios*." Tepoztlan is clearly organized politically in relation to the state by formal institutions representative of village leadership without interposition of extended kinship groups. Yet Tepoztlan faces inward as Rani Khera does not; its principal bonds are centripetal; its people marry within the village. The intervillage networks of relationship are constituted of trade and of pilgrimage to shrines. For northern India, in contrast, we see, from the more inclusive point of vision to which we are led, settlements more diffusely scattered over a landscape. Each village is internally a complex system of heterogeneous parts. While the village has the degree of unity we have come to accept for the other Indian villages reported in this book, each village is connected with many others by networks of a notably different kind from those prevailing in Mexico: intervillage networks arise from the ties of caste connection and of intermarriage. We accept Dr. Lewis' emphasis upon village endogamy versus exogamy in affecting the kinds of countrywide networks, which, it becomes apparent, we are to study and compare if we are to understand peasant village life. The Mexican and North Indian contrast is between two rural social systems, or even village-state systems. And the North Indian instance is indeed remarkable. In Dr. Lewis' view, the importance of kinship and the extension of caste connections in the East Indian case are somehow "primitive"; yet, if an isolable, inward-facing village is primitive, the Indian countryside is less primitive than is Mexico. Lewis refers to these widespread intervillage connections as "rural cosmopolitanism."

As its title announces, McKim Marriott's paper directly raises questions of interrelation of an Indian village with the larger society and with the civilization of which it is a small and local part. The balanced account of the village in Aligarh District both as a unified world in itself and also as a part of communities outside itself treats more fully than do earlier papers this question, recurrent for the book as a whole. But the topic is only introductory here. To Dr. Lewis' characterizations of types of village organization and of countrywide networks Marriott adds a greatly expanded historical dimension: he treats Kishan Garhi as an element in the development of native Indian civilization. Government and culture alike have grown upward from Kishan Garhi and thousands of other villages. And the government and the reflective thought of India have influenced the development of all these Kishan Garhis. Upward from the village to the institutions and ideas of the state and civilization, and downward from the civilization and the state to the village, his mind runs in his efforts to identify some of the characteristic historical processes by which a native civilization, seen through the life of a village, may be understood.

In Part I of his paper (pp. 182–91) this historical interaction is seen as a relation of little community and great community. Here we see government and land tenure, and then caste organization, as products of interaction over many generations. Native Indian government is in part a growth upward from the institutions of the local community. On the other hand, features of the village that appear at first as local developments—elements of kinship structure, village layout, and typical modes of conflict—turn out to be "reflexes of general state policy." And caste relationships too are in part reflexes of institutions of the wider community, "degradations of the royal style." The conclusion is reached that "both little communities and greater communities are mutually necessary conditions of each other's existence in their present forms."

In Part II Marriott makes the same point in terms of culture, content of ideas. To little and great community correspond little and great tradition. The religious life of Kishan Garhi is examined in historical depth. It is asked: "What elements of ritual and belief represent contributions from village life upward to the formation of India's great Sanskritic tradition? What elements are local modifications of elements of that great tradition communicated downward to it?" To the two aspects of the double process of this interaction between little and great traditions Marriott gives names: universalization and parochialization. We are being helped to a viewpoint, a set of concepts, and a way of work that will allow anthropologists to study a village in its generic historic processes of interaction with the civilization of which it is a part. We shall become able to combine "a focus upon the small half-world of the village" with "a perspective upon the universe of Indian civilization." To this combination the anthropologists who study India are moving.

Besides writing this paper, Mr. Marriott performed the arduous and often difficult tasks incident to editing this book. The general editors of the series are very grateful to him. We are also grateful to the other contributors for their help and for their patience with us. The support of the Ford Foundation in making possible first the seminar and now this volume, mentioned by Mr. Marriott in his Preface, is also thankfully acknowledged by us.

ROBERT REDFIELD
MILTON SINGER

CHICAGO, ILLINOIS

PREFACE

THE PAPERS of this volume are products of a seminar in social anthropology entitled "Comparison of Cultures: The Indian Village." The seminar, conceived and organized by Professors Robert Redfield and Milton Singer, was conducted at the University of Chicago during April and May of 1954. Both the seminar and this publication of its results were made possible through a program for the comparative study of cultures and civilizations, directed by Professors Redfield and Singer, and supported by a grant from the Ford Foundation.

The eight authors of this volume focused their attention in the seminar on a dual problem raised by the extension of anthropological methods of holistic analysis to villages in India's complex civilization. Ways of considering small communities as wholes were first surveyed for the seminar by Professor Redfield through his lectures on "The Little Community" (The Gottesman Lectures for 1954 at Uppsala University), of which an outline was circulated among all participants. Two questions were then raised by Professor Singer: How relevant are such holistic methods of analysis for studies of villages in India? And if village studies make use of such holistic methods of analysis, then what relevance do those studies have for understanding problems which concern all of India?

Each paper of this volume, excepting only that of Professor Srinivas, who was unable to attend in person, was presented for a week's discussion in the Chicago seminar. Professors Redfield and Singer there provided for the continuity and cumulation of ideas. Draft versions of most of the papers, together with notes on the seminar discussions, were subsequently circulated among all authors for mutual comment and for revision.

The present papers trespass on the territories of nine languages and dialects of India. Phonetic and phonemic transcriptions being as yet unavailable, the standard taken for romanizing words of these languages and dialects is literary: an attempt has been made to transliterate from the more or less standard forms found in dictionaries of the native character. An attempt has also been made to employ the same romanizations for equivalent characters in each of the different written languages. Bulletin 31 of the Library of Congress Cataloging Service (Washington, D.C.: U.S. Government Printing

Office, 1954) has been found to be a helpful guide. Departures from that guide consist in the replacement of its *sh* by the more precise *ṣ*, and in the replacement of its *ṃ* by *ṉ* as the symbol for nasalization of the preceding vowel, consistent with conventional practice in romanizing Hindi. Final *a* and word-medial, interconsonantal *a* are either represented or not, according to context and common usage. The necessary diacritics are employed on all italicized words, and on italicized words only. Proper names of persons and of geographic features as well as a few nouns of very common occurrence such as "Brahman" (*Brāhmaṇa*) and "panchayat" (*pañcāyat*) are reproduced in popular, anglicized forms in plain type and without diacritics.

The authors wish to record their thanks for the stir and thoughtful seasoning added by Professors Redfield and Singer to each phase of the seminar's progress. They are sensible also of the contributions made to their own thinking by the other faculty members and students who comprised their discerning audience in Chicago. They are grateful to the student recorders who facilitated the early circulation of notes on the papers and discussions.

As editor, I am especially indebted to the India Village Studies Project of the Institute of East Asiatic Studies, University of California, Berkeley, for the freedom to undertake this volume; to Professors Redfield and Singer for their counsel throughout its preparation; to Professor Murray B. Emeneau and Mr. William I. Moore for their linguistic advice; to Miss Anna M. Pikelis for her thorough and energetic devotion to editorial management and process; to Miss Rosemary Witko and Mrs. Janet Seibert for their accurate handling of many exacting stenographic tasks; and to Mr. Harry A. Millman for his preparation of the Index.

McKim Marriott

University of California, Berkeley

THE SOCIAL SYSTEM OF A MYSORE VILLAGE[1]

M. N. SRINIVAS

MY AIM in this essay is to give a brief description of the social system of Rampura (*Rāmpura*), a large, nucleated village in the plains of Mysore District in Mysore State in South India. Rampura is a village of many castes, yet it is also a well-defined structural entity. Comparisons between Rampura and other villages may throw some light on India's rural social systems generally.

With its 1,523 residents in 1948, Rampura must be ranked among the largest 5 per cent of the villages in Mysore State. Seventy-seven per cent of all villages in the state contained less than 500 persons in 1941, while 93 per cent contained less than 1,000 persons (*Census of India* 1942: 12).

Structurally, also, Rampura is much more complex than the average village, for it contains nineteen Hindu castes and Muslims. Each of the four largest castes of Rampura has a strength of more than one hundred persons, and together these four number 1,274 out of the total village population of 1,523. Others are much smaller. Below is a list of all the castes of Rampura, arranged in order of their population strength in the village, together with the traditional calling of each caste (Table 1).

Traditional callings are implied in the vernacular names of most of the castes. For convenience in description, I refer to them by English terms which are equivalent to their vernacular names—"Potter" for *Kumbāra*, "Peasant" for *Okkaliga*, etc. Exceptions are, however, made for the religious terms "Muslim" (*Musalmān*), "Brahman" (*Brāhmaṇa*), and "*Liṅgāyat*," and for the "Untouchable" (*Holeya*).

I. THE CASTES AND THEIR OCCUPATIONS

Each caste in Rampura is traditionally associated with the practice of a particular occupation. This does not mean, however, that

1. I have spent twelve months doing field work in Rampura. An initial stay of ten months in 1948 was made possible by the generosity of the University of Oxford. A second visit of two months in 1952 was financed by the M.S. University of Baroda. I wish to thank the University of Manchester for the award of a Simon Senior Research Fellowship which permitted me to spend nine months during 1953–54 on the analysis of field data.

all the members of a caste or even a majority of them do in fact always follow their traditional calling. And even when they do follow a traditional calling, they need not do so to the exclusion of another calling. In fact, some nontraditional calling may be economically more remunerative than the traditional one.

Older and more conservative persons in each caste tend to regard the traditional calling as the proper one. Each takes pride in the skills which are required for his traditional calling and regards these skills as natural monopolies of his caste. For instance, Brahmans are assumed not to possess agricultural skill. If, in fact, a Brahman villager does show some skill in agriculture, then other villagers may

TABLE 1

POPULATION AND TRADITIONAL CALLINGS OF CASTES IN RAMPURA (1948)

Name of Caste	Traditional Calling	Population
Okkaliga	Peasant	735
Kuruba	Shepherd	235
Musalmān	Artisan and Trader	179
Holeya	Servant and Laborer	125
Gāṇiga	Oilman	37
Ācāri—Kulācāri and *Matācāri*	Smith	35
Liṅgāyat	Non-Brahman Priest	33
Eḍiga	Toddyman	24
Kumbāra	Potter	23
Baṇajiga	Trader	22
Kelasi	Barber	20
Besta	Fisherman	14
Korama	Swineherd	12
Agasa	Washerman	7
Mēda	Basketmaker	7
Brāhmaṇa—Hoysaḷa Karnāṭaka	Priest and Scholar	6
Brāhmaṇa—Mādhva	Priest and Scholar	6
Brāhmaṇa—Śrī Vaiṣṇava	Priest and Scholar	3

express their surprise. The Brahman priest of the *Rāma* temple in Rampura shows such skill and is frequently to be seen carrying a basket and a sickle to the fields. His agricultural skill is admired if not envied, but he is also criticized for alleged neglect of priestly duties in favor of agriculture. On the other hand, the Peasants of nearby Bella village are criticized because of their urban ways and their lack of skill in rice cultivation, to which they are comparative newcomers.

Contrary to popular impression, the traditional calling is not unchangeable. Changes are especially common at the present day when members of all except the lowest caste are seen opening shops and starting rice mills and bus lines. In the recent past, too, castes have changed their occupations, and changes probably took place in the remoter past as well. For instance, the Shepherds of Rampura have changed over from keeping sheep and weaving blankets to farming. In Rampura none of the Fishermen fishes for a living, and in the neighboring village of Kere most of them have taken to agriculture. Only two families of Oilmen still work the traditional bullock-powered mills to extract oil out of oilseeds. The rest of the Oilmen are engaged in petty trade or work in agriculture as tenants, servants, or laborers. During my stay in the village I came across a party of itinerant Washermen who had discarded their traditional occupation in favor of digging wells.

Again, a caste may have more than one traditional occupation. For instance, the Toddyman not only taps toddy from palm trees but also sells it. The Oilman extracts oil from oilseeds and sells oil, oil-soaked cotton torches, and edibles fried in oil. The Fisherman not only catches fish but also sells them. The Shepherds used to keep sheep, make blankets, and sell both sheep and blankets. In brief, division of labor is not highly developed: the specialized caste often performs many operations to produce its special articles and then markets them as well. Furthermore, in addition to their separate traditional occupations, all castes down to the Untouchable have for long commonly practiced agriculture. Even the Brahmans have done so, although there is a scriptural ban against their doing so (Manu X. 84).

The extent of conformity, change, flexibility, and overlapping in the traditional occupations of the castes of Rampura may best be seen from a caste-by-caste review of the actual situation.

A. PEASANTS AND AGRICULTURE

The Peasant caste is the only caste in the area of Rampura which has agriculture as its sole traditional occupation. Peasants are the most numerous caste in Rampura village, numbering as they do nearly half the population. They tend to predominate generally in the districts of Mandya and Mysore. The bulk of the Peasants are actually occupied on the land, either as owners, as tenants, as laborers, or as servants. All the biggest landowners in Rampura are Peasants.

But it may be repeated here that most other people in the village, regardless of their differing traditional occupations, are also engaged in agriculture in one capacity or another. Brahmans were found along with Peasants among the biggest landowners of the area until about thirty years ago. In Rampura at present, only the Traders, Basketmakers, Washermen, Swineherds, and a few Fishermen do not engage in agriculture in any way. The total number of the nonagricultural population in the village does not exceed 100 persons. According to the Harvest Scheme List for 1946–47, more than one-half of the families of Rampura required no grain ration cards. Forty-nine families were reported to be growing enough grain for their own consumption, while 100 families were reported as producing a surplus for government purchase.

The remainder of the agricultural families—132 out of the total number of 281 families—were reported to be marginal agriculturists who did not grow enough grain to subsist without help of a government ration. If any bias exists in these figures, it is probably in the direction of minimizing agricultural production so as to escape giving grain to the government. Agricultural work and income are a substantial element in most villagers' lives, even if many participate in agriculture only as servants or as casual, seasonal laborers.

Like the Brahmans before them, some Peasants and members of other, older, landed castes have been attracted to the city and have given up their lands. Rampura boasts of three Peasant and one *Liṅgāyat* college graduates, three of whom are employed in the government while one works as a lawyer in a nearby town. Between 1948 and 1952 two Peasants started rice mills, and another started two bus services to Mysore. The bus-owner has bought a house in Mysore and has also built a few houses for renting in Bella. Some Peasants are engaged in trade: they keep teashops, sell groceries and cloth, and hire out cycles. A few Peasant youths show a keen awareness of the changed political situation and have ambitions of capturing political power.

B. PRIESTLY CASTES

Brahmans and *Liṅgāyats* are the traditional priestly castes of Rampura. This does not mean that every Brahman or every *Liṅgāyat* in the village is actually a priest. In fact, the bulk of Brahmans and *Liṅgāyats* are engaged in secular occupations primarily, while even those who practice priesthood often also engage in subsidiary occupations such as agriculture and moneylending.

To say that Brahmans and *Liṅgāyats* are priestly castes means only that some individuals from these castes serve as domestic or temple priests. Brahman and *Liṅgāyat* priesthoods are somewhat distinct from one another. *Liṅgāyats* are temple priests only at temples where the god *Siva* in one of his numerous manifestations is worshiped. Brahmans do not in theory enter temples where *Liṅgāyats* are priests; *Liṅgāyats* do not enter temples where Brahmans are priests; but members of other Non-Brahman castes may enter temples where either Brahmans or *Liṅgāyats* are priests. There is a distinction also in domestic priesthood: *Liṅgāyat* priests are called to officiate at births, weddings, or other ritual occasions only in the houses of other *Liṅgāyats*, while Brahman domestic priests may be called by any of the other high Non-Brahman castes.

In addition to Brahman and *Liṅgāyat* priests, there are priests to be found in every other caste. Such priesthood tends to run in certain families, one of the sons being initiated into the priesthood on the death of the father or paternal uncle. Practicing the priesthood might mean conducting regular, i.e., daily or weekly, worship in a temple, or offering worship on certain special occasions. In Rampura, for instance, the biggest lineage among the Peasants has a small temple in which are housed two goddesses who were brought into the village by the founders of the lineage. Two men of the lineage are priests (*guḍḍa*) and offer worship at the temple once a week, besides officiating at the periodical festivals held in the deities' honor. This lineage also supplies a priest to the *Māri* temple in the village. *Māri* is the goddess presiding over plague, smallpox, and cholera, and her propitiation protects the village from the dreaded epidemics. The village as a whole is interested in warding off epidemics. Brahmans residing in the village make offerings to *Māri* when someone in the house is suffering from plague or cholera, or when an epidemic is about. The Untouchables have another separate shrine to *Māri* and have recently established a separate shrine for worshiping the deity *Rāma*. Only Untouchables worship at these shrines. In brief, it is wrong to assume that priests are always recruited from the Brahman and *Liṅgāyat* castes and not from other castes.

Nor are Brahmans of Rampura by any means restricted to practicing some sort of priesthood to earn a living. At the beginning of 1948, one of the three Brahman families of Rampura was the immigrant *Śrī Vaiṣṇava* family of the village doctor. A second was the old native family of the village postmaster, who owned a little land and did contract work on the canal in summer for the government. The third family was that of the priest who had been called by the local elders over twenty-five years ago to come and officiate at the *Rāma* temple. This temple priest gave part of his time to temple work and part to cultivating the lands with which the temple was endowed. The priest also occasionally officiated at a wedding or other ritual occasion in the village if he was invited to do so. But he was really not entitled to do this, as the right belonged to another Brahman who was residing in Hogur, a large village about five miles from Rampura. The joint family of this absent Brahman had the right to provide a priest at weddings or other ritual occasions among all high castes, barring *Liṅgāyats,* in the sixty-five villages forming part of Hogur Hobli. This right is enforceable. Any other Brahman acting in his place without his prior consent might be asked to explain his conduct before the village panchayat. The man employing him would also be liable. In such a case, the panchayat would fine the guilty parties. Such a right would be enforceable also before a government court of law.

In 1948 this domestic priest was acting also as the accountant (*śānabhōg*) of Rampura and of the adjacent village of Gudi in place of the true holder (*barābardār*) of that accountantship. In 1949 a descendant of the joint family of the true holder was able to assert his claim to the office. His ancestors had lived in Rampura and had owned a considerable quantity of land there. But, like many Brahman families in this area, they had left the village for the city to secure Western education and urban jobs. The family had come down in the world, and the return of one of its members to Rampura to take up an extremely ill-paid accountantship was a measure of its fall. The family sold all its land, most of which was bought by rising Peasant families—a familiar sequence of events in the neighborhood. The postmaster, too, had spent some time in Mysore in his youth, and later returned to Rampura only because he could not get a job in the city.

Like the Brahmans, the *Liṅgāyats* of Rampura practice either priestly or secular occupations according to their circumstances. There are two priestly lineages among the local *Liṅgāyats.* One of them, which enjoys the lucrative priesthood of the *Mādēśvara* temple at Gudi, which is about a mile away from Rampura, is split into two joint families, each of which performs the tasks of priesthood in alternate years. One of the two joint families further split up into four families during the latter half of 1948. Each of the four brothers now acts as priest once every eight years. A second *Liṅgāyat* lineage furnishes a priest for the temple of *Basava,* the bull on which the deity *Śiva* rides. The priest cultivates the temple's endowed lands. The other *Liṅgāyats* in the village are engaged in agriculture and in trade.

C. SERVING CASTES PAID AT THE HARVEST

Five castes—the two Smith castes, Potter, Washerman, and Barber—serve the cultivators regularly and are paid a certain quantity of grain at harvest time by those whom they have served during the year.

"Smith" is a blanket term which includes two castes and three groups of occupations in Rampura—working with wood and iron, building houses, and working with precious metals and stones. Generally speaking, the last-mentioned belongs to the *Matācāri* subdivision, and the first two to the *Kulācāri* subdivision. There is, however, one *Matācāri* Smith who works with wood and iron, and one *Kulācāri* Smith who works with wood and iron as well as with precious stones. One Smith who works with wood and iron also occasionally helps a housebuilding Smith in his occupation. The *Matācāris* drink alcoholic beverages while the *Kulācāris* do not. Each is a distinct endogamous group.

The hereditary Potter of Rampura lives in Gudi. He makes pots and pans and supplies them to several families on occasions such as birth, marriage, and death. He does not seem, however, to make tiles for the inhabitants of Rampura. There are, in addition, a few Potter families resident in Rampura, only one of which (composed of a man, his wife, and an immigrant assistant) carries on the traditional occupation. The head of this house owns a little land which he personally cultivates, and during the nonagricultural season he makes pots, pans, and tiles. He makes them, however, not for grain payments but for cash.

The Potters' trade hangs on old tastes. Their traditional products are favored by the bulk of the villagers, who believe that food cooked in earthen pots is "cooling," unlike food cooked in metal vessels, which is "hot." Even in the rich headman's house *rāgi* flour is still cooked in huge earthen pots. But Brahmans and some of the richer persons in other castes now use metal vessels, usually of brass or copper, for the use of metal vessels is thought to confer more prestige on their owners than the use of earthen ones. As the supply of cash in Rampura has increased in the last fifteen years or more, there seems to have been an increasing tendency among the poor to buy metal vessels. Similarly, houses roofed with the traditional Potters' tiles are believed to be cooler in summer than those roofed with factory-made tiles, yet there is a tendency for the richer and more urbanized villagers to use factory-made tiles for prestige reasons. In 1948 three buildings in Rampura had been roofed with factory-made tiles. If this tendency increases, the Potters may be forced in course of time to give up their traditional calling.

While Smiths and Potters serve everyone in the village irrespective of caste, Barbers and Washermen serve only those castes which do not pollute them by contact. A Smith is not polluted by handling an Untouchable's plow, nor is a Potter polluted by giving a pot or a few tiles to an Untouchable. But physical contact with the customer is implied in the services which are rendered by the Barber and Washerman. Swineherds and Untouchables are therefore excluded from the services of the Barber and Washerman castes: they have to provide these services for themselves from within their own respective castes.

The Barber of Rampura shaves his customers once a week or once a fortnight, depending on the amount of grain paid. He does not shave his customers on certain inauspicious days, such as the days of the new and full moon. The Barber provides special services on ritual occasions, such as birth, death, and wedding, in return for extra pay.

Two families of Washermen serve Rampura. One of them which is resident in the neighboring village of Bihalli washes the clothes of only a few Rampura families, notably those of the headman and Barbers. Between 1948 and 1952, however, the Bihalli Washerman lost the custom of the Rampura headman. The headman's reversion to the local Washerman conforms with the common tendency for ties with servicing castes to be confined within the same village. The Barbers' patronage of the Bihalli Washerman is due to a long-standing dispute between themselves and the Washermen of Rampura.

The Washerman washes clothes, returning the clean garments to his customers once a fortnight. Between his visits, his customers wash their own clothes, since it is only the better-off Peasants who own more than one change of clothes. The washing of their customers' menstrual clothes, which women of the Washerman caste do, is regarded as degrading and defiling. Men of the Washerman caste wash only their male customers' clothes.

D. OTHER CASTES

There are nine resident castes which do not provide regular services or receive grain payments at the harvest: Shepherds, Oilmen, Toddymen, Fishermen, Basketmakers, Swineherds, Traders, Untouchables, and Muslims. And there are several other nonresident castes which also enter into the economy of the village.

None of the Shepherds now keeps sheep, but a few of them still make coarse blankets from wool. They obtain this wool either from the few local Peasants who have kept small flocks or from neighboring villages. The wool is "paid for" in blankets, there being a recognized rate of exchange. There is very little pasture land in or around

Rampura, and this is one of the reasons why local Shepherds have had to change to agricultural occupations.

Two Oilman families, the heads of which are brothers, carry on the traditional calling by extracting oil from seeds. They also own some land, which they cultivate. In addition, they go periodically to the great temple of *Mādēśvara* in Kolegol Taluk in Madras State, where they sell torches made of oil-soaked rags tied to lengths of bamboo. Pilgrims go round the temple with torches in their hands. Selling torches is apparently a profitable business: the brothers have bought some riceland, and have saved some money in addition. The other Oilmen in Rampura are mere laborers, servants, or petty traders.

One large joint family of Toddymen owns some riceland and a cloth shop. The head of this joint family also sews on a sewing machine in his shop. He seems, furthermore, to have an interest in a toddy shop in Hogur. A second Toddyman family in the village makes and sells mats made out of toddy palm leaves—a traditional occupation of women of the caste. But some members of this mat-making family also engage in odd coolie work. The toddy shop outside Rampura itself is run by a Toddyman widow. She is the only member of the local caste group who is entirely dependent on this traditional calling, a calling which is considered to be low.

Three of the four Fisherman families in the village live by coolie labor, while the head of the fourth operates a sewing machine.

The Basketmakers are recent immigrants, and they make baskets, screens of split bamboo, winnowing fans, hencoops, etc., for sale either locally or in a nearby weekly market (*sante*). They buy the bamboos in Mysore. Their contact with towns is greater than that of the other castes. They are not regarded as belonging to the village, as every few years one batch of Basketmakers is replaced by another.

The men of the Swineherd caste herd the swine which they own, and the oldest woman among them goes about villages telling fortunes. Both are traditional occupations. The Swineherds speak among themselves a dialect of Telugu, and have a culture which is somewhat different from that of the other castes in the village. They live in huts on the outskirts of the village. From the beginning of the rainy season until the end of paddy harvest they live in the village headman's mango grove to the north of the village; then they spend the summer in the headman's paddy field to the southeast of the village. Their transhumance is due to the headman's desire to have his fields fertilized with pig manure.

There are three joint families of Traders, all of which are engaged in trade. Groceries and fried eatables are sold in their shops. One Trader has also kept a cloth store and a sewing machine which he operates himself. Two other Trader youths are able to sew, and one of them left Rampura some time ago to settle down in Harigolu, his wife's village. It is interesting to note that none of the Traders owns land.

Of thirty Untouchable families, fifteen are cultivators, and fifteen live by coolie work. Some of the cultivators are *cākaras*, or hereditary village servants, whose duty it is to assist the headman and accountant in the collection of land tax. The men of the families which live by coolie work are either agricultural laborers or servants. Most Untouchable women do coolie work. They transplant paddy shoots, weed, help with harvest work, trim the acacia trees during summer, clean grain, grind flour, etc.

In 1948 there were thirty-nine Muslim families in Rampura, of which thirteen owned or cultivated land, fifteen worked as laborers, and seven were engaged in petty trade. The occupations of butcher, shoesmith, tinker, doctor of Unani (Muslim) medicine, and plasterer were each performed by a Muslim. There were, in addition, two Muslim tailors. Some show much enterprise in their commercial activities: though Hindus own the mango groves in this area, the entire trade in mangoes is in the hands of Muslims. The poorest Muslims act as middlemen, borrowing money for short periods at high rates of interest and working on very small margins; it is not surprising that their enterprises collapse occasionally. The Muslims are therefore occupationally as well as spatially mobile. The bulk of the Muslims of Rampura are recent immigrants and are not yet regarded as fully belonging to the village.

Several itinerant castes also visit Rampura and neighboring villages, commonly in the summer. Sawyers from the lowlands of the Tamil country come to saw timber for building. Tilers, Hunters (*Bēḍas*), Well-diggers, and a few castes of entertainers also come—*Gāruḍiga* magicians, Muslim snake charmers, Pipers who play pipes through their nostrils, etc. Shepherds from villages very near Mysore City come to Rampura if a long drought has burned up the grass in their area. They take their flocks along the banks of the Cauvery River. There is a customary arrangement by which the Shepherds stand their flocks so as to manure a man's field at night and receive in return a meal or the raw materials of a meal. Most peripatetic castes wander about only after the agricultural season is over. During the agricultural season they stay at home to raise crops.

II. THE TRADITIONAL ECONOMY OF LAND AND GRAIN

In the traditional economy of this area, money seems to have played a minimal part. Even at the beginning of this century cash was scarce, and the buying power of a rupee was much greater than it is today. Barter still prevails in Rampura, and it was much more widespread in the past. Today, as long ago, a farmer's wife barters paddy for dried fish, vegetables, and betel leaves. Fruit-sellers are frequently paid in paddy. Though the farmer grows paddy, his staple is *rāgi* (finger millet). Before World War II it was not uncommon for villagers of Rampura to drive carts of paddy to Hunsur in the west in order to exchange the paddy which they had grown for the *rāgi* which they would eat.

Within the village of Rampura the usual way of paying for services was and is in grain, or in land, the source of grain. The various kinds of payment may be arranged in a hierarchy of prestige, with payment in land at the top. Land is the most permanent form of payment. A piece of land may be attached to an office, as, for example, to the office of a village servant or of a temple priest; or it may be given to someone for rendering a service, as it has occasionally been given to a servant who had faithfully served his master's family for a long time. The implication of payment in land is that the land is to be held so long as the office is held or the service performed. Prestige is also attached to grain payments, though their prestige is less than the prestige which is attached to payments in land. The prestige of grain payments is understandable, for the ability to pay in grain is the result of rights in land, rights either of ownership or of tenancy. Grain payments also imply enduring relationships, and enduring relationships are valued. The payment of a crop growing on a piece of land is regarded as intermediate in prestige between payments in land and payments in grain. Finally, at the bottom of the hierarchy of prestige are payments in cash.

The principal temples in the village—the temples of *Rāma, Basava, Haṭṭi Māri* and *Kabbāḷa Durgada Māri*—are endowed with agricultural land. Excepting the lands of the *Haṭṭi Māri* temple, all the endowment lands are ricelands. The priests enjoy the fruits of these lands, and the priests of the *Rāma, Basava,* and *Mādēśvara* temples claim, in addition, a headload of paddy with straw from everyone who grows enough to have some to spare.

In the past, three Brahman families, including the hereditary domestic priest of the village, held grants of riceland. The reason for the grant to the priest is clear; the reasons for grants to the others are less clear, though any gift to poor Brahmans has always been regarded as a pious act. I have not made a study of these grants, but I would assume in all these cases that the state was the donor. Where the gift is attached to a temple, or to an office, such as that of a village domestic priest or servant, enjoyment of the land is conditional on performance of the duties of the office. But after the lapse of a generation or two such property tends to be treated as the private property of the donee. The village priest of Rampura, for instance, sold a portion of his land a few months before I started work in the village. And it is very common, if not universal, for such property to be divided, like any other property of a joint family, among the heirs of the deceased person.

In this area it is common for the village servants, like the village priests, to be paid for their services in the form of land. In Rampura these village servants are Untouchables. They are required to assist the headman and the accountant in the discharge of their duties. The land of the village servants, too, has been divided, as if it were joint family property.

There is, however, a difference in responsibility as between priests, on the one hand, and village servants, on the other. Village servants, like the headman and the accountant, are servants of the state government. They are subject to the authority of the revenue officials and, in case of extreme incompetence or corruption, are liable to dismissal by the government. But the priests are responsible only to the village community represented by the elders. If a priest enjoys the fruit of his lands without performing the duties of his office, he may be controlled only by public opinion and by religious sanctions.

The village headman (*paṭēl*) and accountant are paid indirectly from the land. They keep for themselves a cash commission figured as a percentage of the land taxes which they collect. This commission form of payment may have been instituted to encourage them to collect the full tax from the cultivators.

Grain payments, which stand below land payments in point of prestige, are made for rent, for regular services, for charity, and for labor under certain circumstances. Tenants in Rampura universally pay rent (*guttige*) to the landowners in the form of grain. Such a grain payment may be either a fixed share of the harvest—one-half or one-third—or a fixed amount of paddy. Rents vary at present from four to six *khaṇḍis* of paddy per acre, one *khaṇḍi* being equal to 180 seers (about 360 pounds).

The Smith, Potter, Washerman, and Barber are paid a fixed quantity of grain, called *aḍade,* during the paddy harvest of each of their more substantial customers. These four are entitled to receive also small quantities of the pulses, which are harvested in late summer, of the vegetables and chilies grown in the vegetable plot in the paddy land, and a few cubes of jaggery, if jaggery is being made. They are given additional gifts of grain, money, and food for their services on special ritual occasions. When a Washerman or Barber refers to a family as his "*aḍade kuḷa,*" i.e., "grain-paying family," he implies, first, that the family is wealthy enough to pay annually in grain and, second, that the relationship between them is an enduring one. Such grain payments are made only by those farming families which grow a surplus of grain. Cash is paid for every act of service by those who do not grow a surplus. The quality of the service rendered by the Smith, Potter, Washerman, and Barber depends on whether the customer pays annually in grain or not, on the quantity of grain paid, and on the customer's general social position.

There are minute regulations governing the conditions of service of these grain-paid castes. The quantity of grain paid to the Smith varies from family to family, but varies always at a fixed rate according to the number of plows owned. The Smith is not required to make the entire plow anew; he only beats into a plowshare and sharpens the piece of iron brought by the customer. The customer must first buy the piece of iron, either from a local trader, in a weekly market, or in a nearby town. He must take the iron along with a length of acacia wood to the Smith. The customer has in addition to contribute his own labor. The chips from the wood are the Smith's perquisite. The Smith repairs all the agricultural implements as part of his retaining fee, but he has to be paid separately for repairing carts.

While the amount of grain paid to the Smith depends on the number of plows, the Barber's depends on the number of adult males in the houses he serves. The question as to when for purposes of grain payment a boy becomes an adult male is a matter which must be argued between the Barber and the head of a household. The amounts of grain paid to the Washerman and Barber depend upon the total number of adults in the household. Women mean more work for the Washerman, as a woman's saree is a longer garment than a man's lower cloth. Normally, the Washerman and Barbers would exchange their services without pay, but, since a dispute has arisen between them, the Barbers have been getting their clothes washed by the

Bihalli Washerman, while the Rampura Washerman pays the Barber for his shave.

Next in order of importance after the payments to the servicing castes are the payments of headloads of paddy with straw which are given to the priests of the principal temples in the village. These are said to be contributions toward the daily offerings of cooked rice which are made to the deities.

Headloads of paddy with straw are also given to mendicants, agricultural servants, and the importunate poor. The giving of grain at harvest time to the poor and to mendicants is an act of piety. The performance of such a charitable act results in good, both materially and spiritually, here and hereafter.

The richer landowners in Rampura sometimes pay their servants partly in cash and partly in grain. The servant is given the paddy crop growing in three or four plots. He is then required to supply manure to these plots and to do the weeding and harvesting himself. A rich landowner adopts this mode of payment when he wants to be certain of the supply of labor. Such payment is more highly valued than money, as the food-buying power of money varies. Paddy is preferred because it is food, although it may be converted into money if necessary.

Labor is especially scarce during the paddy transplantation season (July–August). At that time the labor of many people, men and women, has to be concentrated in a particular field for a particular day, or two, or three. Villagers are fond of saying that transplantation (*nāṭi*) is like a wedding: by this they mean that it is a collective undertaking which has to be finished within a brief and specified period of time.

Laborers who help at transplantation are usually paid in cash, since grain is scarce at transplantation time. Only when both the landowner and the laborer belong to the same village, and when the landowner is known to be a reliable man, does a laborer agree to be paid in grain at the harvest for the work which he has done at transplantation time. Wages for labor during the harvest are paid in paddy.

Payments in the form of land and grain bring home to everyone in Rampura the interdependence of the castes. The Smith, Potter, Washerman, and Barber, the priests of the principal temples in the village, the laborers who helped during transplantation and harvest, other servants, poor friends, the village sweeper, the butcher—all these and many others may be given gifts of headloads of paddy with straw. In such a traditional economy the divisiveness of caste endogamy and the barriers against commensality and free contact are only a part of the story. Division also implies interdependence. Each caste is aware that it is not self-sufficient. Payments in land and grain may be said to dramatize this fact.

While the traditional economy of Rampura may be described as one of land and grain, a land tax in the form of cash seems to have been paid at least since the time of Chikka Deva Raja Wodeyar (A.D. 1628–1704). The role of money has been increasing, however, in recent times. The prevalence of high prices for food grains during World War II brought large sums of money into Rampura and other villages, especially into the hands of the larger landowners. Some portion of this money was invested in new enterprises such as rice mills, buses, and urban houses for rent, rather than in older forms of investment such as land, usury, rural houses, and women's jewelry.

III. SOURCES OF FLEXIBILITY

Under the caste system the nonagricultural castes are assured not only of a monopoly over their traditional callings but also of the freedom to choose among certain alternatives—especially agriculture and trade on the external market—alternatives which give flexibility to the traditional social system, yet help to preserve its forms.

The stability of caste monopolies is enforced by family inheritance. That is, the right to serve a particular family—the right of making plows for it, or of periodically shaving the heads of its male members, or of washing its clothes—is treated as a heritable and divisible right. Thus the partitioned brothers of a Barber family divide among themselves the families which they were all jointly serving before partition. On the other hand, all the partitioned sons or brothers of a patron family continue to patronize the same Barber, Smith, Potter, and Washerman who used to serve them before partition. A respect for enduring relationships is to be seen everywhere.

But this tendency toward stability does not mean that continued unsatisfactory behavior on either side will be tolerated. After protesting to the village elders, the aggrieved party will break off the old relationship and form a new relationship with another. Shifting relationships may ultimately make one Smith or Potter more popular and therefore richer than others. Such shifting of relationships is also partly responsible for the rivalry which exists between members of the same nonagricultural caste in a village. Each Smith has one eye on the customers of another Smith. Occasionally the elders of the village are called upon to settle a dispute between two Smiths, one of whom alleges that the other is trying to poach on his circle of customers. Such a dispute highlights a feature of the caste system that is normally in abeyance: while there are undoubtedly strong ties binding together the families of any nonagricultural caste in a local area, strong rivalry often also exists among them (cf. Gough 1952: 535). The kinship links, agnatic or affinal, which prevail among them act both as checks and as stimulants to this rivalry.

Rivalry within the caste tends also to encourage the formation of friendships outside the caste (cf. Marriott 1952: 873). Thus the division into castes brings together the various castes in a village or local area by means of two linked processes: first, the existence of occupational specialization brings the different castes together, and, second, the rivalry for customers splits the members of a caste and forces them to seek friends outside.

Occupational specialization has its limits, however, since no single village or group of a few neighboring villages can support an indefinite number of Smiths, Barbers, Potters, Washermen, Oilmen, Fishermen, Shepherds, Traders, Basketmakers, Swineherds, or Priests. It is obvious that the bulk of the people of a village, who live by agriculture, have to "carry," as it were, the nonagricultural castes by their payments of grain and of grain-producing land.

When there are too many persons in a nonagricultural caste group, the excess may migrate to a nearby town. They may stay there practicing their traditional occupation or a new one. Change of occupation is more likely if the town is a Western-type town rather than a traditional one. Movement to a town, if it is also followed by a change of occupation, may lead to the formation of a new caste, and eventually to change of caste rank. Migration to another village may also occur, especially when the migrant has there relatives or a patron who can sponsor him. It is, however, theoretically possible for a nonagricultural caste to live largely independent of the village economy by producing for a weekly market. Thus Basketmakers, Oilmen, Potters, and others might make a living largely outside the village economy. This is, however, infrequent, as a weekly market does not provide the same security of livelihood that grain payments do, unless the market is an exceptionally big one. It is more usual for an artisan to trade at a weekly market simply to supplement his more certain income within the village.

Another alternative for the surplus nonagriculturists is to abandon their traditional callings and to take up agriculture as tenants, as servants, or as laborers.

The rule permitting all castes to take up the common occupation of agriculture keeps the caste system going by drawing off the surplus persons in the nonagricultural castes. If it had not been for the alternative of agriculture, the occupational aspect of the caste system, and with it perhaps the entire caste system, would have broken down under the great increase of population which has occurred during the last hundred years.

Agriculture gives flexibility to the social system in yet another way. In the traditional rural economy, ownership of land is the most important source of wealth, and is the means by which individuals lift themselves up in the local prestige system. If a member of a low caste becomes rich, he invests a good part of his wealth in land. There is, in such a case, an inconsistency between his caste rank and his wealth. This is seen, for instance, in the case of one Toddyman of Rampura, who is better off than many members of higher castes. For purposes of contribution to common village festivals he is put in the second division along with some members of higher castes. The lower divisions also include some who belong to higher castes. Brahmans are in a sense removed from comparison with wealthy members of lower castes, for Brahmans do not contribute to festivals, nor do Muslims or Untouchables.

I suggest that here again is a situation which makes possible both the formation of a new caste and the upward movement of a caste in the hierarchy. When a member of a low caste owns some land, there is a tendency on his part to Sanskritize his ways and customs (cf. Srinivas 1952: 30–31 and *passim*). In the past, a caste's claim to high position went hand in hand with Sanskritization. Nowadays, members of low castes who hold official positions also show a tendency to Sanskritize their ways.

IV. TRADITIONAL POLITICAL ORGANIZATION: THE DOMINANT CASTE

The existence of caste courts has been interpreted as proof of the strength, if not of the autonomy, of a caste. But the separate political strength of the castes, like their occupational specialization, is only a part of the story. The settlement of disputes in the village occasionally brings out the importance of one caste which is locally dominant, and the dependence of the other castes on it. The concept of the dominant caste is important for understanding intercaste relations in any local area, and for understanding the unity of the village.

A caste may be said to be "dominant" when it preponderates numerically over the other castes, and when it also wields preponderant economic and political power. A large and powerful caste group can more easily be dominant if its position in the local caste hierarchy is not too low.

The elders who govern Rampura owe their power not to legal rights derived from the state but to the dominant local position of their Peasant caste group. Their power is so great that it is not unknown for cases pending before the state's official courts to be withdrawn in order to be submitted to their adjudication.

Justice can be swift and cheap in the village, besides also being a justice which is understood as such by the litigants. The litigants either speak for themselves or ask a clever relative or friend to speak on their behalf. There are no hired lawyers arguing in a strange tongue, as in the awe-inspiring atmosphere of the urban state courts. I do not hold that the justice administered by the elders of the dominant caste in Rampura is always or even usually more just than the justice administered by the judges in urban law courts, but only that it is much better understood by the litigants.

The elders of the dominant Peasant caste in Rampura administer justice not only to members of their own caste group but also to all persons of other castes who seek their intervention. Even now, in the rural areas, taking disputes to the local elders is considered to be better than taking them to the urban law courts. Disapproval attaches to the man who goes to the city for justice. Such a man is thought to be flouting the authority of the elders and therefore acting against the solidarity of the village. The few men in Rampura who take disputes to the urban courts are not respected.

The elders of the dominant caste are able to dispense justice to everyone because, where necessary, they apply the code which the disputants recognize and not the code of their own caste. They may regard their own caste code as superior, but they recognize that members of other castes have a right to be governed by their own codes.

The minority castes in Rampura, including the Muslims, seem only too ready to take their disputes to elders of the Peasant caste for settlement. The sentiment that disputes should be settled within the caste does not seem to be very strong. There is, on the other hand, a tendency for the poorer people to take their cases, even quarrels within the joint family, to their patrons, who are usually Peasants. Peasant elders may be called upon to decide cases in which all the litigants are Brahmans, or Untouchables, or Muslims. In one case which I collected from the village of Kere the Peasant elders on appeal set aside a decision given by the elders of the local Fisherman caste to some of their own castemen on the grounds that the decision was unjust and motivated by malice.

Sometimes, however, the elders of the dominant caste either give permission, or actually suggest, that a case be referred to the caste court of the disputants' own caste. They may do so when an intricate point of caste custom is at issue, or when the witnesses are spread over several different villages. Other considerations may also prevail, such as the question of jurisdiction. A general rule is difficult to state, because there is variation from village to village and from caste to caste. On the whole, the elders of the dominant caste show respect for the customs of each minority caste and for its elders, and vice versa.

The elders of the dominant caste are spokesmen for the village. Trouble would ensue for a person who did not show them proper respect. They are able to supply or to withhold information about people living in the area. Their co-operation may be essential for rendering effective a sentence passed against an individual in a caste court. Their friendship may be needed in some future transaction in land or cattle, or in soliciting a loan from someone, or in finding a bride.

By comparison with taking a dispute to the village elders, taking a dispute to the caste court is a procedure not unattended by an element of risk. A man can be certain of receiving consideration, if not kindness, at the hands of the elders of his own village; he cannot be as certain of it at the hands of his caste elders, some of whom belong to different villages and some of whom he does not know well. A caste court is not unlikely to decide a case entirely on a point of law —a thing which is less likely to happen in a court of village elders who are well acquainted both with the persons and with the circumstances of each case.

V. THE CASTE HIERARCHY

The essence of hierarchy is the absence of equality among the units which form the whole: in this sense, the various castes in Rampura do form a hierarchy. The caste units are separated by endogamy and commensality, and they are associated with ranked differences of dietary and occupation. Yet it is difficult, if not impossible, to determine the exact, or even the approximate, place of each caste in the hierarchical system.

Before the castes can be ranked as unequal, they must, of course, exist as separate units. Separation of the castes is achieved, first, through endogamy. The effects of caste endogamy are, on the one hand, to deny a powerful potential means of forging solidarity among different castes and, on the other hand, to increase solidarity within each caste.

Separation of the castes is achieved, second, through restrictions on commensality. Complete commensality may be said to exist only when all persons, men as well as women, accept cooked food and drinking water from each other. Thanks to the pervasive concept of pollution, each person accepts drinking water and cooked food only from castes which he regards as equal or superior to his own. Acceptance from an inferior caste would pollute him and would entail his performing, among other things, a purificatory ceremony to regain his normal ritual status. The pollution conveyed by contact with lower castes is one of several kinds of pollution (cf. Srinivas 1952, chaps. ii, iv).

Women are more particular than men about commensal restrictions. For instance, while the men of equal castes may eat food cooked by each other, women do not do so. Thus the Peasant and Shepherd men eat food cooked by each other, but their women do not. Complete commensality prevails only within a single caste.

There is a hierarchy in diet and occupation to which the caste hierarchy is related. Vegetable food is superior to meat, and there is again a hierarchy in meat. Beef is the lowest of all, while pork, chicken, and mutton follow in order of superiority. Cattle are sacred to all Hindus, and no one kills a live cow or bull for food. Only dead cattle are eaten by Untouchables. Thus beef-eaters are also eaters of carrion. The domesticated pig goes about the village eating, among other things, human ordure, and this is why eating the pig is considered a mark of very low castes. The same consideration applies in a less strict way to fowls which roam about the village lanes; some individuals who eat the flesh of sheep and goats avoid eating fowls. Some of those who avoid eating the domestic pig have no objection to eating wild, jungle pork. Eating flesh is a mark of the lower castes because the taking of life in any form is a sin. The drinking of alcoholic beverages is again a mark of the lower castes. The Brahmans, who occupy the highest position in the caste hierarchy, avoid nonvegetarian food, including eggs, and also abstain from alcoholic drinks.

When a caste wants to rise in the hierarchy, it may adopt the Brahmanical dietary. A striking example of this is provided by the *Liṅgāyats.* Some Smiths also have adopted the Brahmanical dietary, but others have not. The latter are consequently regarded as inferior to the former.

There is a certain amount of surreptitious consumption of non-vegetarian food and alcoholic beverages, but this gets to be known eventually. For instance, one of my informants told me that the Traders in Rampura were vegetarians, but another cut in, "So you think, but I once found a Trader woman throwing out domestic refuse in which there were bones." Again, those who eat mutton would indignantly deny eating animals such as the domestic pig, the field rat, and water snake. It is alleged by some that the Peasants in neighboring villages eat the domestic pig, but any public statement to this effect before a Peasant would lead to unpleasantness. It is also well known that the poorer Peasants in Rampura and around eat the field rat and water snake, but this again would be denied. Only a few of those who drink alcoholic beverages would admit to it.

Occupations also form a hierarchy. Butchery is a low occupation because the butcher kills animals for a living. In this area, only Muslims are butchers. It is true that all the nonvegetarian castes occasionally kill animals, but not for a living. Fishing also involves killing living creatures. Working with leather is a low occupation, because handling hide is defiling; such defilement may be related to the taking of life, and to the messiness of skinning and tanning. Only Untouchables work with leather. Herding swine is a low occupation because swine defile. The tapping and sale of toddy are low occupations because only low castes drink toddy; Western alcoholic drinks, which are consumed only by the wealthy, are not considered low. Although agriculture is an occupation common to all, Manu (X. 84) forbids it for Brahmans because the plow injures the earth and destroys living things. Brahmans in this area do not usually engage personally in agriculture, and even the richer Non-Brahmans have the actual work on the field done by servants.

The work of both the Barber and the Washerman involves handling dirt, and this makes the occupations of both unclean. Handling hair and nails after they are separated from the body defiles the man who handles them. The Barber's touch consequently defiles a member of a higher caste. The Washerman handles soiled clothes, including menstrual clothes. It is interesting to note that both the Barber and the Washerman refuse to serve the Untouchables. On the other hand, the Brahman is extremely particular about purification after being shaved by the Barber. The spot where he and the Barber sat is washed with a solution of the purifying cowdung. Then a member of the Brahman's family pours several vesselfuls of water over him, wetting him thoroughly. The Brahman himself may not touch a bathing vessel before this. But some of the lower Non-Brahmanical castes are not very particular about taking a bath after being shaved by the Barber.

The clean clothes brought by the Washerman are purer than soiled clothes, but they are not pure enough for the Brahman to wear during worship. For this, either a silk cloth, or a cloth washed by a member of the Brahman's family, or a cloth washed by a Non-Brahman servant but subsequently dipped in water by a Brahman, is necessary.

Ideas of pollution do not attach themselves to working with iron, making pottery, basketmaking, shepherding, or trade, excepting trade in low articles such as toddy and meat. There is no inherent reason why these occupations should be regarded as low. But the fact remains that they are, and the castes practicing them are unequal.

Castes in Rampura may claim higher rank not only by reference to the criteria of dietary and occupation but also by reference to myths and to particular caste customs. Some identify themselves with positions in the order of *varṇa*, which sorts out castes into *Brāhmaṇa*, *Kṣatriya*, *Vaiśya*, *Śudra*, and Untouchables. Unfortunately, however, the sociologist can take little comfort in these identifications, for the hierarchical situation in any village or local area is quite unlike the *varṇa* view of the hierarchy. Nebulousness as to mutual position is one of the features of the caste system as it exists in fact, as distinct from the neat view which the traditional Brahmanical writers have put forth (see Srinivas n.d.).

Any attempt to arrange the castes of a village or local area into a hierarchy is therefore both difficult and fraught with risk. Any hierarchical list is necessarily tentative and arguable. But these considerations should not prevent an attempt, for the existence of a hierarchy and the preoccupation of village people with it are beyond doubt. The list in Table 2 represents an attempt to arrange the castes of Rampura in a hierarchy based on mutual ritual rank. Table 2 omits Muslims entirely, because their membership in another religion raises excessive uncertainties as to their hierarchical position.

Other ambiguities require that Smiths and *Liṅgāyats* be placed in separate columns rather than in one column with the other castes.

Thus the Smiths of Rampura claim, on the one hand, that they will accept cooked food only from Brahmans. Smith men accept cooked food also from *Liṅgāyats*, but their women do not. On the other hand, most, if not all, of the other Hindu castes say that Smiths are inferior to them and, in support of this contention, point out that other castes do not accept cooked food and drinking water from Smiths. Even the Untouchables do not take food and water from Smiths. One reason for the Smiths' strange position is that they are said to belong to the Left-hand (*eḍagai*) division, while the bulk of the Non-Brahmanical castes, including the *Holeya* Untouchables, belong to the Right-hand (*balagai*) division. The Brahmans, and probably the

TABLE 2

Hierarchical List of Castes in Rampura

Rank Group	Caste		
I	Brahman (A) *Hoysala Karnāṭaka* (B) *Mādhva*	*Liṅgāyat*	Smith
II	(A) Peasant—Shepherd—Trader—Oilman—Potter—Fisherman—Washerman—Barber—Basketmaker—Toddyman		
	(B) Swineherd		
III	Untouchable		

Liṅgāyats as well, are in neither division. In those areas of peninsular India where Tamil, Kannada, and Telugu are spoken, the Non-Brahmanical castes are commonly grouped into Right- and Left-hand divisions, which were formerly bitter rivals (Thurston 1909, III: 117, 143; IV: 252). Castes belonging to the Left-hand division, such as the Smiths and the *Mādiga* Untouchables, were subjected to certain disabilities. For instance, Smiths in this area formerly could not perform their weddings within the village except in those villages where there was a temple to *Kāḷi*. The wedding procession of the Smiths was not allowed to pass through those areas where the high castes lived. No Smith was allowed to wear red slippers (*caḍāvu*). The marriage canopy of the Smiths was required to have one pillar less than the canopies of the others. The Smith is even today said to have "one color less" (*ondu baṇṇa kaḍime*) than the Right-hand castes, and there are myths which try to account for this saying.

Discrimination against the Smiths occurs everywhere in peninsular India, possibly as a result of their attempts in the past to rise high in the caste hierarchy by means of a thorough Sanskritization of their customs. Of the *Kammāḷans* (Smiths) of the Tamil country, Thurston writes (1909, III: 118):

> The Kammālans call themselves Achāri and Paththar, which are equivalent to the Brahman titles Ācharya and Bhatta, and claim a knowledge of the Vēdas. Their own priests officiate at marriages, funerals, and on other ceremonial occasions. They wear the sacred thread. . . . Most of them claim to be vegetarians. Non-Brāhmans do not treat them as Brāhmans, and do not salute them with namaskāram (obeisance).

The Madras Census of 1871 notes that the *Kammāḷans* " 'have always maintained a struggle for a higher place in the social scale than that allowed to them by Brahmanical authority. . . . There is no doubt as to the fact that the members of this great caste dispute the supremacy of the Brahmins, and that they hold themselves to be equal in rank with them.' John Fryer, who visited India in 1670, seems to refer to this attitude" (cited in Ghurye 1932: 6). The Smiths' attempt to rise to the top of the hierarchy in the Tamil country by Sanskritizing their customs seems, as in Mysore, to have earned them only the combined hostility of most of the other castes.

The *Liṅgāyats* are another Non-Brahmanical caste of Rampura who question the supremacy of the Brahmans. They worship the deity *Śiva* in his several manifestations, are strict vegetarians, and abstain from alcoholic beverages. They have their own priests and do not call in the Brahman priest. Some of them refuse to eat food cooked by Brahmans. Most Non-Brahman castes eat food cooked by the *Liṅgāyats*. The Brahmans do not, however, accept cooked food or water at the hands of *Liṅgāyats*.

The other castes in the village may be put approximately into a hierarchy as is shown in Table 2, but I am convinced that such a ladder-like arrangement is not a perfect way of representing the situation. For instance, in Table 2 the *Holeya* Untouchable is shown as occupying the bottom of the hierarchy. But he would claim that he was not inferior to the Smith and to the *Mārka* Brahman. In support of his claim he would point out that he belongs to the Right-hand division, while the Smith belongs to the Left-hand division, and that he does not accept cooked food and water either from the Smith or from the *Mārka* Brahmans of neighboring villages (cf. Thurston 1909, I: 367–68).

Frequently the position claimed by a caste differs from the position conceded to it by others, and the sociologist has either to accept one of these claims or to construct his own picture of the hierarchy. The sociologist's construction cannot claim complete objectivity, for it involves the evaluation of statements made by his informants. But it is less subjective than the claims of any one of the castes themselves. The sociologist, for instance, points out that, while the *Holeya* Untouchable claims to be superior to the Smith, the former has certain disabilities which the Smith does not have. The Untouchable has to live apart from the other castes, and he may not bathe or take water in a river at a point higher than that utilized by a member of the other castes. Similarly, he may not take water from or bathe in the tank but must use the tiny canals on the other side of the road which take water away from the tank into the fields. The Untouchable may not come into the temples of the higher castes, while the Smith may. And so on. But it must be noted here that the Smith too has, or had, certain other disabilities which have already been mentioned. The sociologist evaluates these two kinds of disabilities and says that one kind puts a caste into a lower position than the other. Of course, he is not bound to make such an evaluation.

The castes of the middle group II(A) span a considerable structural distance without definite lines between any two of them. Some pollution is involved in the work of Washermen and Barbers, and also in the work of those Toddymen who handle toddy or the leaves of the toddy palm. Washermen, Barbers, and Toddymen are therefore placed near the bottom of the II(A) group of castes. No such pollution is involved in the work of any of the other castes of this subdivision.

Peasants and Shepherds in Rampura regard themselves as standing higher than every other caste except Brahmans and *Liṅgāyats*, and they are accordingly placed at the top of the middle group of castes. Here we come across an important principle of caste hierarchy that is not sufficiently, if at all, acknowledged—the presence of local factors which influence the structure of the hierarchy. In Rampura the Peasants are the dominant landed caste, and the Shepherds are only next to them in strength and importance. This local dominance gives the Peasants a high status among the castes in the middle division. The local numerical strength of a caste and the amount of land it owns are not the only factors, however. The actual occupation locally pursued and the extent of Sanskritization are also important. Thus there is one Toddyman of Rampura who occupies a higher position by virtue of having given up the direct handling of toddy and having taken to new occupations. This underlines the fact that the hierarchy is everywhere influenced by local factors: since local factors may change over a period of time, the hierarchy is also dynamic.

Definitely beneath these castes, but above the Untouchables, are the Swineherds, who are consequently put into a lower subdivision, II(B). The Swineherds herd swine, eat pork, and drink toddy. Their touch defiles. The Peasant headman once refused to cut a mango fruit with a Swineherd's knife because he feared that the knife might have been used to cut slices of pork. No one eats food cooked by the Swineherds, or drinks water from a vessel touched by them.

There is one final and complex point. The hierarchy which is presented in Table 2 has ritual considerations as its basis. That is, the castes are arranged in a particular order on the basis of ideas regarding pollution. But there is, at least nowadays, a certain discrepancy between the hierarchy as it is conceptualized by the people and as it exists in behavior. Discrepancy is due to the fact that, in conceptualizing the hierarchy, ritual considerations are dominant, while in the day-to-day relationships between castes economic, political, and "Western" factors also play an important part. Thus the relation between the poor Brahman priest and the rich Peasant headman of the village is a complicated one, the Brahman being aware of the secular power of the headman, and the headman showing deference to the Brahman's ritual position. The local Untouchable servant or tenant is treated as an inferior by a Peasant, but, when the same Peasant meets an Untouchable official, he shows respect, although grudgingly. Thus there are ritual, economic, political, and "Western" axes of power, and any single point of contact between individuals belonging to different castes is governed by all these axes which are present in the point. All the axes may be said to be implicit in any single act of contact.

VI. PATRONS AND CLIENTS

No account of a village social system in this part of Mysore State can be complete without reference to certain institutionalized vertical relationships between individuals and, through them, between families. These relationships include the relationships of master and servant, landowner and tenant, and creditor and debtor; they may be viewed collectively as the relationships of patrons and clients.

Some of these relationships link persons of different castes, and others may link persons who are rich with persons who are poor, but all these relationships are essentially unequal.

One of these vertical relationships is now defunct, although it was an important part of Rampura's social system before World War I. This is the relation of traditional servantship which prevailed between Untouchables and Peasants. The traditional Untouchable servant was called the "old son" (*haḷemaga*) of the particular Peasant whom he served. This traditional servant had certain well-defined duties and rights in relation to the master and his family. For instance, when a wedding occurred in the master's family, the men of the servant family were required to repair and whitewash the wedding house, put up the marriage canopy before it, chop wood to be used as fuel for cooking the wedding feasts, and do odd jobs. The servant was also required to present a pair of leather sandals (*cammāḷige*) to the bridegroom. Women of the servant's family were required to clean the grain, grind it into flour in the rotary quern, grind chilies and turmeric, and do several other jobs. In return for these services, the master made presents of money and of cooked food to the servant family. When an ox or a buffalo died in the master's household, the servant took it home, skinned it, and ate the meat. He was required, however, to make out of the hide a pair of sandals and a length of plaited rope for presentation to the master.

Many Untouchable families and Peasant families were bound together in enduring ways by the institution of traditional servantship, despite the wide separation of the two castes in the hierarchy. Since the Untouchables are and were very poor, it is likely that some of the traditional servant-master relationships were reinforced by tenancy, contractual servantship, debtorship, and other ties as well.

Jīta servantship may be termed "contractual" servantship, to mark it off from traditional servantship. Under it a poor man contracts to serve a wealthier man for one to three years. The terms of the service, including the wages to be paid by the master, are usually reduced to writing. The master advances, at the beginning of the service, a certain sum of money to the servant or his guardian, and this is worked off by the servant. Usually no interest is charged on the advance unless the servant tries to run away or otherwise break the contract. The sum paid is exclusive of food and clothing, which it is the master's duty to provide. Frequently, before the period of the service runs out, the servant or his guardian borrows another sum of money and thus prolongs the service. Formerly it was not unknown for a man to spend all his working life between ten and seventy years of age in the service of one master. In one case a servant lived with his joint family, numbering over a dozen, in the house of his master, who was also an agnatic kinsman. On the death of the servant the corpse was accorded the honor of a burial in the master's land, near the graves of the master's ancestors.

Some members of most castes in Rampura are involved in contractual servantship, either as servants or as masters. In 1948 there were fifty-eight servants in Rampura. These servants came from every caste except the Brahman and *Lingāyat* castes, and included fourteen Untouchables. Masters were found in every caste excepting in the Untouchable caste, which ranks at the bottom, and in the Smith castes, whose members are assisted at their work by relatives and customers. Hindus and Muslims are bound together by contractual servantship, for Muslim masters invariably employed Hindus as servants, while Muslim servants served only Hindu masters.

The bond between master and servant is intimate. Contractual servantship is often only one of the bonds prevailing between the two families. Sometimes a master employs a man as tenant on condition that he agrees to having his son or younger brother work as servant in the master's house. Caste, kin, and other ties frequently strengthen the tie between master and servant. When a servant works for a master long enough, he tends to be treated as a member of the family. It is not unknown for even an Untouchable servant to fondle his Peasant master's child, in spite of the theoretical ban against such contact. In fact, the conditions of service frequently require the violation of rules regarding pollution.

The master is, in certain circumstances, regarded as responsible for the acts and omissions of the servant, though there is no clear and explicit formulation of the doctrine of vicarious responsibility. An Untouchable servant of the headman was once accused of being abusive to a Peasant. The servant said in defense of his conduct that the Peasant had been diverting water which ought to have gone to the headman's field. When the headman's second son was called to arbitrate the case, it was clear that he secretly approved of what his servant had done. But he had to appear impartial, and the wrong of which his servant had been accused was a serious one. Had the Untouchable been acting in his own right, it is likely that he would have been belabored by the Peasant. But, as things stood, the Peasant had to rest content with simply lodging a complaint.

A rich man does not personally cultivate but has his young sons or servants or tenants manage the agricultural work. In the few top families in the village, even the young sons do not personally handle the plow, though they regularly go to the fields to supervise the work of servants. Servants are cheaper than tenants, but they require close and regular supervision; tenants require no supervision and possess their own plows and oxen. Landowners who are resident in Rampura exact a day's *corvée* from their tenants during the transplantation season. A landowner may also demand his tenants' labor and support on other occasions.

The landowner-tenant relationship occasionally cuts across caste barriers, and this is more common when the landowners are permanently absent from the village. The relationship between landowner and tenant is also an intimate one. Like all intimate relationships, it is frequently marked by conflict. Tenants are heard complaining against the exploitation of the resident landowners; they have begun to feel that absentee landowners have no right to receive income from the land. There is an acute shortage of riceland in this area, and where landowner and tenant, or competing tenants, belong to different castes, the struggle over land may be seen as a clash of castes.

Seasonal fluctuations in the demand for labor in this rice-growing area contribute to the forging of other interpersonal ties which may ignore the barriers of caste. A man finds it difficult to obtain labor when he wants to, especially during transplantation and harvest. Time and numbers are both crucial factors on these occasions. Then the village puts into the field all its available labor force, including men and women. During the harvest, men and women come also from a few neighboring villages to cut the stalks, thresh the grain, rick the straw, and cart the grain away for storage.

Servants, and even tenants, help a man in coping with the work of transplantation and harvest, but they are not enough. Extra labor has to be employed. This may be either paid for in cash or secured on the basis of a reciprocal arrangement with other cultivating families. But securing labor on the basis of reciprocity depends on the ties of kinship, caste, neighborliness, and friendship. A man must be friendly and ready to help another with his labor, time, resources, and money, if he wants others to help him.

A word that is constantly heard in the village is *dākṣiṇya*, which may be translated as "obligation." Because of "obligation," one is frequently called upon to do things one does not want to. Every relationship between two human beings or groups is productive of "obligation," and gives each of them a claim, however vague, on the other. If A once refuses to do what B wants him to do, then B may sometime refuse to do what A wants him to do. A poor man can put others under his obligation only by giving his personal labor and skill. But a rich man has many devices: he can oblige others by lending them money, by letting them land, by speaking to an official or big man on their behalf, or by performing acts of generosity. Thus a rich man is able to put many persons under his obligation. Every rich man tries to "invest in people," so that he can on occasion turn his following to political or economic advantage.

The several relationships between a master and his *jīta* servants, a landowner and his tenants, a creditor and his debtors, and finally between a rich man and his dependents, may all be subsumed under a single relationship: patron and client. I use the term "patron" in its loose, dictionary sense to mean "one who countenances, or gives influential support to person, cause, art, etc." Such a subsumption is legitimate, as, usually, it is a rich landowner who employs *jīta* servants, lets some of his land to tenants, lends money, and otherwise helps people. Every important man gathers around him a number of people, who may be his relatives, caste-folk, tenants, servants, debtors or potential debtors, those who vaguely hope to receive some advantage from him, and those who just enjoy basking in the warmth of a patron's power. The following of a patron crosses to some extent the barriers of caste. The relation between patrons is frequently one of rivalry, and such rivalry is expressed on various occasions, ritual as well as secular.

During the summer of 1952 I tried to sort out the following of each major patron in Rampura. This was a delicate task and had to be conducted with a good deal of caution. Any open inquiry into the following of each patron was bound to be interpreted as an attempt to expose the seamy side of village life. Not only would such an attempt have been resented, but the majority of people would have refused to label themselves as clients of any one patron, fearing that this would make enemies of other powerful people. I was forced to rely on my own knowledge, supplemented by questioning a few trusted informants. The result is not wholly satisfactory, but I am presenting it here for what it is worth.

My list accounts only for a part of the population of Rampura. I was told that the Untouchables were all clients of the village headman, who may be called Patron I. While they all do follow him in a general way, I am aware that a few Untouchables have also special relationships of dependence upon other patrons. Such other relationships are bound to affect adversely their clientship under Patron I. Multiple relationships of dependence also create one of the chief difficulties in ascertaining clientship. Only the hard core of a patron's following is willing clearly to declare its allegiance to one patron, while many clients have a marginal affiliation to more than one patron. Marginal clients give fluidity to the followings of the various patrons as they shift their allegiance from one to another over a period of time.

In the list which follows, only the most important patrons are mentioned. Minor patrons who are themselves the clients of greater patrons are ignored.

In addition to his Untouchable clients, the headman (Patron I) has a following of fifty-eight families. These comprise twenty-one Peasants, eight Shepherds, ten Muslims, five Potters, three each from Trader, Smith, and *Lingāyat* castes, two Oilmen, and one each from Brahman, Washerman, and Toddyman castes. Patron II has a following of nineteen Peasants, five Shepherds, three Oilmen, two Muslims, and one Smith. Patron III, who is a junior member of the same lineage as Patron II, has sixteen Peasants, one Brahman, and one Muslim as clients. Patrons IV and V have followings of six and four Peasants, respectively.

There is a wide gulf between Patron I and the other patrons, a gulf which has increased since 1949 as a result of a split in the biggest Peasant lineage in Rampura. One part of this lineage is led by Patron II and the other by Patron III. Patron I, as the official headman of the village, has some influence with government officials and Congress leaders. He is far wealthier than the other patrons, and his joint family has the tradition of leadership of the village since its founding. As a result of his dominance, Rampura shows a measure of unity and harmony which does not prevail in neighboring villages.

The word "party" has become a Kannada word. Every administrator and politician speaks of "party politics" in villages, and even villagers are often heard saying, "There is too much 'party' in such-and-such a village." The coming of elections has given fresh opportunities for the crystallization of parties around patrons. Each patron may be said to have a "vote bank" which he can place at the disposal of a provincial or national party for a consideration which is nonetheless real because it is not mentioned. The secret ballot helps to preserve the marginal affiliation of the marginal clients.

VII. STRUCTURAL UNITY OF THE VILLAGE

Rampura is a well-defined structural entity which commands the loyalty of all who live there, irrespective of their affiliation to different castes.

There are many bonds opposing the divisiveness of caste in Rampura. One is physical: like other villages in the plains of eastern Mysore, Rampura is a close cluster of huts surrounded by fields. Each such village is cut off from other villages and from towns owing to the lack of roads. The degree of isolation was even greater in the past, when government was mainly a tax-collecting body.

Each village is a tight little community in which everyone is known to everyone else and in which a great deal of experience is common to all. Agricultural activities in which the vast majority of the villagers are engaged impose the same activity upon all of them at any given period in the year. Hindu festivals are common to the bulk of the inhabitants. A drought or excess of rain is of common concern to all. Formerly, during an epidemic of plague, or cholera or smallpox, the village was evacuated, and temporary huts were put up at some distance. Everyone returned to the village only after the epidemic had died out.

Patriotism for one's village is common. Patriotism finds expression positively in the enumeration of Rampura's virtues, and negatively in the criticism of neighboring villages. It also manifests itself occasionally in opposition to the government. During the summer of 1948 the agriculturai department passed an order stating that fishing rights in village tanks would be auctioned thenceforth. This produced a protest at once from everyone, including the headman, and a petition was immediately drawn up and dispatched to the government. The villagers felt that the government was encroaching on their rights to fish in the village tank when they wanted to. An auction was held a few days later, but no one bid. Care had been taken also to send word to neighboring villages not to bid. Thus a silent act of non-co-operation nullified a government order.

The unity and solidarity of the village emerge most clearly in relation to the government. A criminal from the village is afforded protection as long as he operates outside the village, and as long as it is not too risky to hide him. There are occasionally fights between villages, but these are limited by the fact that individuals and families in the quarreling villages have numerous contacts with each other. A fight causes hardship to many.

The unity of the village finds further expression in ritual contexts.

The entrance to a village (*rāḍu bāgilu*), usually unmarked, receives ritual attention on certain occasions. Every village has a temple to the goddess *Māri*, who presides over epidemics, and she is propitiated in order to drive an epidemic out of the village. It is believed that if the corpse of a man or woman suffering from leucoderma is buried in the ground, a long drought will result. Such corpses are either floated down a river or exposed in stone structures (*kallu sēve*) on hilltops. It is believed that the misconduct of a priest may result in the deity's leaving the local temple and settling down in some other village.

Every village has a hereditary headman, an accountant, servants belonging to the Untouchable castes, and watchmen (*kāvulu*). These functionaries act for the whole village and not for any one section of it.

The village may, then, be described as a vertical entity made up of several horizontal layers each of which is a caste. Yet I believe that the physical imagery involved in this description may be a handicap in thinking about intercaste relations. For testing the vertical unity of the village a crucial question is, "How far does the unity of the village really include polar groups like the Brahmans and Untouchables, and a peripheral group like the Muslims?" Much to my regret the importance of this question did not occur to me until I had started to write up my field data.

In October, 1947, a fight occurred between Kere and Bihalli at Gudi, at the annual festival of *Mādēśvara*. I have an account of the fight, obtained about six months later, but it never occurred to me to ask to which castes the participants belonged. I know that the bulk of them were Peasants and members of other castes of the middle range. But I do not know if Brahmans, *Liṅgāyats*, Untouchables, and Muslims were also involved in it. The question which is important to ask is, "Would a Brahman, Untouchable, or Muslim from either village be attacked merely by virtue of his belonging to it?" My own guess is that a Brahman would not be attacked, because of his position in the hierarchy. An Untouchable would be involved more because of his position as client to a high-caste patron than by virtue of his membership in the village. A Muslim would be in a similar position.

In the Non-Brahmanical village festivals, the Brahmans, Untouchables, and Muslims play at best an unimportant part. The co-operation of the Untouchables and Muslims is, however, sought in the work of the festival, and the Brahman is paid rice, lentils, salt, chilies, tamarinds, and vegetables—the ingredients of a meal.

VIII. SUMMARY AND CONCLUSION

I hope that I have given some idea of the nature of the ties that run across the lines of caste in a multicaste village. While the divisive features of caste have previously received notice, the links that bind together the members of different castes who inhabit a village, or a small local area, have not been adequately emphasized. Many features of village life tend to insulate castes from each other: endogamy, the ban on commensality, the existence of occupational specialization, distinctive cultural traditions, separate caste courts, and the concepts of pollution, *karma* and *dharma*. But there are counteracting tendencies too.

Occupational specialization requires interdependence among the castes, a fact which is dramatized in the annual grain payments made to the serving castes. Yet the availability of agricultural occupations as alternatives for members of all castes at the same time serves to underwrite occupational specialization. Along with migration and production for sale in weekly markets, the alternative of agriculture offers a means for absorbing excess persons from the nonagricultural castes. It makes possible the opening of new land by any caste group, and during times of increasing population it prevents widespread confusion by keeping the surplus population alive. Finally, acquisition of land, along with Sanskritization, makes mobility in the system possible.

Occupational specialization is important in other ways too. It gives each group a vested interest in the system as a whole, because under it each group enjoys security in its monopoly. Monopolies are jealously safeguarded by various means. But the families enjoying a monopoly are also competitors, which means that kinship tensions and economic rivalries may drive each family to seek friends outside the caste.

There are vertical institutions which bring together families and individuals belonging to different castes. Such institutions are *jīta* service, tenantship, debtorship, and clientship. As land was the principal form of wealth in the traditional economy, all these institutions eventually depend upon the private ownership of arable land.

Local methods for settling disputes reveal the part played by the elders of the dominant caste. These elders, standing in an intermediate caste position, wield economic and political power over all the minor castes. These elders are the guardians of the social and ethical code of the entire village society. They represent the vertical unity of the village against the separatism of caste.

In sum, the village is a community which commands loyalty from all who live in it, irrespective of caste affiliation. Some are first-class members of the village community, and others are second-class members, but all are members.

REFERENCES CITED

CENSUS OF INDIA
1942 *Census of India, 1941*. Vol. XXIII: *Mysore, Part II—Tables*. Bangalore, Government Press.

GHURYE, G. S.
1932 *Caste and Race in India*. London, Kegan Paul & Co.

GOUGH, E. KATHLEEN
1952 "The Social Structure of a Tanjore Village," *Economic Weekly* **4**:531–36. Bombay.

MARRIOTT, MCKIM
1952 "Social Structure and Change in a U.P. Village," *Economic Weekly* **4**:869–74. Bombay.

SRINIVAS, M. N.
1952 *Religion and Society among the Coorgs of South India*. Oxford, Clarendon Press.
n.d. "Varna and Caste," in *Essays in Honour of Professor A. R. Wadia*. (Forthcoming.)

THURSTON, EDGAR
1909 *Castes and Tribes of Southern India*. 7 vols. Madras, Madras Government Press.

THE SOCIAL STRUCTURE OF A TANJORE VILLAGE[1]

E. KATHLEEN GOUGH

I. TANJORE DISTRICT

TANJORE DISTRICT of Madras State lies on the southeastern tip of India. It is a green, fertile country, dead flat, the delta of the Cauvery. This river, rising in the Western Ghats in Coorg, flows southeast through Mysore, Salem, and Trichinopoly, to be dispersed throughout Tanjore in a network of small irrigation channels which finally reach the sea. In the northern half of the district most of these channels were built by the Tamil Chola kings, sometime before the eleventh century. British irrigation projects watered the southern half of the district, and culminated in the building in 1934 of the Mettur Dam in Salem District, about one hundred miles northwest of Tanjore. Tanjore's water supply is now controlled from this dam. During March to May, after the second paddy harvest in February, the water is conserved at Mettur for the summer months; it is released again in late May for the sowing of the first crop, which is harvested in September. These irrigation devices have for the most part obviated the former evils of periodic drought and flooding. Tanjore's increased fertility over the last fifty years has attracted many immigrants from the neighboring deficit districts of Ramnad, Trichinopoly, and Madura. In fact, with an area of 3,600 square miles and a population of about three million, Tanjore is now one of the most densely populated parts of India. Wet paddy and coconuts are the chief crops, paddy being exported to neighboring areas. Though there are a number of large market towns, machine industry is almost entirely undeveloped.

1. This paper reports some results of field work in Tanjore District from October, 1951, to April, 1953, which was supported by a British Treasury Studentship in Foreign Languages and Cultures. The village of Kumbapettai was intensively studied from October, 1951, to August, 1952. The analysis presented here was undertaken on a Visiting Research Fellowship at Radcliffe College, with assistance from the Wenner-Gren Foundation for Anthropological Research, Inc.

The Hindu population of Tanjore falls into three broad sets of castes: Brahman, Non-Brahman, and Adi Dravida. Their language is Tamil, though certain immigrant Telugu, Maratha, and Saurashtrian trading castes speak their own languages in the home. The Brahmans, whose ancestors must have come to South India at least early in the Christian Era, number about 200,000 in this district. They own the land and have administrative rights in about 900 out of a total of 2,611 villages. These "Brahman villages" lie scattered mainly along the banks of the sacred Cauvery and its major tributary, the Coleroon, in the northern half of the district.

The many Non-Brahman castes may be divided into higher castes, who traditionally own land and, like Brahmans, administer villages, and lower castes, who for the most part live as tenants, artisans, and specialized laborers under landlords of higher caste. In the former category come the Tamil *Veḷḷāḷaṉs;* several Telugu-speaking castes whose ancestors came with the conquering Nayak armies from Vijayanagar in the late fourteenth century, several castes of Marathas, descendants of the armies and royal family who took over Tanjore from the Nayaks in 1675; and the Tamil *Kaḷḷaṉs,* formerly highwaymen, most of whose ancestors swept up from Madura and Ramnad into the south of the district in the seventeenth century, and who now predominate in the southwest of the district.

In the second category of tenant cultivators and laborers come *Kōṉaṉs,* traditionally Cowherds for the higher castes; *Mūppaṉs,* tenant farmers who work mainly for *Veḷḷāḷaṉs; Paṭaiyāṭcis,* believed to have been once foot soldiers but now tenant cultivators; *Ahambaṭiyaṉs,* who were perhaps once house servants of the Chola kings but are now also cultivators; *Nāṭāṉs,* or Toddy-tappers; *Aṇṭis,* or low-caste Temple Priests; *Kuśavaṉs,* or Potters; Blacksmiths, Goldsmiths, Stonemasons, and Carpenters, all of whom intermarry and choose their trades at will; Washermen and Barbers; *Ambalakkāraṉs* and *Cembaṭavaṉs,* castes of inland Fishermen; and *Kuṛavaṉs* or Gypsies.

Adi Dravidas, or "original Dravidians," are the lowest group, the so-called "exterior castes" of Tanjore. They include *Paḷḷaṉs, Parayaṉs,* and *Cakkiliyaṉs. Paḷḷaṉs* and *Parayaṉs* were formerly the agricultural serfs of the landowning castes and still do the bulk of agricultural labor. *Parayaṉs* rank below *Paḷḷaṉs* because they eat beef, have the task of removing dead cattle, beat tom-toms for Non-Brahman funerals, and tend cremation grounds. *Cakkiliyaṉs* are a small caste of Leatherworkers, usually with one family to about six villages, who buy the cowhides from *Parayaṉs* and make them into shoes.

Tanjore was of interest to me because it is, for South India, one of the main centers of the Saivite religion and of orthodox Brahmanical culture. Its magnificent temples, the best of which were built by Chola kings in the tenth and eleventh centuries, are famous throughout India. The Cholas, who ruled in Tanjore from the eighth to the early fourteenth centuries, patronized the Brahmans, settled them as exclusive landlords in many villages, and encouraged the teaching of Sanskrit philosophy and vedic ritual in schools. The later, conquering Telugu and Maratha kings continued this patronage. Today, Brahman boys who wish to become household priests may still be taught to recite by heart one or more of the Vedas, in privately endowed vedic schools or by a Sanskrit *guru*. *Yāgas*, or vedic sacrifices of goats, are still periodically carried out by Brahman sacrificial priests on the banks of the Cauvery as offerings to the vedic gods on behalf of mankind at large. Public recitations of the *Rāmāyaṇa* and the *Mahābhārata* in Sanskrit and their explication in Tamil draw vast crowds in the summer season. In Kumbakonam, the second town of the district, a richly endowed monastery is maintained for Brahman ascetics. These, instructed by their *guru* who is believed descended by a direct line of disciples from the eighth-century philosopher, Sankaracarya, dedicate their lives to the worship of *Śiva* and to the understanding of the *Advaita* or monistic metaphysic to which South Indian Saivite Brahmans subscribe. Religious instrumental music and singing are much patronized: thousands flock annually to the musical festival in honor of Tyaga Raja Bhagavatar, a famous Brahman songster. The Tanjore *Tēvaṭiyaṉs*, or temple dancers, until recently carried on a magnificant tradition of *Bhārata Nāṭya* dancing in the larger temples dedicated to *Viṣṇu* or to *Śiva*. Though public temple dancing was prohibited about fifteen years ago because of its association with prostitution, it is exhibited at private concerts, and several Tanjore dancing girls are now film stars well known in the Tamil country. In some areas the land in whole groups of villages, comprising up to six thousand acres, is owned by important temples, dedicated chiefly to *Śiva* and managed by Brahman trustees. Altogether the Brahmans, who number about one-fifteenth of the population, are in this district more numerous, wealthy, and influential than elsewhere in the Tamil country.

While Sanskrit learning has been conserved by the Brahmans, Tanjore shares with the neighboring district of Madura an illustrious heritage of Tamil religious literature extending back to the pre-Christian Era and developed by both Brahman and Non-Brahman castes. The best-known works are the *Tirukkuṟal*, or sacred utterances of *Tiruvaḷḷuvar*, probably pre-Christian; the epics, *Cilappatikāram* and *Maṇimēkalai*, believed to have been written in the early Christian Era; the devotional hymns, or *Tēvāram*, of the Saivite saints, Appar, Sundarar, and Tirunanasambandar, of the seventh to ninth centuries; the devotional poems to *Śiva*, or *Tiruvācakam*, of Manikkavacakar, an eighth-century saint; and, most popular, the legendary life-histories of the sixty-three *Nāyaṉmārs*, or saints of *Śiva*, recorded in the *Periya Purāṇam*, or great epic of Cekkilar, in the twelfth century. In the last twenty years much animosity has arisen between Brahman and higher-caste Non-Brahman scholars, professional men, politicians, and also landowners, so that an attempt is often made to divide into two traditions the literary and religious heritage of the Tamil country. The higher Non-Brahmans and particularly the *Veḷḷāḷaṉs* claim honor for indigenous Tamil literature, ignoring its debt to *Vedānta* philosophy and the Sanskrit Saivite texts, or *Āgamas*. These favor the *Śaiva Siddhānta* philosophy in which God and the soul are regarded as separate entities; the work of the soul is to escape bondage in the material world and approach God in positive, blissful communion. The Saivite Brahmans, by contrast, tend to emphasize their unique heritage of the Vedas and *Vedānta* philosophy, to some extent neglect those Tamil saints who were not Brahmans, and favor the monistic *Advaita* metaphysic. This proclaims that God and the soul are one, that the bondage of the material world is an illusion, and that the work of the individual, by asceticism, is to lose individual consciousness and to realize the union of his soul with the divine.

While so famous in religious and literary history, Tanjore is today looked down on by the more "progressive" Western-educated Tamils of neighboring districts. Having no machine industries, Tanjore town lacks the amenities of other more industrialized district capitals such as Trichinopoly, Coimbatore, and, of course, Madras. The old-fashioned religious orthodoxy of Tanjore Brahmans, their stranglehold on much of the land, their general opposition to land reform and welfare movements among the lowest castes, and their apparent arrogance, cunning, and tortuousness in philosophical argument are mocked in other districts. The word "Kumbakonam," the name of the second town of the district, where orthodox Brahmans are particularly influential, has come to mean "humbug" or "bunkum" among the educated in Madras. The wealthier *Veḷḷāḷaṉ*, *Kaḷḷaṉ*, and immigrant Telugu Non-Brahman landowners of the district have a similar reputation for backwardness in social reforms. Among these higher castes in general (though many, since independence, pay lip service to Congress ideology) it is probably true to say that very few are ardent in implementing its policies. The comparative lethargy of the higher castes with regard to economic development, coupled with a general increase in the population over the last hundred years and a particularly marked increase owing to immigration from the neighboring famine areas during the bad harvests of the last five, have recently created acute economic distress among landless laborers and small tenant farmers of the lower castes. The spectacular rise of the Communist party in the last five years issues partly from these circumstances. In response to angry rebellion among laborers, the Madras government passed an emergency ordinance in September, 1952, requiring security of tenure for share-cropping tenants, an increase in the tenant's share of paddy crops from approximately one-fifth to two-fifths, and, for permanently employed, tied laborers, an increase in wages which in some villages amounted to a doubling of the traditional rates of pay. This ordinance, while it appeared temporarily to appease the small tenant and the permanent laborer, did nothing to change conditions for the ever increasing number of Adi Dravidas and low-caste Non-Brahman landless coolies who are hired by the day. Labor relations were still exceedingly tense when I left the district in April, 1953, and the Communist party appeared by that date to have enrolled most of the Adi Dravidas as members.

II. KUMBAPETTAI, A TANJORE VILLAGE

Kumbapeṭṭai, the Brahman village studied, lies eight miles north of Tanjore town, about two hundred miles southwest of Madras, and three miles west of the Madras to Tanjore railway. In the center of the village is a single street containing thirty-six occupied and twelve unoccupied Brahman houses. The Brahmans living in the village are small landowners, apart from six families who have recently sold their lands. Holdings of wet paddy on the outskirts of the village range from three to thirty acres per family. Near the Brahman street are three streets of Non-Brahman tenants and servant castes, comprising twenty houses of *Kōṉaṉ* tenants and cowherds; seven of *Kaḷḷaṉ* paddy merchants and small cultivators; twelve of Toddy-tappers, cultivators since prohibition; six of recently arrived *Ahambaṭiyaṉ* and *Paṭaiyāṭci* tenants; four of *Āṇṭi* Temple Priests; three of Potters; one of *Tēvaṭiyaṉ* prostitutes and low-caste temple dancers; four of *Ambalakkāraṉ* fishermen; two of Maratha coolies;

one of Blacksmiths, one of Goldsmiths, and one of Carpenters; two of Barbers; one of Washermen; one of Muslim watchmen; and one of Gypsies, who are now employed by the government as road-sweepers.

The bulk of agricultural labor is done by landless laborers, formerly serfs, of the *Paḷḷaṉ* caste, who live, in eighty-nine houses in five streets, beyond paddy fields, outside the village proper. Kumbapettai has no *Parayaṉs* but employs two families from the next village to remove dead cattle and beat drums at funerals.

In considering the structure of social relations within this village, we may take as our central problem: To what extent is Kumbapettai an isolable social unit? And to what extent is it changing in this respect? I propose to discuss this problem briefly with reference to economic organization, local administration, ritual practices at the village level, intercaste relations of a social nature within the village, and some general relations of the village to the wider community.

It is questionable whether the Tanjore village has ever been economically entirely self-sufficient within the period of written history. Certainly Brahman landowners and priests have for at least a century participated in a wider cash economy, selling their surplus paddy to urban traders and buying cloth from weavers in the towns. But within living memory, and I take as my date line the period between forty and fifty years ago, it is clear that Kumbapettai has been much more self-sufficient than it is today. Until about twenty years ago Brahman families living in the village owned all the village lands and held economic control over their tenants and Adi Dravida laborers. Forty years ago, all Non-Brahmans of Kumbapettai were either tenants of Brahmans or specialized village servants working for Brahmans and each other. *Kōṉaṉs*, the dominant Non-Brahman caste of the village at that date, leased land on an annual share-cropping tenure from Brahmans, from which they retained roughly one-fifth of the crop for their maintenance and cultivation expenses. In addition, some worked as cowherds and gardeners for Brahmans and were paid monthly in paddy. Those fields not given over to tenants, that is to say, about two-thirds of the village land, were cultivated directly by Adi Dravidas, among whom each man was attached as a tied laborer, or *paṇṇaiyāḷ*, to a Brahman landlord. He was paid daily in paddy and, in addition, was perpetually in debt to the landlord for extra amounts granted at marriages, births, and funerals. Both tenants and laborers received annual gifts of clothing, materials to re-thatch their huts, built on sites owned by the landlords, and extra food in time of sickness or in the summer famine months. Part of the laborer's paddy was exchanged for toddy, tapped by the Toddy-tappers, who leased their coconut gardens from Brahmans. The village servant castes of Barbers, Washermen, Goldsmiths, Blacksmiths, and Temple Priests, and the village watchmen appointed by the landlords, were paid in kind by both landlords and tenants twice annually after each harvest.

Today, Kumbapettai has moved about halfway in the transition from this relatively stationary feudal subsistence economy to a much wider-scale, expanding capitalist economy. First, one-third of the land has in the last twenty years been sold by impoverished Brahmans to more prosperous traders or professional men of Tanjore and neighboring towns. Some of these belong to a modern bourgeoisie of Muslim businessmen from the town three miles away, who originally acquired cash as coolies in Malaya. Others include a Brahman lawyer, a Non-Brahman cinema owner, and a wealthy Brahman landlord of a nearby village. Further, twelve Brahman families who have houses and own lands in the village have temporarily emigrated to towns, some to Madras, where they work as clerks in government offices, as teachers, or as vegetarian restaurant owners. Some of these absentee landowners come home twice annually at harvest to receive rent in kind from their tenants; others give their land on subtenure to Brahman kinsmen within the village, who make a small profit on the rent they receive from tenants. Nine out of sixty-seven Non-Brahman men now lease land from landlords living outside the village and are no longer under the economic control of their traditional administrators.

Other Non-Brahmans have become partly or totally emancipated from the feudal system in modern forms of work. Most of the seven *Kaḷḷan̲* households, descendants of one man who came fifty years ago, earn a living as paddy merchants, buying paddy from Brahmans and carting it to the mill three miles away. Two *Kaḷḷan̲s*, two Toddy-tappers, one Potter, and five *Kōn̲an̲s*—that is to say, ten out of sixty-seven Non-Brahman men—have managed to buy between one and four acres of land from Brahmans, which they cultivate themselves. Nine out of sixty-seven men work in other ways independently of Brahmans: three have teashops, and two have small grocery shops in the village; one has a teashop in the town three miles away; one Muslim is the watchman of some coconut gardens in the village which have been bought by another Muslim of Tanjore; and two men are wage-earners in a cigar factory in the nearby town. Only eleven men lease land from owners within the village, while nine are tied laborers, and ten are daily coolies. Thus, altogether, only 63 per cent of Non-Brahman men are now economically dependent on Brahman landowners within the village.

Among Adi Dravidas, too, revolutionary changes have taken place. Only 22 per cent now work as tied laborers for payment in kind. One family now owns one acre of land, 38 per cent have in the last ten years become share croppers on the same terms as the Non-Brahmans, while 39 per cent work as daily coolies for whoever—Brahman, Non-Brahman, or outsider—will employ them, and receive their wages in cash. Even tied laborers, since paddy rationing was instituted in the war and landlords were subject to procurement regulations, are obliged to receive part of their pay in cash.

These economic changes within the village are accompanied by a great increase in economic transactions outside it. Members of all castes, when they can afford it, now patronize the cinema in Tanjore and in the nearby town; all travel on buses and trains to buy clothing or household goods, which have increased both in amount and in kind. Few families now receive clothing from their landlords; most are required to buy it from the town themselves. Most important, the village as a whole is now in debt to the town. All except eight Brahman landowners owe money, ranging from 1,000 to 10,000 rupees, to wealthier kinsmen or to moneylenders from the town; most, in turn, are creditors to their tenants and laborers. In short, the village is annually participating to an increasing extent in the wider urban economy. This change, as everywhere in India, is part of the over-all change from a feudal to an expanding capitalist economic system, and is the fundamental prerequisite, in my view, for most other modern changes in the pattern of social relations within the village.

Before British rule, the Tanjore village was to a large extent an administrative isolate: its allegiance to the kingdom appears to have been slight. In contrast to Malabar, there was, for example, no village headman appointed by and responsible to government, nor was there a permanent military caste residing in villages. In 1816 the institution of village headman was created by the British government; today, his duties are to collect revenue from landowners, to record births, marriages, and deaths, and to settle cases of debt involving not more than fifty rupees. Though appointed by government, the headman of Kumbapettai is of necessity a Brahman landowner; he could not otherwise assert authority in the village. Within his caste, he is not an authority but *primus inter pares:* he could not, for example, try cases arising between his own kinsmen, who would not submit to his jurisdiction. By common consent his function is in fact restricted to revenue collection, for the village has a traditional administrative system of its own in which a headman's role is superfluous.

In this traditional system Brahmans have administrative rights over all the lower castes. Among themselves Brahmans have no elected leaders; as we shall see later, such a system would be alien to their value orientations. Within each patrilineal extended family all submit to the oldest man; between families, quarrels drag on in a desultory manner for months, sometimes years, until both parties are weary or kinship or ceremonial obligations draw them together again. In recent years a few suits against kinsmen, concerning land disputes, have been filed in Tanjore by Brahmans, but all of these were withdrawn because the parties felt that to go to court would involve loss of dignity in the eyes of their kin and their villagers. In general, fear of losing dignity before the lower castes, coupled with the belief in *ahiṉsa,* chiefly toward peers and elders, prevents Brahman quarrels from ending in physical combat.

Among their Non-Brahman and Adi Dravida servants, Brahmans have the power forcibly to interfere in disputes which threaten the peace of the village and to punish rebellion in any form against their own authority. In such cases the offenders or the disputants are summoned to the courtyard of the central village temple. The facts are then elicited by an assembly of Brahman elders, and punishments are meted out. These vary between fines, paid to the temple funds; beating with sticks, administered by Brahmans; in more serious cases, the penalty of forcing the culprit to drink a pint of cowdung or even human dung dissolved in water; and, in the most serious cases, eviction from the land. Sometimes whole streets or caste groups offend against village custom. Such an offense was committed at *Puṅgal,* the annual harvest festival, two years ago. *Paḷḷaṉs,* as the personal laborers of Brahmans in their own unleased fields, have in many ways a closer bond with them than have Non-Brahmans, and are as a caste jealous of Non-Brahman power in the village. Non-Brahmans, on the other hand, make efforts to crush *Paḷḷaṉs,* confine them to their own streets, and prevent them from gaining special favors from the landlords. At this *Puṅgal* festival, on the second day when the Brahman cattle had been driven out in display, the *Paḷḷaṉs,* without waiting for the Non-Brahman display as they should by custom have done, went home and drove out their own cattle through their streets. Approached by irate Non-Brahmans, the Brahmans were obliged to recall the recalcitrants, and fined each street one hundred rupees in the village temple yard.

Among Non-Brahmans and *Paḷḷaṉs*, married men of each street periodically elect their own leaders to settle private disputes within the street. Non-Brahmans elect two equal headmen; *Paḷḷaṉs* elect one headman, one treasurer, and one messenger to call offenders to assemblies or to carry news of deaths, marriages, or assemblies to members of other streets. These leaders, in the company of all married men of the street, have the duty of hearing and adjudicating between private disputants concerning debts, adultery, small thefts, or assault. They are usually men of above-average intelligence, often somewhat wealthier than the majority of their fellows. Their job is to settle quarrels according to traditional custom and to fine offenders. Among Non-Brahmans fines are paid to the village temple fund and retained by the headmen to help in financing a private annual Non-Brahman festival to the deity. Among *Paḷḷaṉs* fines are retained for the *Paḷḷaṉs'* own temple, dedicated to a goddess who is believed to be the younger sister of the village deity.

In connection with the unity of the village, the important point is that Brahmans were until recently, by reason of their economic power, able to prevent disputes within their village from passing into the hands of the local police, or, alternatively, to negotiate with the police in such a way that their own authority, and traditional custom, were upheld. An example of this took place one year before my arrival. When prohibition came under Congress rule in 1947, the tenor of *Paḷḷaṉ* life was gravely disrupted. All *Paḷḷaṉ* men had been heavy drinkers, often taking toddy instead of food at midday. Individual offenses of illicit tapping and distilling have been numerous. Brahmans often turn a blind eye, but sometimes, when the offense is too blatant, they encourage the police to make arrests. About a year before I arrived, the *Paḷḷaṉs* could bear it no longer and broke out in unison. Large fires were built one night, and huge pots of water, French polish, tree bark, limefruits, and coconut flowers were boiled. All five streets were gloriously, hilariously drunk for the next three days, totally irresponsible and totally incapable of work. When the bout subsided, the Brahman village headman, after consulting his kinsmen, conducted the local police to the streets and made select arrests. The whole *Paḷḷaṉ* male population was then marched to the temple yard, harangued by Brahmans, and fined two hundred rupees.

In the past the village has also acted as a political unit in battles with neighboring villages. Sometimes battles arose as a result of boundary disputes between landlords of adjacent villages; in that case, Brahmans themselves did not fight, but bands of Non-Brahman lessees and *Pallan* laborers of the two villages were assembled by their respective landlords and fought on the boundary. In other cases quarrels arose, sometimes concerning adultery, between individuals of different villages from the lower castes. Then *Pallans* and Non-Brahmans of each village again assembled to fight on behalf of their co-villagers. Four such intervillage battles were reported over the last twenty years, the last having taken place five years ago.

But today Brahmans complain that with the gradual loss of their economic power over the lower castes the loyalty of tenants and laborers is no longer what it was, and the unity of the village is declining. During my stay a poor Brahman of the next village, with kin in Kumbapettai, set up a "meals' hotel" on the main roadside of the village. A *Kallan* of a third village ran up a bill there and was one day asked to pay. When he refused, promising to pay later, the Brahman slapped his face. The *Kallan* at once cracked the Brahman's head open with a staff and walked coolly out of the village. Streaming with blood, the Brahman was rushed by bullock-cart to the Tanjore hospital, and came home vowing to file a suit against his aggressor. He did not do so, however, for he was too poor to risk losing the costs. Asked why an intervillage fight did not ensue, Brahmans replied gloomily that there was no longer any unity in Kumbapettai. The offended Brahman, landless, had no tenants to fight on his behalf. If a fight were organized, a few cowherds and *Pallans* of the Brahman street might join, but the odds were that the independent, trading *Kallans* of Kumbapettai and their own *Pallan* coolies might join the enemy side, glad to defend their castefellows and score off their rivals, the Brahmans.

In other ways, the breakdown of the feudal economic system, the emergence of lower-caste groups in economic rivalry rather than cooperation, and the widening range of social relations beyond the village have endangered the power of the Brahmans and the unity of Kumbapettai. In the past, though the headmen of each lower-caste street were elected by street members, Brahmans reserved the right to depose a low-caste headman if he displeased them in any way. Five years ago they had in fact deposed the headman of one of the *Pallan* streets, after a festival in which, while drunk, the headman had been heard to ask one of his kinsmen if he could tell him what use Brahmans were to the village. But in recent years it has been impossible for Brahmans to interfere in the street administration of the two newest Non-Brahman streets. In these two streets the *Kaḷḷaṉ*, *Kōṉaṉ*, and Toddy-tapper households are almost all economically independent of Brahmans and conduct their street affairs without consulting Brahman opinion. During my stay, when the all-India elections took place, only members of these streets dared openly to admit that they had voted for the Communists, against the Congress-supporting Brahmans. Their own Non-Brahman tenants and *Paḷḷaṉ* laborers were marshaled by the Brahmans on voting day and instructed to vote for Congress, though it was doubted whether all had complied. Shortly after I left the village, however, in September, 1952, the Tanjore Tenants' and Laborers' Ordinance increased the economic strength of tenants and *Paḷḷaṉs* and removed from them the fear of eviction by their landlords. At the next harvest, in February, 1953, I heard, while working in a second village sixty miles away, that Kumbapettai *Paḷḷaṉs* had emerged in a body against their landlords, hoisted the Communist flag in their street, and refused to thresh the village paddy until higher wages were promised for daily coolies as well as for tied laborers of the village to whom the act strictly applied. In the area where I was then working in the east of the district, the Adi Dravidas of twelve neighboring villages had already three years ago formed a Communist-controlled union in open opposition to their landlords, along the lines of their traditional street assemblies.

The unity of the village was formerly dramatized in ritual at the annual temple festival to *Ūritaicciyammaṉ*, the mother-goddess of the village. This goddess, like all village deities, is a Non-Brahman deity; though she is worshiped by Brahmans and is regarded by them as an aspect of *Śakti*, the consort of *Śiva*, it is clear that she is not one of the Sanskrit pantheon. Her temple stands between two Non-Brahman streets in the center of the village, and she is worshiped daily by a Non-Brahman priest. She is believed to protect or to harm crops and cattle and to be responsible for smallpox and cholera in the village and for barrenness among women. She is properly the traditional goddess of the *Kōṉaṉ* and throughout the year is worshiped mainly by Non-Brahmans. Brahmans for the most part worship their own deities, *Śiva* and *Viṣṇu*, in two temples, one at either end of their street. *Paḷḷaṉs* again have a separate deity, *Kāḷiyammaṉ*, whose shrine stands at the head of the *Paḷḷaṉ* streets. Annually, however, at the large temple festival, all castes combine in rituals which are sponsored by the Brahmans and conducted by both Brahman and Non-Brahman temple priests. At the start of the festival, in April to May, the Non-Brahman priest walks round the village boundaries ringing a bell; the whole village is then believed to enter a state of ritual purity, and sexual intercourse within it is forbidden for seventeen days. During this period nightly processions of the deity are conducted through all streets of the village, and offerings are made to her by the several castes—incense, food, and vegetables by the Brahmans, and goats by the lower castes. This festival dramatizes the unity of the village and also the separateness and ritual rank of each caste within it.

But in the year of my stay this festival was for the first time not conducted. Brahmans, who are responsible for organizing and collecting funds from villagers, complained that their several families, many of whose more influential members have left the village, would not co-operate together and that the state of unrest among tenants and laborers made them fear disputes and possibly violence if they attempted to enforce the traditional ranked participation of all the castes. I heard that the festival was, however, conducted the following year, but that not all castes had taken part. It is clear that village festivals of this type are dying out all over the district; in many villages in the eastern part of Tanjore District they were abandoned five years ago. At the same time, the last twenty years have seen a growth in importance of the large temple festivals to Sanskrit deities, formerly managed by Brahmans, in the major towns of the district. To these festivals, where, since the Temple Entry Act of 1947, caste rank is no longer emphasized, thousands flock by bus and train to witness the spectacle of the processions and the firework displays. Even these festivals, however, are now losing their appeal for the lower castes, among whom they are associated with the supremacy of Brahmans and with religious doctrines in which they no longer have faith. Changes in ritual co-operation thus show a widening of social relations and a tendency toward new homogeneity in ritual practices of Brahmans and the higher Non-Brahman castes, yet at the same time the emergence of a new, low class of unbelievers who pin their faith rather to rebellious political action. Among organized Communist groups of Adi Dravidas in the east of the district the younger leaders pursue an active policy of antireligious and anti-Brahman propaganda, and here ritual co-operation within the village is almost confined to the higher castes.

The vertical unity of the village has always been counterbalanced by the horizontal unity of each endogamous subcaste. Traditionally, each caste group of the village appears to have belonged to an endogamous subcaste extending over some fifteen to thirty villages. For at least forty to fifty years, however, with the vast increase in population and the influx of newcomers and movement of small Brahman and Non-Brahman groups over all parts of the district, whole streets or individual families of the endogamous subcaste have become very widely scattered. The Brahmans of Kumbapettai thus today belong to a subcaste of eighteen villages fairly widely scattered round the North Tanjore and Trichinopoly boundary. Many of their individual families are also now settled in towns up to one hundred miles away. Members of each of the several Non-Brahman caste groups have kin up to sixty miles away who are visited by bus or train at family ceremonies. The *Paḷḷaṉ* endogamous caste group is still confined largely to villages within a radius of twenty miles, but isolated families are scattered farther afield. In Kumbapettai no intercaste marriages have yet taken place, but in other respects accidental contiguity and similarity of economic status are replacing kinship ties as organizing principles within and between villages. Thus the three traditional Non-Brahman streets, once occupied respectively by Cowherds, various servant castes, and Toddy-tappers, now each contains immigrant families of other castes who dine with the traditional occupants at ceremonies and combine to elect the street headman. A fourth most modern street on the main roadside, sprung up in the last eighty years, contains families of six Non-Brahman castes, about two-thirds of whom are independent of the traditional landowners, and most of whom dine together at each other's ceremonies. *Paḷḷaṉs* and Brahmans, at the two extremes, are still isolated in their streets, but each group contains two or three families of recent immigrants, of other endogamous subcastes within the same broad caste, to whom dining rights are extended. In each wider endogamous caste, by contrast, all but the closest kinship ties are gradually being weakened by the increasing heterogeneity of wealth, education, and occupation.

All these changes in the broad pattern of village organization have their effect on everyday social relations between the several castes. In Kumbapettai the fact that two-thirds of the land is still owned by Brahmans and that about 75 per cent of the population is still employed in traditional ways accounts, in contrast to some other villages, for the comparatively orthodox etiquette still preserved in relations between members of different castes. Thus Non-Brahman and Adi Dravida laborers still come to the back door of a house to receive their wages, and Adi Dravidas still do not enter the Brahman street or, of course, the Brahman temples. Brahmans and most Non-Brahmans do not enter the Adi Dravida streets. Not only do they not wish to, because of ritual pollution; they also say that the *Paḷḷaṉs* would not permit them, since it is believed that if a Brahman entered an Adi Dravida street the whole street would fall prey to disease, famine, and sexual sterility. Adi Dravidas, though they may walk in the Non-Brahman streets, may not enter Non-Brahman houses. I myself was on my second day refused the use of the local well after I had received *Paḷḷaṉs* into my house and distributed betel and areca nuts among them. Brahmans may enter Non-Brahman houses and, in fact, rather frequently have sex relations with their Non-Brahman lessees' wives, but they may not eat there and must bathe before re-entering their homes. A few Brahmans do, however, occasionally take tea or lemonade from one of the five small Non-Brahman shops, and many Non-Brahmans eat vegetarian food from the new Brahman "meals' hotel," though they eat in a room separate from Brahmans. Similarly, since the toddy shops were closed, Adi Dravida men now drink tea in Non-Brahman teashops, but they are served separately behind a wall at the back, with separate glasses. In other directions, in the last twenty years, a considerable relaxing of caste restrictions has taken place. Non-Brahmans were formerly forbidden to enter Brahman houses; both men and women now work as house servants for their landlords, though they may not enter the kitchen. Non-Brahmans were formerly forbidden to wear shoes while walking in the Brahman street or standing before a Brahman. But today two Non-Brahman boys whose fathers are independent of the landlords walk deliberately in their shoes down the Brahman street to post letters in the mailbox. These boys, one Adi Dravida, and thirteen Brahman boys attend high school three miles away, where caste discrimination is forbidden. In particular, no group now has power to excommunicate serious offenders against caste law. In the past, though Brahman men were freed from the pollution of illicit sex relations with Non-Brahman women after taking a purifying bath, men who had intercourse with Adi Dravida women, or Brahman women who committed adultery at all, were driven from their caste. Even thirty years ago, one Brahman who had sexual relations with a *Paḷḷaṉ* woman was ostracized by his street and asked to leave the village, which he did after selling his lands. But, today, at least two men regularly have relations with *Paḷḷaṉ* servant women in empty houses of the Brahman street; they are condemned but not ostracized. If excommunication were attempted, the offending family would refuse to move, using the modern argument, derived from the modern secular law, that unless he is taken by the police no man can be forced to leave his property. Similarly, adultery on the part of Brahman women, even with lower-caste men, tends nowadays to be hidden by their husbands and kinsfolk, and only private vengeance is exacted.

In the east of the district it is among Communist groups and particularly Adi Dravidas that caste restrictions have broken down most completely. Non-Brahman Communist leaders go freely into Adi Dravida streets, eat with them, and spend the night in their huts. In the second village where I worked, *Paḷḷaṉs* and *Parayaṉs* of twelve villages had in the last five years completely abandoned their age-long dispute for precedence, ate freely together, assembled together at large areal Communist meetings, supported each other in strikes to gain higher wages from landlords, and, within each village, together settled their disputes concerning debt and adultery. In this district, in fact, so weak is the propagation of Congress policy regarding caste, and so strong the Communist, that any person who attempts to defy caste laws is promptly hailed as a Communist. Among some Adi Dravidas, the Communist party is regarded as another foreign power, comparable to the British, whose aim is to break the sway of high-caste landlords and to establish equal rights for all castes. A few I met, indeed, thought in a vague way that all the British, being foreigners and white men, were Communists; one old man actually asked me, "But is not Russia in London?"

III. CONCLUSION

It is clear that, in general, the social structure of the Tanjore village is changing from a relatively closed, stationary system, with a feudal economy and co-operation between ranked castes in ways ordained by religious law, to a relatively "open," changing system, governed by secular law, with an expanding capitalist economy and competition between castes which is sometimes reinforced and sometimes obscured by the new struggle between economic classes. In perhaps ten years, even if there is no Communist revolution in the meantime, it is questionable whether the village will any longer be a useful isolate for study. Certainly, it is difficult even now to speak meaningfully of modern economic relations within the village without reference to broader government policies—for example, of rice rationing, procurement of surplus paddy, admittance of students to high schools and colleges, communal representation in government employment, and government attempts to readjust the relations between landlords and tenants. It is equally difficult to speak of social and administrative relations between castes without reference to the rise of the Communist party since 1947 or to the earlier development of anti-Brahman political movements. All the more need, therefore, to record what we can of the traditional structure of villages before this has quite decayed.

THE CHANGING STATUS OF A DEPRESSED CASTE[1]

BERNARD S. COHN[2]

THIS PAPER describes attempts by the members of one "untouchable" caste in one village to raise their social status. The caste is the *Camārs,* traditionally Leatherworkers and agricultural laborers, who have long stood near the bottom of the regional society of Uttar Pradesh in wealth, power, and caste position. Attempts by the *Camārs* of Madhopur (*Mādhopūr*) village to achieve a higher status must be understood in relation to changes both in the village and in the outside world as well as in relation to the *Camārs'* own internal social and religious organization. This paper offers a preliminary analysis of some of the complex processes which are involved.

I. THE VILLAGE AND ITS ECONOMY

Madhopur is a large, *Rājpūt*-owned village of 1,047 acres on the level Ganges-Gomti plain. It is located in Kerakat Tahsil in the southeastern part of Jaunpur District, U.P. Like most of the eastern districts of U.P., Jaunpur is densely populated, overwhelmingly agricultural, and relatively poor as compared with the western districts of U.P. In Madhopur village the agricultural lands are about equally divided between the production of rice and the production of other grains such as barley and millets, with sugar cane as a leading cash crop. The village is two miles from an all-weather road and bus route which connects it with the cities of Banaras and Azamgarh, twenty-five and thirty-eight miles distant, respectively. It is four

1. Field work in Madhopur from September, 1952, to August, 1953, was supported by an Area Research Training Fellowship of the Social Science Research Council and by a scholarship grant from the United States Educational Foundation under the Fulbright Act. The author would like to express his appreciation to Prof. Morris E. Opler and to Mr. Rudra Datt Singh for their direction and encouragement during the field study; to the Cornell University India Project for the use of its facilities in the field and at Cornell; and to Mr. James Michael Mahar for his comments.

2. In the original edition, authorship of this article appeared as "Based on Reports by Bernard S. Cohn." Shortly after presenting two reports to the seminar and writing a preliminary draft of the article, I was inducted into the U.S. Army and was unable to prepare a final draft of the article; hence McKim Marriott graciously and effectively prepared the material for publication. A footnote is an inadequate place to express my deep appreciation to McKim Marriott for the sensitivity, skill, and dedication with which he edited the materials that were available to him.

miles from the nearest railway, which provides transportation to Jaunpur, the ancient district center (Nevill 1908: 1–3). Kerakat town, the subdivisional headquarters for Madhopur, having a population of about 5,000 persons, is four miles away. Descriptions of the traditional village of Madhopur and of recent changes there have been published previously by Opler and Singh (1948, 1952*a*, 1952*b*).

The *Camārs* of Madhopur are the most numerous of the twenty-three principal caste groups which are resident there. Among the 1,852 persons enumerated by the village accountant in his census of 1948, five castes were represented by more than 50 members each: *Camārs* (636), *Rājpūt "Ṭhākurs,"* or "Lords" (436), *Noniyās* (239), *Ahīrs* (116), and *Lohārs* (67). Eleven other local caste groups had less than 20 members each.

The twenty-three local caste groups of Madhopur are distributed in one main settlement and in nine hamlets in a manner which approximately symbolizes their relative standings in Madhopur society. Twenty caste groups are represented in the main settlement together with one of its hamlets. The houses of the dominant *Ṭhākurs* and other high castes tend to be located at the center, while others circle the peripheries. Two other hamlets are the residences mainly of *Noniyās* and *Ahīrs,* independent tenants who have settled near their tillage. No *Camārs* are permitted to make their residences in any of these higher-caste settlements. Instead, their houses are found clustered in six outlying hamlets on all sides of the settlements of the other castes.

Camārs, like all other castes of Madhopur, have long been subordinate in all economic and political affairs to the *Ṭhākur* landlords (*zamīndārs*) of the village. These *Ṭhākurs, Rājpūts* of the *Raghubaṉśī* clan, have held predominant economic and political power in Madhopur since the conquest of the village and the region by their ancestors in the sixteenth century. All *Ṭhākurs* of Madhopur today trace their descent to Ganesh Rai, who conquered a fourteen-square-mile area around Madhopur which is now known as Dobhi Taluka. The two sons, and later the twelve grandsons, of Ganesh Rai divided this area among themselves into shares (*mahāls*). These twelve shares still constitute the largest landholding divisions of the taluka.

The village which I have called Madhopur fell to the lot of Madhoram, the eldest grandson of Ganesh Rai. Within the village, his share was again divided for management among his six sons and their heirs into sections which are known as *paṭṭīs* or *thoks*. Each section of the village has its revenue headman (*lambardār*), who is charged with the duty of depositing the land tax of his section twice each year at the Kerakat Tahsil treasury. By 1934, the landlord holdings of Madhopur had been partitioned into twenty-eight smaller shares by ownership, although the original six *paṭṭīs* continued as tax-collection units up until the implementation of the U.P. Zamindari Abolition Act on July 1, 1952. Until that time, every non-*Ṭhākur* family cultivating land in Madhopur did so only as the tenant or through the tenant of a *Ṭhākur* family or a *Ṭhākur* lineage (also called a *paṭṭī*).

Zamindari Abolition in 1952 did little to affect the economic and political dominance of the *Ṭhākurs* either in Madhopur or in the immediate region, for it expropriated the landlords only from that part of their tenanted lands which had not previously been registered as being under their own personal cultivation. As long ago as 1906, half the lands of Chandwak Pargana, of which Madhopur is part, had been recorded as being under the landlords' own cultivation. In 1953, after landlord abolition, *Ṭhākur* ex-landlords still owned and cultivated approximately 70 per cent of the lands of Madhopur. The few permanent tenants in the village were enabled to buy out their parts of the *Ṭhākurs'* landlord holdings by payment to the state government of ten times the annual rent, but the landlords who lost land thereby are to be compensated by the government. Some ex-landlords, moreover, continue to receive rent from their now protected tenants-at-will. Although the old legal bases of tenancy under landlords ceased to exist in 1952, most non-*Ṭhākur* families continue to gain access to land only as lessees under *Ṭhākurs*.

The relationships which were traditional between landlord and tenant tend still to survive in Madhopur. These relationships involve much more than strictly economic considerations. The lessee of a *Ṭhākur* is called a "*prajā*," literally a "subject," "dependent," or "child." While a man may farm the lands of several *Ṭhākurs*, he has a primary and lasting socioeconomic tie with the *Ṭhākur* on whose land he had originally built his house. The *Ṭhākur* is considered to be responsible for the welfare of his tenants, and responsible for their care in need and ill health. Each tenant in turn owes allegiance and support to his *Ṭhākur*. The landlord-tenant tie is dramatized at life-cycle ceremonials, when the tenant performs ceremonial services and is fed in return by his *Ṭhākur*. At festivals, too, the tenant receives gifts of food from his *Ṭhākur*. The tenant's tie with his *Ṭhākur* is clear also in disputes: the tenants of each *Ṭhākur* support him, even to the extent of doing violence to his adversary.

Much like the traditional relationship between a landlord and his tenant is the relationship between a *Ṭhākur* and his agricultural laborers. Permanent "plowmen" (*halvāhās*), who do every sort of agricultural work, are the most subordinate of the kinds of agricultural laborers. In Madhopur these laborers are usually *Camārs*. Members of other caste groups in the village also do agricultural work, but, since the *Camārs* are the most numerous of the impoverished lower castes, an employer talking about his "laborers" is most likely to be referring to his *Camārs*.

Besides its tenants and laborers, every *Ṭhākur* family, acting as patron (*jajmān*), also has traditional workers (*parjūniyas*), who provide specialized goods and services. Among the traditional workers of each *Ṭhākur* family are the *Kahār* (Water Carrier), *Nāī* (Barber), Brahman priest, *Lohār* (Carpenter-Blacksmith), *Kohār* (Potter), *Camār* (Leatherworker and midwife), *Bārī* (Betel Leaf Distributor) and *Dhobī* (Washerman). In return for their services, the traditional workers are given biannual payments in grain and are sometimes given the use of a piece of land. The patron-worker tie is a hereditary one: a patron cannot arbitrarily change a traditional worker, and no one other than the hereditary worker will perform the traditional work for a patron, under threat of outcasting. Similarly, a traditional worker cannot change a patron without the permission of the patron and of his own caste. Members of castes other than the *Ṭhākurs* have their traditional worker families also, usually four: Barber, Carpenter-Blacksmith, Potter, and *Camār*. Members of low castes usually employ the same traditional worker families which are employed by their own respective *Ṭhākurs*.

II. THE *Camārs* THEMSELVES

A. KINSHIP ORGANIZATION

Within this complex village of Madhopur, with its elaborate intercaste connections, are found 122 joint households of *Camārs*. Each joint household (*ghar*) is conceived as a group of related persons who eat from the same hearth and share all of their property and labor. *Camār* joint households contain on the average a fraction over five persons each. The joint household group tends to be composed of a nuclear family, eighty of the *Camār* families being nuclear family groups with but a single living married couple, while only forty-two are extended family groups with two or more couples each.

Beyond their families and households, *Camārs* are organized into lineage groups composed of persons related through the male line, usually residing together in one part of a single hamlet. A lineage group usually has as its headman the oldest active male and is usually identified by his personal name. The headman of a lineage group advises members, arbitrates disputes among them, sets the dates for group activities, and intercedes for members with other groups in the village. If there is a meeting of all the *Camārs* of a hamlet or of the village, these lineage headmen take the most active parts.

Camārs reside in six hamlets composed of six, eight, fifteen, fifteen, thirty, and forty-eight families, respectively. Non-*Camār* villagers refer to each of these hamlets as a "place of the *Camārs*" (*Camarautī*); they distinguish one *Camār* hamlet from another either by its direction from the main village settlement or, as do the *Camārs* themselves, by the name of one of its leading residents. In five of the six hamlets there is a single leading resident who is known as its "headman" (*caudharī*).

Hamlet unity is strong. The *Camār* men of one hamlet often work together in groups when they work for *Ṭhākurs*. A gang of *Camārs* may be recruited under one contract from a single hamlet to do jobs such as well-digging, brickmaking, or house construction. A *Camār* uses kinship terms when addressing a *Camār* older than himself from his own hamlet, but he uses a personal name when addressing a *Camār* from another hamlet, whether older or younger. A *Camār* will willingly lend his brass water pot (*loṭā*) within the hamlet, is leery of doing so in other hamlets of Madhopur, and will not do so outside the village.

Eighty-five per cent of all *Camār* men in Madhopur were born there and, in accordance with the preferred pattern of virilocal residence, have brought their wives to live in Madhopur. Mothers' and wives' relatives outside the village nevertheless remain very important to every *Camār* man, both socially and politically. Visits between affinal relatives are frequent and may be long. Often a child spends two or three years with his mother on a visit to his mother's father's household in another village. Members of the mother's family, the wife's family, and the sister's husband's family are invited to attend all major feasts and ceremonies such as those at the time of marriage and on the thirteenth day after death. Outside ties are annually renewed at the festival of *Makar Saṅkrānti*, when men send presents to their daughters-in-law's and sisters' husband's families.

Visiting and ceremonial participation with affinal relatives serve to maintain important political and economic channels for *Camārs*. If a *Camār* gets into trouble with a *Ṭhākur* in his own village, he may still take refuge with his mother's, his wife's, or his sister's relatives in another village. He cannot so easily turn to his paternal relatives for help against a local *Ṭhākur*, since they usually live in the same hamlet with him and are themselves subordinate to the same *Ṭhākur*. Partly due to such political circumstances, 15 per cent of the *Camār* men living in Madhopur today are connected with the village through a wife or a mother rather than through a father. Over the years, migration among affinal relatives' villages has continued to the point that one-half of the *Camār* families of Madhopur are remembered to have come as "outsiders" in past generations.

B. RELIGIOUS CUSTOMS

The traditional part of *Camār* religion is typical of the religion of the low castes in that it is composed mainly of pre-Aryan and non-Brahmanical elements (cf. Crooke 1896, II: 184–85). Two generations ago, *Camār* rituals, both public and domestic, were sharply differentiated from those of the upper castes. Exorcists and mediums (*ojhās*) dealt dramatically with the spirit world. Among traditional ceremonies for propitiation of the village godlings, the most spectacular were the fire sacrifices (*havans*) conducted by the *Camārs* of a whole hamlet at a time. These sacrifices were dedicated to *Bhagautī* and her followers, godlings thought to be responsible for epidemic diseases. They continue to be performed to the present day.

Domestic ceremonies of the *Camārs* also differed greatly from those of the upper castes. When a marriage was settled, for example, the father of the boy and the father of the girl jointly sacrificed a pig to *Paramesarī Devī*, the patron goddess of the *Camārs* and of their marriages. After the sacrifice, the pig was cooked and eaten by the members of both households. In the marriage bargain, furthermore, unlike the upper castes, *Camārs* paid no dowry, not even in symbolic form. The wedding ritual itself was also simpler than that of the higher castes: the groom, accompanied by his father and a wedding party, went to the bride's house for a single day. The father of the groom there simply presented the father of the bride-to-be with ten seers (about twenty pounds) of flour, one saree, and five rupees. Brahman priests had no direct participation in any rituals of the *Camār* wedding but merely determined an auspicious day on which the ceremonies might be held.

For several generations, however, while most of the *Camārs* of Madhopur have followed their old, distinctive lower-caste religious customs, some others have attempted indirectly to "Sanskritize" (Srinivas 1952: 30–31, 212–27) their customs through adherence to the *Śiva Nārāyaṇ* sect. This Vaisnava reform sect is less than two hundred years old, although its roots go back for five hundred years to the time of Ramananda. Ramananda was born about the beginning of the fifteenth century (Farquhar 1920: 323; Bhandarkar 1913; Macauliffe 1909, IV: 101), and himself became a member of the South Indian *Rāmānuja* sect which worshiped *Rām*, hero of the *Rāmāyaṇa.* Ramananda lived in years of religious and intellectual ferment under Muslim rule (Tara Chand 1946: 130–42) when, much as during the nineteenth and twentieth centuries, Hindu social institutions were suffering attack. Ramananda taught the doctrine that emancipation (*mokṣa*) could be attained through devotion (*bhakti*) to *Rām* by anyone, rather than only by men or by persons of high caste. Though he did not oppose caste as a social institution or attempt to overturn the priestly functions of the Brahmans (Farquhar 1920: 325), he did include among his disciples a *Camār*, a *Jāṭ*, a *Lohār*, a Muslim, and a woman. And the influential sects which sprang from among Ramananda's followers emphasized the use of vernaculars rather than Sanskrit for religious purposes.

The *Camārs* of Madhopur nominally recognized and still recognize their spiritual descent from Raidas, the *Camār* shoemaker disciple of Ramananda, by calling themselves "*Raidāsīs.*" While the stories and sayings of Raidas were preserved in the seventeenth-century *Bhakta Māla* (Farquhar 1920: 317; Grierson 1909: 607; 1910: 210) and in the Sikh holy book, the *Granth Sāhab* (Macauliffe 1909: 316–42), and while stories of his abilities and saintliness are widely current among *Camārs* (Wilson 1861, I: 113–18; Grierson 1919: 560; Macauliffe 1909: 316–21), Raidas himself does not seem to have founded an organized and enduring sect (Briggs 1920: 210; cf. Grierson 1921: 579).

Some *Camārs* of Madhopur have for several generations been more directly and institutionally connected with the tradition of Ramananda through the *Śiva Nārāyaṇ* sect. This sect was founded by Siva Narayan, a *Rājpūt* follower of Ramananda who lived in Ghazipur, a district adjacent to Jaunpur, in the eighteenth century. Siva Narayan preached the worship of one God, who is truth; he preached temperance and mercy. He left sixteen volumes of his writings and sayings and established a sect with four monasteries (*maths*) (Grierson 1921: 579; Farquhar 1920: 345; Wilson 1861, I: 358–59). His sect was and is open to members of all castes, but in recent generations the majority of its adherents have been *Camārs* and *Dusādhs*, a low caste of menials and cultivators in Bihar and Bengal. In Jaunpur District the bulk of the adherents to the *Śiva Nārāyaṇ* sect are *Camārs*, although in Azamgarh District some adherents are said to be found among Brahmans and *Rājpūts*. The *Śiva Nārāyaṇ* sect is organized in small houses of worship. Each house has a leader (*mahant*), an assistant leader, a messenger, and a council of five. The leader is generally hereditary but is also educated in the sixteen holy books—especially in one of them, the *Guru Nyās*—and in the rituals of the *Śiva Nārāyaṇ* sect. The leader of the *Śiva Nārāyaṇ* sect for Madhopur is also the leader for six or seven other villages surrounding Madhopur. An individual who desires to become a full-fledged devotee comes to the leader and signifies his desire. On the festival of *Kṛṣṇa*'s Birthday the intended devotee receives lectures from the leader on the tenets of the religion as well as a Sanskrit formula (*mantra*) to be learned by heart. He is then considered to be a devotee and a full member of the sect.

The main local activity of the *Śiva Nārāyaṇ* sect is the holding of public ceremonies (*gādīs*), with singing and rituals for the worship of Siva Narayan and his holy books. Such ceremonies must be held at least twice a year, on the festivals of *Kṛṣṇa*'s Birthday and *Basant Pañcamī*. The forms of worship used in these public ceremonies are very much like Brahmanical forms of worship, although no Brahman priest actually officiates. Members of the *Śiva Nārāyaṇ* sect, while making use of vernacular language, have generally stood for the use of more Sanskritic forms of religious worship and for more Sanskritic ways in every sphere of life.

Up until about fifty years ago, along with the traditional *Camār* religion and the Sanskritized sect of *Śiva Nārāyaṇ*, the *Camārs* of Madhopur also included many adherents of a cult called the *Pāñcoṉ Pīr*. This cult combined Hindu and Muslim elements and had the allegiance of members of many castes besides the *Camārs*. The cult of *Pāñcoṉ Pīr* has since been fought both by members of the *Śiva Nārāyaṇ* sect and by the higher-caste members of the Hindu reformist Arya Samaj movement.

III. POSITION OF THE *Camārs* IN MADHOPUR

Because of their low-caste status, *Camārs* are in some senses less a part of the community of Madhopur than are most of the other, higher castes. But the community also incorporates them in certain central ways and could not do without them.

A. CASTE AND SOCIAL STATUS

The status of the *Camār* caste has generally been described as "untouchable." In eastern U.P. they are often dubbed with a vernacular term, "*achūt*," which means just that. Elsewhere, too, their status has been said to be actually untouchable: Bhattacharya says that being touched by a *Camār* requires a good Hindu to bathe with his clothes on (1896: 267). Risley places the *Camārs* of Bengal in the lowest grade of the Hindu social system, among those "whose touch pollutes, whom no Brahman, however degraded will serve, and for whom barber nor washerman will work" (1908: 117). In Madhopur at the present time, however, a *Camār*'s touch does not ordinarily carry defilement to the body of another. When most high-caste persons refer to a *Camār* as "untouchable," they mean only that they cannot take food or water from him, and that his touch will pollute food, water, and the utensils used for food and water. *Camārs* are regarded as defiled especially because of their repugnant traditional occupations of skinning, tanning, and midwifery, and because of their reputation for eating carrion beef.

Since the name "*Camār*" has accumulated abusive connotations, as in the phrases "dirty as a *Camār*," "black as a *Camār*," etc., the *Camārs* of Madhopur prefer to designate themselves by other names. Some *Camārs* call themselves "*Raidāsī*," taking the name of their most famous saint, Raidas. Other *Camārs*, of whom there are many in the next district of Azamgarh, style themselves "*Harijan Ṭhākurs*," literally, "Children of God-" or "Untouchable-Lords." But the *Camārs* of Madhopur prefer to be called by the name of their subcaste, "*Jaisvārā*." According to local reckoning *Jaisvārās* are the highest subcaste of the *Camārs;* they will not take water or food from or marry with any of the other subcastes. Other subcastes of *Camārs* are looked down on by them for doing jobs which *Jaisvārās* will not consider doing. For example, *Jhusiyā Camārs* will carry palanquins and bear heavy burdens on carrying poles. Any *Jaisvārā* who did either of these jobs would be summarily outcasted.

Toward members of higher castes and especially toward *Ṭhākurs* the behavior of *Camārs* shows formal respect and deference. A *Camār* lets a *Ṭhākur* precede him on a path. If he meets a *Ṭhākur* coming toward him on a path, a *Camār* will step off the path, bow, and salute him by folding his hands together. A *Camār* will let a *Ṭhākur* start the conversation even if he goes to a *Ṭhākur*'s house with a specific request. The *Camār*'s inferior social position is shown also in the rules of seating arrangements by which the *Camār* is required to sit on the ground while the *Ṭhākur* sits on a string cot (*cārpāī*). If a *Camār* is seated on a string cot when a *Ṭhākur* passes by, the *Camār* rises until the *Ṭhākur* passes. If the *Ṭhākur* stays to talk with the

Camār, he is given the string cot, and the *Camār* squats on the ground.

Older *Camārs* extend some kinship terminology and behavior to their *Ṭhākurs*. Some address *Ṭhākurs* even of their own age as "father's father" (*bābā*). Older *Camārs* feel that a *Ṭhākur* should receive the same respect as a father or grandfather. One informant, when retelling an incident in which his *Ṭhākur* had beaten him, asked, "How could I have struck him back? He is my *Ṭhākur*, and a *Ṭhākur* is respected like a father." Older *Ṭhākurs* often address their *Camārs* as their "children." *Ṭhākurs* and members of other high castes also formerly used familiar forms of verbs and pronouns in addressing *Camārs*—forms appropriate only for children. Now fewer persons use these forms, and their use is generally resented by *Camārs*.

Camārs' caste-status relations with Brahmans are much like their relations with *Ṭhākurs*. In the use of titles and other polite forms of speech, in differences of dress and in the handling of food, *Camārs*' lower status is constantly symbolized. Even in these matters, however, there are wide variations in the details of behavior depending on the individual *Ṭhākurs*, Brahmans, and *Camārs* who are involved. Thus some high-caste persons say that *Camārs* are forbidden to use the wells from which high-caste persons draw their drinking water; actually *Camārs* do use the drinking-water wells of the higher castes, and little objection is raised.

With castes below the Brahmans and *Ṭhākurs*, *Camārs*' relationships are somewhat less clearly structured. Food, water, and vessels are still kept strictly separate, and a *Camār* is never permitted to enter the kitchen of another caste. If a man of *Lohār* or *Kohār* caste is working at a *Camār*'s house, he will have his own drinking vessel and will draw his own water from the well. But the gaps are less severe among these castes than is the gap between *Camārs* and *Ṭhākurs:* in ordinary day-to-day relations, respect behavior is determined less by caste than by individual identity. An elderly *Camār* who is respected within his own caste may be treated with deference also by some persons of castes higher than the *Camārs*.

There is a potential bond among the *Camārs* and all other low-caste people, no matter what their relative status. They are all low in caste in relation to the *Ṭhākurs:* all are tenants or are in other ways economically dependent upon the *Ṭhākurs*. Friendships exist between people of different low castes, so that occasionally a *Camār* will count a *Noniyā*, a *Kohār*, or a *Kahār* as a close friend. In all but very formal situations they treat each other as equals. It would appear that, although castes stand in a graduated hierarchy, the difference of status between *Ṭhākurs* and all other castes of Madhopur is greater than any differences of status among the low castes themselves.

For the last fifteen years *Camār* children have attended the local primary school. There children of all castes study and play together. But, at the two school dramas which were performed while I was in Madhopur, no *Camār* child was given an acting part.

B. CEREMONIAL STATUS

Camārs occupy a subordinate and partly excluded position in the ceremonial life of Madhopur. They do follow the custom of members of all the higher castes and do separately worship the village gods at times of stress in their own households or hamlets. But they do not join simultaneously with members of the higher castes in all-village rituals such as those held for the propitiation of *Kālī* at times of cholera epidemics. As traditional workers of the families of *Ṭhākurs* and other high castes, the *Camārs* receive food at such festivals as *Holī, Divālī, Makar Saṅkrāntī,* and *Nāg Pañcamī,* but they do not celebrate these festivals on equal terms with members of the other castes. Their role in the annual pageant of the *Rām Līlā* is that of bystanders.

C. ECONOMIC STATUS

Camārs are economically tied to the village, especially to its *Ṭhākurs,* as tenants, as traditional workers, and as laborers.

As the tenant of a *Ṭhākur,* the average *Camār* family cultivates only a little more than one acre of land. (The average *Ṭhākur* family cultivates six times as much.) Out of the total of 107 acres which the *Camārs* cultivate as tenants, only 9 acres are lands on which they hold permanent tenancy rights; on the rest of their tenancy holdings in Madhopur they are temporary tenants-at-will. *Camārs* of Madhopur therefore stood to gain ownership of very little land under the Zamindari Abolition Act effected in 1952. Their only gain was to increase the security of their tenure as tenants-at-will. The grain which the *Camārs* grow by their own cultivation still lasts them on the average for only four months of the year.

The average *Camār* family attaches great subjective importance to any lands which it holds as tenant but depends for a much larger part of its subsistence and for most of the year on the wages which its members receive as laborers. Since *Ṭhākurs* are prohibited by their own caste rules from plowing, every *Ṭhākur* family, no matter how poor, has to employ at least one permanent "plowman," usually a *Camār*. Those *Camār* laborers who are not permanent plowmen generally work as manual laborers by the day in local agriculture. The usual daily wage for agricultural labor in the village is two seers (about four pounds) of grain plus breakfast.

The *Camārs'* traditional work is of less direct economic profit to them than is agricultural labor, but nevertheless it connects them broadly with other villagers. Skinning and tanning are no longer done in Madhopur. *Camārs* are, however, obliged still to cart off the dead animals of their patrons of several castes. *Camār* women also serve as midwives for families of all other castes in the village. In turn, the local *Camārs* are served traditionally by Carpenter-Blacksmiths, Potters, Barbers, and Washermen.

The *Camārs* of Madhopur also function as part of a village economy which for at least two hundred years has been partially integrated with the wider economy of northern India. Outside employment is not a recent phenomenon among *Camārs* of the area: some fought with Clive at Plassey; others have been noted as grooms and servants of British residents; and seventy or eighty years ago large numbers of *Camārs* started to work in the cotton and jute mills, in the mines, and in the cities as coolies and rickshaw-pullers.

The trend toward outside and urban employment has been further accelerated in recent years as land has become scarce in the village. While the village population has steadily risen, the rise of agricultural prices during and after World War II has induced the *Ṭhākurs* of Madhopur themselves to farm more and more of their landlord holdings. Some of the lands which are now being cultivated under personal direction of *Ṭhākurs* is waste land which has been brought only recently under cultivation, but the bulk of it is land from which the landlords have ejected tenants. The increase in population and the resumption of more land by the *Ṭhākurs* have created a steadily deteriorating economic position for the *Camārs* within Madhopur.

Outside employment has gradually increased until in December, 1952, there were thirty-six *Camārs* of Madhopur residing and working outside the village. With the exception of two or three families which have sufficient land, every *Camār* household at one time or another sends members out to work in the cities. Although there is much temporary geographic mobility of *Camārs* from the village to the city, over the last three generations only one family of *Camārs* from Madhopur is known to have settled permanently in a city.

D. POLITICAL STATUS

Until the middle of the nineteenth century the *Ṭhākurs*, as landlords, were *de facto* rulers, judges, and arbitrators for the *Camārs*, for the village of Madhopur, and for the whole taluka of Dobhi. Each of the twelve hereditary divisions of the taluka was led by a chief (*sarganā*)—a man noted for his honesty and wisdom, who could influence people through these characteristics and through his economic and social power. The twelve chiefs met as a panchayat to discuss matters of interest to the *Ṭhākurs* themselves and to the taluka, and to arbitrate disputes of every nature that might arise within or between any of the 110 villages of the taluka. The panchayat members, knowing the villages and the villagers intimately and priding themselves on their own integrity, could find the facts, make honest decisions, and enforce their decisions. Their penalties included fines, banishment, and—in the case of *Ṭhākur* offenders—outcasting. Decisions of this panchayat of chiefs were not subject to appeal before any higher authority. Up until 1906 not a single case went up to a British-established court from Dobhi Taluka, once a final decision had been given by this panchayat of chiefs.

Beneath the taluka and within Madhopur itself, four or five *Ṭhākurs* were usually recognized by all castes as informal headmen (*caudharīs*) of the whole village. Occasionally these informal headmen sat together as a village panchayat. They tended to be selected from leading families in each of the six *Ṭhākur* lineages, which were simultaneously sections for land management. The actual selection of informal headmen shifted over the years along with changing economic fortunes and changing personalities in the several lineages. Behind each informal headman and his family was the physical power of those tenants and servants who could be depended upon to follow him, with quarter-staff in hand, if necessary. Either through fear, through satisfaction with the system, or through ignorance of alternative systems, *Camārs* and other low-caste people were quiet and followed the political leadership of their *Ṭhākur* landlords. Through their respective caste panchayats, too, people of the lower castes handled some of their own crimes and disputes, aided by their control of the fearsome sanction of outcasting.

The picture which I have described thus far of nineteenth-century political organization is a somewhat idealized one. The panchayat of chiefs and the government of informal headmen in the village did not always function well. There was no lack of rivalry, jealousy, and friction. The bane of Indian villages, factionalism, did exist in the nineteenth century, and there were fights, killings, and house burnings, usually involving land and arguments over land. Jonathan Duncan, British Resident in nearby Banaras from 1787 to 1795, reports that intravillage fights and bloodshed were common even in his day (Shakespear 1873, I: 47). Given the organization of the village and of the landholding system, fights in the village over land were almost inevitable. Relatives held land jointly, so that divisions often fell between brothers, cousins, or other agnatic kin.

From the early part of the nineteenth century there existed alongside this informal structure of power a formal, semihereditary village administration of dual nature. There was, first, the land revenue administration contacting the village, as described above, through the revenue headman of each *Ṭhākur* lineage. Appointments of these revenue headmen were confirmed by the district magistrate. Imposed on top of this village revenue administration there was, second, the police administration of the village, answerable to the subinspector of police and operating through an appointed police headman (*mukhya*), who was usually one of the revenue headmen.

An attempt was made in the twentieth century to introduce a formal system of local self-government through the appointment of official village panchayats by the district magistrate. In Madhopur this appointed panchayat consisted of three *Ṭhākurs*, one *Ahīr*, and one *Noniyā*. It was effectively dominated by the families of the *Ṭhākurs*, and thus failed to provide representative government for the village. It had little effect on the traditional structure of power.

Not until after 1906 did that plague of lawsuits begin in Dobhi Taluka which is so typical of modern Indian villages. As more and more *Ṭhākurs* learned the written law and learned how to manipulate the outside legal system, they turned more and more to the British-established courts to pursue their interests rather than compromising them through traditional means nearer home. When people learned that there were outside legal agencies to which they could turn and which could enforce decisions through the official revenue and police administration, the traditional panchayats of the village and of the taluka began to wither.

Until recent years, however, most *Camārs* have remained very much under the control of their *Ṭhākurs*, and most continue to identify their own interests closely with those of their Lords and of the *Ṭhākurs* of Madhopur in general. The *Ṭhākurs* of Madhopur protect the *Camārs* of Madhopur from the *Ṭhākurs* of other villages, from the police, and from any other outside interference. A *Ṭhākur* of

Madhopur will become incensed if a *Ṭhākur* of another village comes to Madhopur and tries to hire or to discipline a local *Camār*. Even though a *Camār* may feel that he is abused and exploited in Madhopur, still he feels deeply that Madhopur is his village and that it will remain his home no matter where he goes. This feeling of identification with the village was exemplified by one *Camār* whom I questioned about a despised form of marriage: "We are the *Camārs* of Madhopur and we wouldn't do a thing like that," he said.

IV. RECENT CHANGE

By the early part of the twentieth century the seeds of social change had been extensively sown: a railroad had been built near Madhopur, affording wider geographic mobility; boys had left the village to go to colleges and universities; the official courts settled more and more village disputes; the Arya Samaj movement of religious reform grew strong; elections brought political competition on a wider scale; and the nationalist struggle became a reality for the villagers. Along with these outside influences, population in the village and surrounding area steadily rose. Because of strains on the village economy, more and more residents from all castes began to seek work in the cities. Family structure, political behavior, attitudes toward caste status, and religious customs have all undergone notable change. All these happenings are summed up by the remark often heard in the village, "A new wind is blowing."

A. CHANGE IN FAMILY STRUCTURE

The *Ṭhākurs* of Madhopur, and following them at some distance the *Camārs*, have been slowly reshaping their respective family structures. Among the *Ṭhākurs*, family ties have grown looser and the importance of clan and village has declined. *Ṭhākurs* are tending to move in the direction of less formality and respect for the father, more freedom between husband and wife, and smaller household units. The stimuli of Western education and urban living have been strongly felt among them.

The small changes in family structure that can be noted among the *Camārs*, especially among *Camārs* who have attained some education, are not changes in the direction of a Western-influenced family but changes in the direction of a more orthodox "Hindu" family. *Camārs* are trying to tighten the authority of the father and place restrictions on the wife. While the *Ṭhākur* wife is coming out of seclusion, the *Camār* wife is being put into seclusion. The *Ṭhākur* model for the family appears to be influenced by the urban, Western family, while the *Camār* model is based on the family of the *Ṭhākurs* fifty years ago. A similar chronological sequence and typological discrepancy is evident between *Ṭhākur* and *Camār* models for caste observances, religion, food habits, and many other aspects of social life.

B. POLITICAL CHANGES

The twentieth century saw the breakup of the *Ṭhākur* panchayats which had once dominated both the village of Madhopur and the whole taluka of Dobhi. The decline of these panchayats may be related to changes throughout the whole social fabric, but may be attributed particularly to changes in the prestige system of the *Ṭhākurs* and in the formal superstructure of government.

Since 1900 more and more *Ṭhākurs* had begun to derive incomes and prestige from working outside the village as teachers, police inspectors, printers, and businessmen rather than from the traditional sources of landownership and from agnatic and affinal family ties. Such externally oriented persons were much less at the mercy of the sanctioning pressures which any rural panchayats could apply. Outcasting lost its sting for the *Ṭhākurs,* for an outcaste *Ṭhākur* family could with increasing ease make marriage alliances with other outcaste families or with families in good standing whose desire to establish marriage ties with a *Raghubaṉśī* family outweighed their scruples about the stigma of outcasting. The legal, economic, and prestige structures of the village and taluka were ceasing to exist as a closed and integrated system, but the *Ṭhākurs* were at the same time learning how to exercise their power at new and higher levels. The higher administrators, if they are not *Ṭhākurs* themselves, tend to be of high caste and often of landowning backgrounds, so that their sympathies generally lie with landlords rather than with tenants.

While the authority of *Ṭhākur* panchayats began to grow weaker, caste organization among the *Camārs* if anything grew stronger. As patron-client and landlord-tenant ties have weakened, *Camārs* have come to depend more upon themselves for the settlement of their own disputes. *Camārs* have also grown more sensitive about their collective good name. It was a commonplace a generation ago for a *Ṭhākur* man to have sexual relations with a *Camār* woman. This still occurs, but the caste is now trying to punish offenders. Eating and drinking restrictions for the *Camārs* have been tightened and are strictly enforced. Although *Camārs* formerly would eat with and take water from other untouchables, they now punish such acts by outcasting. As the *Camār* caste has grown stronger, outcasting by the *Camār* panchayat has actually become more frequent.

The beginnings of elections, first for the District Board in the twenties, later for the legislative positions of the provincial and central governments in the thirties, helped further to weaken the *Ṭhākurs*' local and taluka panchayats, while they gave still further stimulus to action by *Camārs* and other lower castes.

District boards had been set up in India in the eighties to give the people some small measure of self-government. The initial electorates for these boards were very small, however, and many members of the boards were either officials or appointees of officials. Only in the twenties, when elective representation was increased, did there begin to be competition among some of the Dobhi *Ṭhākurs* for election to positions on the Jaunpur District Board. To secure votes, candidates had to promise help and support to factions among the chiefs of the Dobhi Taluka panchayat. Both the *Ṭhākurs* who were candidates and the chiefs of the panchayat who were allied with them lost their reputations for honesty and impartiality in these elections. Like outside employment and litigation, election to the District Board offered an extravillage and extrataluka source of power and prestige. Members had control of rural education, sanitation, and roads as well as access to higher government officials whom they could influence to the advantage of themselves and their friends and supporters. Village and taluka panchayats became small matters by comparison, and fell into desuetude.

Provincial elections in 1937, which were won by the Congress party after an intensive political campaign, helped to stimulate subsequent political action by tenants against the *Ṭhākurs* of Madhopur. Although the electorate was closely limited by criteria of property and education, a few low-caste people were entitled to vote. One of these was a *Noniyā*, who not only voted but also actively supported the Congress candidate. The *Noniyā* was an exceptional individual. As a boy, he had struggled to get himself an education through the eighth grade. He put his education to use by learning and studying the land laws. He quickly realized that, even before the formation of a Congress ministry, the permanent tenants had possessed guaranteed rights which the *Ṭhākurs* were ignoring. The tenants were so cowed and were kept in such a state of ignorance by the *Ṭhākurs* that the more powerful and clever *Ṭhākurs* could successfully evict even tenants who had legal right to permanency. The *Noniyā* first defended his own lands against seizure by the *Ṭhākurs* and then began to advise the other *Noniyās*, as well as the *Camārs* who lived near the *Noniyā* hamlet, as to their rights.

Not long after the elections, in 1938 the *Camārs* made their first large-scale attack upon the *Ṭhākurs'* position of power. They did so by supporting some *Noniyās* rather than their own *Ṭhākurs* in a dispute over land. This alliance of *Noniyās* and *Camārs* gave one of the first indications of the growing solidarity of the lower castes in opposition to the *Ṭhākurs*. To punish them for joining the *Noniyās*, the *Ṭhākurs* decided to prevent the rebellious *Camārs* from sowing their winter crop. A gang of *Ṭhākurs* went to the fields where the *Camārs* were working, drove off their cattle, beat the *Camārs*, and then went to the *Camārs'* hamlet where they ripped down the thatched roofs of the *Camārs'* houses.

The *Camārs* held council with the *Noniyā* who was their ally. He advised them to complain directly to the district magistrate in Jaunpur, while he himself wrote letters on their behalf to various officials in Lucknow, the state capital. The *Camārs*, preparing for a difficult siege, took their cattle and all that they could carry of their belongings and went to Jaunpur. There the District Congress Committee fed and housed them. The *Camārs* immediately hired a lawyer to prosecute the *Ṭhākurs* who had beaten them.

The *Ṭhākurs* of Madhopur supposed that the beaten *Camārs* had simply run off to another village. When word reached them of the *Camārs'* legal and political action, they were thunderstruck. A few of the more influential *Ṭhākurs* went at once to Banaras, where they contacted a relative who was an employee in the courts. Through him they were able to reach the officials in Jaunpur who would deal directly with the case which the *Camārs* were bringing against them. The *Ṭhākurs* were successful in having the case delayed and then in having it taken out of the courts in Jaunpur and sent to the more pliable subdistrict officer's court in Kerakat. The *Ṭhākurs* next bribed the police subinspector of Kerakat to delay his report to that court for several months. Meanwhile, the court ordered that no one must cultivate the land in dispute in order to prevent further trouble. During all this time the *Camārs* had to pay a lawyer, court fees, and other expenses, while they were deprived of income from their cultivation. After more than six months of postponements, the *Camārs* agreed to a compromise with the *Ṭhākurs*. They dropped their case against the *Ṭhākurs*, took back their lands, and obtained a written guarantee from the *Ṭhākurs* that the *Ṭhākurs* would not beat them.

The *Ṭhākurs* had nevertheless caused the *Camārs* great loss by attrition.

The "Quit India" movement in 1942 and the independence agitation of 1946–47 reached the village of Madhopur and even touched the *Camārs*. These political actions were but distractions, however, from the *Camārs*' own drive for power.

The next principal episode in the *Camārs*' struggle and their second major defeat came about after the passing of the U.P. Panchayat Raj Act of 1947. Under this act, which replaced the previous official, appointed panchayat, a village council (gaon sabha) and a rural court (panchayati adalat) were to be elected by universal adult suffrage. The village council, with thirty-six members, was to take over a large number of local governmental powers and responsibilities regarding land, sanitation, roadways, rationing, etc. The rural court was to try all minor cases from Madhopur and from several nearby villages.

Elections for these new panchayats in 1948 provided the occasion for the first successful organization of all the lower castes of Madhopur against the *Ṭhākurs*. The party of the lower castes was called the "Tenant [*Prajā*] party." Its leadership was provided by an *Ahīr*, a Brahman who had been a political thug, a *Kāndū* who had lived many years in Bombay, a *Telī* who prided himself on his part in the independence movement, and the *Noniyā* who had stimulated previous legal action against the *Ṭhākurs*. Several of the lower castes were brought into the Tenant party by their own caste headmen. Secret meetings were then held in the *Camār* hamlets. When protection was promised them against possible reprisals by the *Ṭhākurs*, the *Camārs* joined the party wholeheartedly. Some *Ṭhākurs* even associated themselves with the Tenant party from the beginning, partly through friendship with its Brahman leader and partly through a desire to strike back at old enemies within their own caste.

As the time for the panchayat elections drew near, the *Ṭhākurs* who had been the traditional leaders of the village saw that the Tenant party controlled the bulk of the electorate. The influential *Ṭhākur* who had been the chairman of the old appointed panchayat declined to stand at all in the election lest he be defeated. Other influential *Thākurs* likewise withdrew from candidacy. In a final gesture of dissociation, the majority of the *Ṭhākurs* refused even to vote against the Tenant majority.

The lower castes' Tenant party thus succeeded in electing both a village council and a rural court made up wholly of its own candidates or sympathizers. *Camārs* were elected to both bodies. The traditional village leadership of the *Ṭhākurs* had been completely routed from formal control of Madhopur. What was more, the Tenant party's strength and its connections with the district Congress party at first prevented the *Ṭhākurs* from moving directly against it.

After its initial success in winning the panchayat elections, however, the Tenant party rapidly declined in power and organization. The viilage council whose offices had been won proved unwieldy. Ordinances which the council passed to promote cleaning of the village paths, proper drainage, and removal of manure piles could not be made effective because of the opposition of the traditional leaders who were *Ṭhākurs* and of persons of other high castes. An attempt by *Camārs* to force compliance by court action proved too expensive. The village council found itself unable even to collect its own tax. Its meetings, scheduled to be held monthly, became less and less frequent. The Tenant party was disrupted through the bribing of some of its leaders, and through lawsuits brought against its members individually by certain *Ṭhākurs*. The low castes, and particularly the *Camārs*, lacked the economic base for a long-term fight against the *Ṭhākurs*, on whom they were dependent for a livelihood. The final act in the dissolution of the Tenant party was the murder of one of its leaders by a *Ṭhākur*.

Thus, although the *Camārs* found that with their allies they could elect a village government and for a short time could even coerce the upper castes, they found also that they could not sustain themselves in a position of effective dominance. Today, political solidarity among the lower castes of Madhopur has vanished, and there is much discouragement.

C. EFFORTS TO RAISE SOCIAL STATUS

For the last thirty years the *Camārs* of Madhopur have struggled consciously to raise their status on another, related front—that of the caste hierarchy—but with scarcely greater outward success than they achieved on the political front.

At least two generations ago *Jaisvārā Camārs* in the vicinity of Madhopur began to outlaw the eating of beef and the carting of manure in what proved a futile attempt to gain greater respect for the caste. Previously *Camārs* had been thought degraded because of their eating of carrion beef; they often had been accused of poisoning cattle in order to obtain the meat. Somewhat more than thirty years ago, beef eating was banned by the *Camārs*. Although some *Ṭhākurs* suspect that a few *Camār* women still eat beef, *Camārs* maintain that beef eaters would be outcasted immediately. Thirty years ago, in opposition to their own *Ṭhākurs*, some *Camārs* of Madhopur declared also that they would no longer carry manure to the *Ṭhākurs*' fields. They were compelled to leave the village to escape the *Ṭhākurs*' wrath. When ultimately these *Camārs* were permitted to return to the village and were excused from the manure work which they had perceived as degrading, *Camār* women in general took a further step: they refused any longer to make dung cakes for the *Ṭhākurs*' households. Ultimately, they, too, secured a grudging acquiescence from the *Ṭhākurs*. As for inspiring greater respect from the higher castes, such changes of caste behavior receive at best passive recognition, certainly not approval. The gain to the *Camārs* from these changes has been chiefly a gain in the vital dimension of self-respect.

Camārs are not alone in trying to elevate their caste status. Fifteen years ago representatives of most of the *Bhars* of Kerakat Tahsil met to plan ways to raise their status. Several educated *Bhars* who were government officials addressed the meeting and told them that they were lowly and despised because they raised pigs. The *Bhars* gave up pig-raising, yet it is difficult to say that they have improved their status in the eyes of other castes. They are still regarded as "untouchable," although they are held in better regard than are the *Khaṭīks* and *Pāsīs* of the area, who still herd swine.

Other castes have made more extreme efforts to raise their status. Fifteen years ago the *Noniyās* of Madhopur went so far as to put on the sacred thread and call themselves by their long-claimed title of "*Cauhān Rājpūts*." Their action was met with violence by the Lords of the village, who beat the *Noniyās*, broke their threads, and threatened further violence if the act was repeated. Five years ago the *Noniyās* again put on their sacred threads, this time without overt reaction on the part of the Lords. Now the *Ahīrs* and the *Lohārs* of Madhopur also wear the thread of the twice-born, the *Ahīrs* calling themselves "*Yādav Rājpūts*" and the *Lohārs* claiming to be "*Viśvakarmā Brāhmaṇs*." *Camārs* in nearby villages of Jaunpur District and also in Azamgarh District have started wearing sacred threads, calling themselves "*Harijan Ṭhākurs*," but so far the *Camārs* of Madhopur have not joined them.

Such attempts by *Camārs* to raise their caste status are not individual in character or effect, nor are they necessarily legislated by large, formal gatherings. Rather, a leader or group of leaders in the caste in one village may feel that some traditional behavior should be changed, and the change is talked over in the village. Relatives and others who are visiting hear about the proposed change and carry the news to their home villages. If a local group of *Camārs* decides to initiate the change, it decrees that any *Camār* who fails to conform to the new pattern will be outcasted. Active propagandizing follows from the initiating village or villages. Ultimately, the initiating *Camārs* determine that they will no longer give daughters to or accept daughters-in-law from *Camārs* who do not conform to the change.

While the *Camārs* are becoming stricter about their habits of diet, dress, and occupation, the higher castes are becoming less strict. *Camārs* have become very sensitive about such matters as accepting food from castes whom they consider to be their inferiors, while at the same time some of the *Ṭhākurs* are relaxing their conformity to commensal prohibitions. Younger *Camārs* are less prone to give outward signs of respect to *Ṭhākurs*, and the younger *Ṭhākurs* seem to expect such signs less.

Quite apart from changes in traditional symbols of caste status, modern secular education is playing a central role in *Camārs'* efforts to improve their position. *Camārs* constantly verbalize a desire for more education, and many attribute their low position to a lack of education. But those two *Camārs* who have achieved the most education—the two *Camār* schoolteachers—have not been accorded the full degree of respect which is granted to teachers of higher caste. Teachers of higher caste are called "Master" (*Māsṭar*), while these *Camār* teachers are merely called "Writer" (*Muṇśī*). Teachers of higher caste are given a string cot or chair to sit on when they visit a *Ṭhākur*'s house, while these *Camār* teachers are given instead a stool or an overturned basket only—a better seat, however, than the floor, which is the only place for an uneducated *Camār*. One of these schoolteachers is among the leaders who are most actively attempting to make *Camār* behavior accord more with the traditional behavior of the higher castes. Education is an individual achievement, but even educated *Camārs* cannot escape an awareness that mobility for them, too, must be a group phenomenon.

D. RELIGIOUS CHANGES

Consistent with efforts to raise their caste status and to gain power, the *Camārs* of Madhopur have in recent years also made conscious efforts to suppress their distinctive traditional religion, to Sanskritize their rituals still further, and to emulate the specific religious forms of the higher castes. Although they continue to propitiate the goddess *Bhagautī* jointly in ceremonies of the whole hamlet, and although they continue to worship the other village deities as do members of higher castes, yet they have made many changes in the rest of their religious practice. *Camār* schoolteachers, leading families, and especially members of the *Śiva Nārāyaṇ* sect, rather than the traditional *Camār* panchayat, have been the principal agents of these changes. At the same time that the *Camārs* are becoming more concerned with the forms of their religion, however, many persons of the upper castes, most notably the *Ṭhākurs*, are being drawn into a more secular culture.

Domestic ceremonies of the *Camārs* have been modeled increasingly upon domestic ceremonies of the *Ṭhākurs* and Brahmans, especially under the influence of leaders and devotees of the *Śiva Nārāyaṇ* sect. The sacrifice of a pig which formerly began the *Camār* wedding ceremony has now been given up and replaced by the cutting of a nutmeg. The practice of giving dowry has been introduced, although the boy's father still gives a token payment to the girl's father: here the transition between bride price and dowry can be seen in progress. *Camār* weddings have now been lengthened from one day to three days, so as to resemble Brahman weddings. A Brahman priest now conducts every ceremony of the wedding except the final rites. While *Ṭhākurs* now marry at higher ages, *Camārs* are marrying at lower ages: *Camārs* of Madhopur now marry at from five to seven years of age, whereas they had previously married at from twelve to sixteen years of age. Horoscopes are now cast by Brahmans for *Camār* babies at the ceremony of naming, and death rituals have been altered in several ways so as to conform more closely with the practices of the higher castes. Adherence to the cult of *Pāñcoṉ Pīr* has been eliminated. A new emphasis on pilgrimages has helped to Sanskritize *Camār* religion even more fully. If the older cult of *Śiva Nārāyaṇ* may be said to have paralleled Sanskritic religion, recent changes have moved *Camār* religion directly toward the main stream of the great tradition of orthodox Hinduism.

Parts of the religious ideology of the *Śiva Nārāyaṇ* sect recently have been fused with the social and political aspirations of the *Camārs* in annual celebrations of the birthday of the *Camār* saint, Raidas, in the month of *Māgh* (January–February). Educated *Camārs* have played an important part in the revival and transformation of these birthday celebrations. In 1953 the procession and meeting were organized by a *Camār* member of the Legislative Assembly, by several of the *Camār* schoolteachers in the area of Madhopur, and by *Camār* students from Ganesh Rai Intermediate College and from the Banaras Hindu University. *Camārs* from all of Dobhi Taluka attended the celebration. The speakers, who included a *Ṭhākur* schoolteacher, spoke of Raidas as a saint and pointed out the *Camārs*' contribution to the culture and religion of India. Several of the speakers used Raidas as an example of a *Camār* who, through leading a "good life," gained the respect of the rest of the community. Other speakers used the opportunity to preach political action to the *Camārs*. Saints and devotees such as Raidas are important to the *Camārs* because they reaffirm the *Camārs*' belief that members of their caste at one time were the equals or in some senses the superiors of the Brahmans and other high castes. The stories reaffirm the belief that it is not a person's caste status but his devotion that counts.

V. SUMMARY

The *Camārs* of Madhopur, like many other peoples of the Indian subcontinent, are in the midst of processes of change. These processes of change are complex and even contradictory. While the *Camārs* are organizing and fighting for social, political, and economic equality with the higher castes, they are also trying to borrow and to revive for themselves elements of a culture that the higher castes are shedding. As the higher castes of Madhopur become secularized and are increasingly drawn into an urban economy and culture, the *Camārs* seem to be trying not only to benefit by the loosening of some old restrictions but also to buttress their own position by adapting these old restrictions to new uses.

REFERENCES CITED

BHANDARKAR, R. G.
1913 *Vaisnavism, Saivism and Minor Religious Systems.* Grundriss der Indo-Arischen Philologie und Altertumskunde, ed. GEORG BÜHLER, III Band, 6 Heft. Strassburg, Trübner.

BHATTACHARYA, JOGENDRANATH
1896 *Hindu Castes and Sects.* Calcutta, Thacker, Spink.

BRIGGS, GEORGE W.
1920 *The Chamārs.* Calcutta, Association Press.

CROOKE, WILLIAM
1896 *The Tribes and Castes of the North-Western Provinces and Oudh.* 4 vols. Calcutta, Superintendent of Government Printing.

FARQUHAR, JOHN N.
1920 *An Outline of the Religious Literature of India.* London, H. Milford, Oxford University Press.

GRIERSON, GEORGE A.

1909–10 "Gleanings from the Bhakta-mala," *Journal of the Royal Asiatic Society* 1909: 607–44; 1910: 87–109. London.

1919 "Rai Dāsīs," in *Encyclopedia of Religion and Ethics*, ed. JAMES HASTINGS, Vol. 10, pp. 560–61. New York, Charles Scribner's Sons.

1921 "Śiva Nārāyaṇīs," in *Encyclopedia of Religion and Ethics*, ed. JAMES HASTINGS, Vol. 11, p. 579. New York, Charles Scribner's Sons.

MACAULIFFE, MAX ARTHUR

1909 *The Sikh Religion*. 6 vols. Oxford, Clarendon Press.

NEVILL, H. R.

1908 *Jaunpur: A Gazetteer*. District Gazetteers of the United Provinces of Agra and Oudh **28**. Allahabad, Government Press.

OPLER, MORRIS E. and RUDRA DATT SINGH

1948 "The Division of Labor in an Indian Village," in *A Reader in General Anthropology*, ed. C. S. COON, pp. 464–96. New York, Henry Holt.

1952*a* "Two Villages of Eastern Uttar Pradesh (U.P.), India: An Analysis of Similarities and Differences," *American Anthropologist* **54**:179–90. Menasha, Wisconsin.

1952*b* "Economic, Political and Social Change in a Village of North Central India," *Human Organization* **11**:5–12. New York.

RISLEY, HERBERT H.

1908 *The People of India*. Calcutta, Thacker, Spink.

SHAKESPEAR, ALEXANDER (ed.)

1873 *Selections from the Duncan Records*. 2 vols. Banaras, Medical Hall Press.

SRINIVAS, M. N.

1952 *Religion and Society among the Coorgs of South India*. Oxford, Clarendon Press.

TARA CHAND

1946 *The Influence of Islam on Indian Culture*. Allahabad, Indian Press.

WILSON, HORACE H.

1861–62 *Essays and Lectures on the Religions of the Hindus*, ed. REINHOLD ROST. 2 vols. London, Trübner.

INTERPLAY AMONG FACTORS OF CHANGE IN A MYSORE VILLAGE[1]

ALAN R. BEALS

BANGALORE, the largest city in Mysore State, is a major center of foreign and urban influence in southern India. The city's streets are crowded by nearly 800,000 people speaking many different languages. In its motion-picture theaters epics written in Kannada, the regional language, compete with Tamil, Sanskrit, and Hindi epics, and with stories drawn from Muslim and Christian holy books. A candy store run by Sindhis may be found between a Chinese restaurant and an American-style milk bar. On the sidewalks tribesmen carrying bows and arrows are jostled by pedigreed Guernsey and Holstein cows. In one corner of the city a statue of Queen Victoria gazes uncomprehendingly down Mahatma Gandhi Road.

Bangalore City is a changing confusion of cultures with an influence radiating over many miles of rural Mysore. Acts and regulations of the state government in Bangalore affect the economic and social life of villagers 150 miles away. The city's insatiable demand for firewood brings a livelihood to villagers in distant forests. Buses, motor trucks, and railroads carry thousands of villagers to Bangalore every day. Many of them leave with urban gimcracks in their shopping bags and new ideas in their heads. Millions regard Bangalore as the cultural, economic, and political center of their world. It is the place where all roads lead.

An hour's bus ride from the shops and factories of Bangalore is a rural village which I shall call *Nāmhaḷḷi* (cf. Beals 1953, 1954*a*, *b*). Although most people who live in Namhalli continue to work in agriculture or in a related occupation, growing external and urban influences over the last one hundred and fifty years have been sufficient to change almost every aspect of Namhalli's way of life. This

1. This paper is based on field work in Namhalli from May, 1952, to January, 1953, and from March to August, 1953. Field work was supported by the Social Science Research Council. Writing was undertaken in association with the India Village Studies Project of the Institute of East Asiatic Studies, University of California, Berkeley. Grateful acknowledgment is made to the Department of Anthropology, University of California, Berkeley, for assistance during writing, and to Prof. David G. Mandelbaum and Dr. McKim Marriott for their comments.

paper attempts to describe and to explain the interplay of these influences upon the social and economic life of one village.

One of the problems encountered in attempting to explain what has happened in Namhalli is that of relating external influences to internal changes. Typically, a wide variety of changes in Namhalli has been paralleled by an equally wide variety of changes in the external situation. Changes in the caste system of Namhalli, for example, have occurred congruently with many aspects of urban development, including changes in the school curriculum, the introduction of motion pictures, and improvements in transportation. Specific changes in the village are usually the result of complex external pressures; it is rarely possible to infer that a particular external influence has stimulated a particular internal change.

A more fruitful approach is to examine the changing interrelationships of the external factors over a period of time. Study of the interplay of external factors reveals the development of external stresses or crises which are followed by comparatively rapid changes within the village.

The problem of relating changes in Namhalli to the influence of external factors is further complicated by the paucity of reliable data concerning Namhalli's history. Documents concerning Namhalli itself are limited to a few censuses and land records made at intervals over the last fifty years. Moreover, most of these documents were prepared by untrained village officials and cannot be accepted at their face value. I obtained further information from accounts given by elderly villagers in 1953. This material ranges from mythological, for the period between 1800 and 1876, to half-remembered, for the period between 1876 and World War I, and to reasonably well-remembered for the period following World War I. Less specific materials dealing with changes in the political and social life of Mysore State as a whole are to be found in a few histories, autobiographical accounts, and government records.

I. CHANGE-PRODUCING FACTORS

Although the British conquered Mysore in 1799, rapid changes do not appear to have begun until after the inauguration of the "regulation" system of government in 1860. Before 1860, administrators had regarded themselves as caretakers and had avoided altering local customs. After 1860, administrators sought to introduce sweeping social reforms (Shama Rao 1936, I: 513–14). The regulation system had as its goals the introduction of "modern" techniques of law enforcement and civil government. It sought to increase the revenues of the government by reorganizing administrative systems and by stimulating economic production.

The regulation system, together with other Western influences, induced a pattern of consistent changes in Mysore State. These changes included (1) continued expansion of the authority of the state government at the expense of local and traditional systems of authority; (2) expansion and improvement of systems of transportation, communication, and trade; (3) development of urban manufacturing, trading, and political centers; (4) diffusion of European-style systems of education, public health and welfare; (5) rapid increase of population, continuing a pattern established in 1800; and (6) increasing emphasis on a cash economy.

These external changes include many of the factors of change within Namhalli. The first four factors listed are what might be called "developmental" or "growth" factors. The city and the government have grown larger and more complicated over the years. At times their growth has slowed and at times their influence upon the village has decreased, but their positive Westernizing or modernizing aspects have always been present. With only minor exceptions in the years following 1860, the government has grown increasingly complicated and has employed an increasing number of people; transportation has consistently improved; and Bangalore has steadily increased in size.

To some extent population growth has paralleled these other developmental factors, but with less consistency. Widespread depopulation occurred in Mysore shortly before 1800, and again in 1876–78 and in 1918–19. The effects of fluctuating population will be considered later.

The sixth factor listed above, increasing emphasis on a cash economy, is intended to include factors of deflation and inflation which influence the ability of the villager to purchase urban goods and services. This factor does not vary consistently with population growth or with the first four factors. There is an over-all pattern of increase in the cash value of agricultural produce relative to the cash value of urban goods and services, but this increase is by no means steady. From time to time the villager has found himself partially excluded from the urban cash economy and compelled to purchase locally made goods by means of barter. The interplay among population growth, inflation, and the first four factors mentioned has an interesting relationship to the rate, periodicity, and direction of culture change in Namhalli.

II. NAMHALLI: 1800–1876

Between 1800 and 1876 Namhalli was comparatively unaffected by the external influences described above. The village appears to have been founded shortly after 1800 by a *Jaṅgama* (a member of the priestly caste of the *Liṅgāyat* sect) who had come from a neighboring village. Although the recent origin of Namhalli should be taken into account in any comparisons made between it and other villages, such recency of origin is probably not exceptional in Mysore. The wars between Mysore and England, which ended in 1799, had produced widespread disorder and depopulation in the state, and the estimated population of two million in 1800 may have represented a reduction of one-half (Rice 1897, I: 218). Villages in the path of invading or defending armies had been destroyed and large areas virtually deserted (Buchanan 1807, I: 271). A ruined settlement at the site of modern Namhalli indicates that the same area had been occupied before the wars.

The reoccupation of Namhalli can be explained in terms of the government land-revenue policy of the period. Until 1830 Mysore was governed by a puppet government composed of Mysoreans. The government was required to pay an annual "subsidy" to the British and was therefore under pressure to expand the acreage of cultivated lands. To accomplish this, the government introduced the *śarat*, or auction system of revenue collection (Shama Rao 1936, I: 409–11). Under this system the revenue to be paid on portions of land ranging in size from villages to districts was determined annually by competitive bidding. It can be assumed that the *Jaṅgama* who founded Namhalli had made a successful bid for the privilege of collecting revenue from what had previously been waste lands. As the local collector of revenue, he would have been given the position of village headman (*paṭēl*) and a commission on the revenues he collected.

When the auctioning of village revenues was abandoned in 1830 in favor of a return to the traditional system of revenue collection (Shama Rao 1936, I: 478), it is probable that the *Jaṅgama* retained his position as headman. Under the traditional system of revenue collection, the position of headman was hereditary. Each year the headman, the accountant (*śānabhōg*), and a government representative from outside the village negotiated with the farmers and determined the total acreage of land to be cultivated. Harvested grain was piled in a heap and divided among the farmer, various village officials and servants, and the state government. Usually, the share of the state government amounted to one-third of the harvest less portions of grain given to village and provincial officials. The farmer usually netted one-third of the harvested grain. Sometimes grain was sold by the headman, and cash, rather than grain, was paid into the government treasury. Under such conditions the cash tax paid by the headman was dependent upon the quantity of grain collected.

Under both the auction system and the traditional system of collecting land revenue, the headman was important as a mediator between the villager and the state government. The headman's position did not depend upon landownership per se, although British officials sometimes referred to the headman as a "landlord." For at least one hundred years after the British conquest, land was available to almost anyone who wanted it. Hence landownership was far less important than was the ability to procure farmers to plow the land and capital to purchase bullocks and grain. The role of the headman was to bring together capital and labor. The headman purchased protection from bandits and from rapacious government officials and offered financial credit for the maintenance of resident agriculturalists and for the attraction of immigrants.

For example, suppose that Basappa, a young man of good caste, finds the dry climate and the many bandits of Kolar District oppressive and comes to live with his brother-in-law in Namhalli. Basappa would receive support and assistance from his brother-in-law, but his brother-in-law would be unable to supply him with plow bullocks and seed. If the headman were favorably impressed with Basappa's character, Basappa might obtain a gift of grain and sufficient cash to purchase a pair of bullocks. In April or May, when arrangements were being made to cultivate the village lands, Basappa would offer to cultivate and pay revenue upon a "plow" (about five acres) of land. Before cultivating his own land, Basappa and other villagers would cultivate certain lands for the benefit of the headman. And after the harvest, if it can be assumed that conditions in Namhalli paralleled those in certain mountain villages which I observed in 1952, Basappa and other villagers would deposit all surplus grain with the headman. He would use this grain to pay the revenue assessment of the village, and also to contribute to the costs of marriages, festivals, bribes, and the support of his own family.

An immigrant of poor social standing, who had no relatives or belonged to a low-ranking caste, might not obtain credit or undertake cultivation with such ease. Immigrants of this sort would probably become *jīta* servants. Under the *jīta* system, a servant was given a certain sum of money, clothing, and food. In exchange the servant farmed land for the headman. After a period of service, the headman was expected to arrange a marriage for the servant and, if the servant belonged to an agricultural caste and had made a favorable impression in the village, to permit him to farm lands of his own. Most *jīta* servants appear to have belonged to the *Mādiga* caste (traditionally laborers and serfs), and few were permitted to become landowners.

The history of Namhalli between 1800 and 1876 would appear to have been one of gradual development along essentially traditional lines. The village probably started as a one-household settlement consisting of the headman and his family and servants. Members of cultivating castes and of various servant and artisan castes gradually moved in until the village had a full complement of cultivators, Blacksmiths, Washermen, Barbers, Shepherds, Weavers, and other servants. At that point, the village could have been regarded as an extension of a single family—that of the headman. Nearly all the families in the village were economically dependent upon the headman, and nearly all regarded him as their benefactor, "the mother of the village."

III. EARLY CRISES AND ALTERED INFLUENCES: 1876–1900

The famine of 1876–78 marks the beginning of a period of shifting external influences upon the village. The famine compounded the chronic labor shortage in Mysore. Population fell from 5,055,412 in 1871 to 4,186,000 in 1881 (Rice 1897, I: 218). To counteract the effects of the famine, the government built railroads and irrigation works, but these projects had the effect of intensifying the labor shortage. Irrigation works in Namhalli provided twenty acres of riceland adjoining the village. The land surplus and labor shortage created by the famine and consequent government projects left large acreages of uncultivated land in Namhalli. Although the addition of ricelands might have been expected to have a great impact on the village, the new lands were farmed only reluctantly for a number of years after they had been made available. In the beginning the villagers appear to have experienced difficulty in producing sufficient rice to do much more than pay the high taxes on the new land.

The famine also had the effect of reducing the capital available to the headman and at the same time of increasing the villagers' need for capital. Mortality among plow bullocks, one of the most important items of capital investment, was high, and this must have raised the value of plow bullocks to a point where neither the headman nor the villagers could readily purchase additional stock. Scarcity of capital made it difficult for the headman to play his traditional role as "mother of the village." This role was assumed by the state government, which bypassed the headman and distributed food, clothing, and bullocks directly to the villagers. This had the effect of weakening the bonds of social and economic indebtedness which once had validated the position of the headman in the village.

A further blow to the power and prestige of the headman came in 1886 with the introduction of the *rayatvārī* land settlement. The goal of this land settlement, which was one of the changes made under the "regulation" system of government, was to establish a tax system based upon the acreage of land owned, not upon the quantity of grain harvested. Taxes were to be collected directly from the owners of the land, and all middlemen were to be eliminated. The headman was regarded as such a middleman. By the terms of this land settlement the headman seems to have been allowed to claim only those lands on which he was capable of paying cash taxes. All other lands were regarded as belonging to those who actually farmed them.

The effects of *rayatvārī* land tenure and cash taxation are described by Bell (1885: 127):

> Our first act in a newly acquired district was to decree that the land revenue should henceforth be paid in coin, without having previously ascertained if there was sufficient coin in circulation to allow such a sudden and drastic change. There was not, and the consequence of our ill-judged and precipitate action was a ruinous derangement of values. A pressing demand for specie glutted the markets with an immense quantity of produce which had to be sold for whatever it would bring.

The effect of the land settlement, then, was to reduce the cash value of grain drastically and at the same time to compel farmers to pay a fixed annual cash tax instead of a fixed proportion of the grain harvested. As most farmers could not pay cash taxes, their land automatically became the property of the government. Theoretically, the government should then have auctioned the land to the highest bidder. Actually, such land was rarely auctioned off. Instead, because of lack of purchasers, it had to be given away or given out for cultivation on a crop-sharing basis. Under most of these sharecropping arrangements, the government took half the crop and the cultivator kept half.

Under the traditional system of revenue collection the state government had taken one-third of the crop, while the farmer had used one-third of the crop to pay his expenses and retained a net profit of one-third. A considerable percentage of the crop, including part of the government's share and part of the farmer's share, went to village servants and to intermediate government officials such as the headman and the accountant. Under the new land settlement, the headman and the accountant remained as government officials, but their share of the village harvest was taken by the government, and they received, instead, a small annual salary. In this way the headman became a minor government pensioner where previously he had been the social and economic leader of the village.

Other village officials also suffered a loss of prestige and income during the latter part of the nineteenth century. Most of the lands which had been given to them rent-free by the villagers were either taken away entirely or made taxable, which amounted to the same thing. In Namhalli, the only holders of *inām*, or tax-exempt, nontransferable lands, in 1953 were temple priests, the accountant, and members of the *Mādiga* caste who served as village watchmen and menials. The barber and washerman now own no lands, and the blacksmith and other artisans must pay taxes on their holdings. The aftermath of the famine and the subsequent land settlement thus effected a moderate decentralization of authority and of economic power in the village.

Construction of a railroad near Namhalli is another external event which occurred at about this time, but it had less effect upon village life than might have been anticipated. Villagers were afraid of the railroads. They looked on them as objects worthy of worship and made offerings to the locomotive at each stop. Anglo-Indian engineers acted as the high priests of the locomotives and waxed fat upon offerings of bananas and betel leaves. Furthermore, there were few passenger cars on the trains, and the average citizen of Namhalli, if he had to go to Bangalore, continued to travel on foot, carrying his merchandise upon his head.

It might have been expected that the need for cash with which to pay taxes would compel the villagers to participate increasingly in the urban market. In one sense this was true. The villagers sold more and more products for cash, but, as a rule, they did not enter the city. Usually, tradesmen came to the village, purchased grain, and carried the grain to the city. When villagers did go to Bangalore, they were afraid to enter the modern portions of the city. Muslims there used to cut the villagers' waist cords with knives, tear off their loincloths, and shout insults at them. Because most of the villagers' cash earnings went to pay taxes, most of their needs continued to be filled by local people who provided goods and services in exchange for grain.

The effectiveness of the external influences connected with the famine and the land settlement was apparently limited, not by internal factors such as the "innate conservatism" of the villager, but by contradictions inherent in the external influences themselves. For example, the famine reduced the population of Mysore and thereby reduced the cash value of land. The *rayatvārī* system of land tenure, on the other hand, was based upon the typically European assumption that the land possessed a high cash value. Actually, few farmers had either the desire or the ability to pay high cash taxes on land which had a low cash value. Under these circumstances, the revolutionary effects of a system of taxation based upon landownership and high land value could not be felt until an actual shortage of land produced an increase in land value. As things stood in the years following the famine, there was little that the government could do beyond assuming ownership of land and then redistributing it on a sharecropping basis. There was a tendency, despite the land settlement, for taxes to continue to be collected in a manner closely paralleling the traditional system.

Another contradiction among the external factors influencing the village was the low cash value of grain. The railroad, the land settlement, and other factors could be expected to increase the involvement of Namhalli with urban and European culture, but lack of cash made it difficult for the villager to make sweeping changes in his traditional culture. Without money, the villager could not patronize law courts, purchase bicycles, or send his children to school. Without money, the economic interests of the villager continued to be focused in the village. Most of his other interests remained there as well.

IV. THE YEARS OF STABILITY: 1900–1914

In the early years of the twentieth century, urban influences became increasingly important in the external environment of the village. But, having little cash, low population, and surplus land, the people of Namhalli lacked both means and incentives for carrying out extensive innovations. There is little evidence that potentially modernizing and urbanizing influences were effective in the village during these years.

The social and economic role of the headman had been filled by a group of six large families. Some of these large families were single commensal groups composed of male descendants of a common ancestor and their wives and children; others may have had a more diffuse organization. Thus the propriety of referring to these groups as "large families" or "joint families" is open to question. The main point, however, is that each of these groups consisted of more than thirty members, each formed an economic unit, and each was under the leadership of a single headman. The functions of family leadership were, to some extent, shared by the brothers of the family head. The family head was in charge of finances. He sat on the village panchayat, or council, and represented the family in dealings with consanguineal and affinal relatives living outside the village. Of the brothers of the family head, one was usually in charge of dry-land agriculture; another managed the garden lands, the cattle, or the family industry. Such a division of labor persisted in large families even in 1953, although the largest families of 1953 could count only twelve to fifteen members.

Allied with each of the six large families in 1900 were a number of small households composed of distant relatives and dependents, such as widows and impoverished brothers-in-law, as well as servants and debtors of other castes. In this manner, the six large families included many other families within their respective spheres of influence. Competition was minimal among the six families, for they were reciprocally related by differences of caste and united by a common political organization, the village panchayat.

In 1900 about 15 per cent of the population belonged to the *Mādiga* caste. *Mādigas* were excluded from many forms of social participation. They lived separately, owned a negligible quantity of land, and performed various menial services for other villagers. Most of the *Mādigas* were *jīta* servants. They were punished severely if they attempted to run away. If they obtained money, they were relieved of it in one way or another. The *Mādigas* also enjoyed certain privileges. A *Mādiga*'s relationship with his high-caste master was frequently familial in nature, and he worked side by side with his master in the fields. Masters were required by tradition and public opinion to reward faithful servants by arranging their marriages. *Mādigas* had monopolies on a number of important occupations. They made sandals; they were charged with removing dead animals from the village streets and were permitted to use or sell the flesh and hides. *Mādigas* were given lands and grain in return for their services as village watchmen and village menials. One of the village menials, the *tōṭi*, was important in the collection of land revenue and was a member of the village panchayat.

With the exception of a few individuals like the *tōṭi*, members of the *Mādiga* caste can be placed at the bottom of the ceremonial, social, economic, and political hierarchy of the village. Other castes cannot so easily be placed in a hierarchical relationship.

In general, the important differences among the "middle-class" castes, which made up 70 per cent of the village population, would appear to be occupational. The "middle-class" castes observed few forms of segregation in relation to one another, and informal relationships often crossed caste lines. Differences of rank among these castes appear to have been important only on specified ceremonial occasions. On other occasions, such as meetings of the panchayat, co-operation in village labor, dramatic performances, and gymnastic training, there is little evidence that importance was attached to caste membership. For example, lists of the actors performing in village dramas during this period reveal no connection between caste rank and casting. Likewise, leading roles on the village panchayat have been played by individuals whose caste occupies a low place in the hierarchy of "middle-class" castes.

The monopoly of the headman and accountant positions, held by members of the *Jaṅgama* and Brahman castes, respectively, was an exception to this, but these positions had lost many of their advantages by 1900. In the formation of friendship groups among the "middle-class" castes, age ranking appears to have been more important than caste ranking; that is, people often chose as their friends persons of the same age regardless of caste. In stories which old men in Namhalli in 1953 told concerning the "good old days," a "friend" from another caste figures frequently as an ally in time of trouble, as a companion on expeditions to other villages, or as a fellow-planner who assisted in the execution of a scheme or project.

Economic interdependency of the different castes was connected with the differentiation of occupations inherent in the caste system. While all the castes in Namhalli follow various pastoral or agricultural pursuits, each of the principal castes has a number of special occupations and ritual prerogatives which are usually performed by members of that caste only. The distribution of families in 1900 was such that only one caste contained two large families. There were two large families of *Liṅgāyat* cultivators, one family of Weavers, one of Blacksmiths, one of Shepherds, and one of *Mādigas*.

If the head of a *Liṅgāyat* family in Namhalli did not want to do business with the Blacksmith family in his own village, he could not easily go elsewhere. If he went to a neighboring village, the blacksmith there would almost certainly be a relative, and therefore not a willing competitor, of the blacksmith in Namhalli. This is a result of exogamy from the patrilineage and of endogamy within the caste. Local caste groups tended to be composed of members of a single patrilineage, so that most marriages had to be made outside the village. But the endogamous groups within castes tended also to be rather narrowly localized in nearby villages of a small region. Repeated marriages among nearby villages thus tended to reduce inter-village competition. Even beyond the fact of real or imaginary relationship within a regional caste group, it was neither customary nor practical to patronize artisans living outside one's own village.

The interdependency of the different castes in Namhalli was confirmed and reinforced by ceremonial relationships. The goldsmith, who belonged to the same caste as the blacksmith and the carpenter, made the jewelry for weddings. His prediction as to the success of the marriage—based upon the difficulties he encountered while making the jewelry—was indispensable. Members of the vegetarian castes, particularly Brahmans and *Jaṅgamas*, performed important priestly functions. Equally, *Mādigas*, who played drums for religious processions, were indispensable.

The village panchayat, composed of representatives from every important caste, was the principal administrative, executive, and judicial institution in the village. Nearly all the organized activities of the village were based upon the unanimous agreement of the panchayat members. This is another reflection of the strong village unity required by the mutual indispensability of the different castes to each other. The panchayat maintained smooth relationships among the different castes in the village and arbitrated disputes between castes, families, and individuals.

The relationship of the panchayat to sources of authority outside the village has varied considerably in Namhalli over the years. Until the introduction of the "regulation" system of government in 1860, the village panchayat had been an important part of the government machinery. The traditional role of the panchayat in village affairs appears to have been that of dealing with nearly all legal cases and problems which arose in the village. The ability of the headman to collect revenue and to insure the cultivation of village lands was based upon his leadership of the panchayat. When a problem could not be settled to everybody's satisfaction, it was referred to external authority. The indigenous governments and the early British governments had not been particularly interested in technical legal aspects of village affairs and had rarely interfered unless they were called upon to do so. Thus, the traditional system of authority appears to have allowed the panchayat wide latitude in its handling of village affairs. Later, the government became increasingly interested in the internal problems of villages and attempted to regulate the panchayat and to limit its authority (Buchanan 1807, I: 81; Shama Rao 1936, I: 398–99; Rice 1897, I: 611).

Between 1900 and 1914, Namhalli's panchayat functioned, for the most part, in the traditional manner. Occasionally police officials from outside the village intervened when there were major crimes in the village, but the effects of such intervention appear to have been slight. On several occasions the village elders paid off the police and thus maintained their authority. A man who committed murder was rescued from the police and was punished by means thought appropriate by the panchayat members. According to the technicalities of the "regulation" system the village panchayat's legal authority had been greatly reduced, but, so long as the village kept its private life to itself, the panchayat remained comparatively undisturbed by external governmental agencies.

V. MODERNIZATION AND URBANIZATION: 1914–53

Changes in the relationship of the village to the world outside became increasingly significant following World War I. The chronic shortage of cash which previously had made the adoption of new ways of life difficult was alleviated by the wartime inflation. The cash price of *rāgi*, the principal food grain, increased to four times the prewar price. The price of labor tripled, and the price of land doubled. The cash price of gold and the land tax remained relatively constant. Trade between village and city increased greatly. And in the cities there appeared many small hotels and coffee shops where members of many castes and villages mingled.

A form of "modern" prose drama became common during this period and influenced the dress and manners of villagers. The public school system and other government services were considerably expanded. During 1918 and 1919 there was an influenza epidemic, known locally as the "plague-coming-out-of-black-gunpowder," which wiped out seventy persons in the village, including all but one of the village panchayat members.

Although the influenza epidemic created a temporary shortage of manpower, the value of land does not appear to have declined consistently with the temporary decline in population. Probably this reflects a change in patterns of land use. Formerly, land was valuable in so far as it supported the family and provided sufficient additional income to pay the land tax. In the period following the war, many families felt an increased need for urban products such as machine-made cloth and factory-made roofing tiles. Some of the cash earnings of villagers went to support urban coffee shops, theatrical performances, and, later, cinemas. The village lands had to provide not only for the support of villagers and the government but for the burgeoning urban population as well. More land, more intensively cultivated, was required to support the farmer. During the war and for a few years after it, cash crops such as bananas, potatoes, and peanuts received greater emphasis.

As land increased in value, some of the economic aspects of political power in the village shifted. Instead of demanding free labor, village moneylenders began charging interest on loans. Many of the appurtenances of a European-style financial system began to make their appearance. Stockpiles of grain and hoards of jewelry began to give way to cast-iron safes stuffed with title deeds, promissory notes, and mortgages.

For the first time, villagers began to make use of urban law courts to settle disputes among themselves. Some villagers had been involved in legal cases before 1920, but, in the two cases described by villagers, the government figured as the plaintiff and the villagers as defendants. After 1920, a number of individuals in Namhalli used the law courts to acquire land or to bring about the economic ruin of their enemies. Some of the factors which encouraged increased use of the law courts were better education (middle-school fees were abolished in 1919), increased ability to imitate urban people in dress and mannerisms and thus avoid ridicule and discriminatory treatment, and the necessity for expressing landownership in terms of the British Indian legal system.

The law courts had been in existence for nearly one hundred years, but, as long as they were avoided by villagers, their capacity for influencing the village was comparatively small. As soon as even a few villagers resorted to the devices of the law court, the authority of the panchayat was likely to be reduced. This eventuality might have been postponed for several years if most of the members of Namhalli's village panchayat had not died in the influenza epidemic and left control of the village in the hands of younger men who were less oriented to tradition and more aware of the possibilities of urban law.

As external governmental authority expanded and the police and the law courts became increasingly concerned with happenings in the village, one of the bases of the family structure, namely, rules concerning the inheritance of property within the family, was altered. Dominance of a few elders in the traditional family was maintained by refusing to make any division of the property on the demands of younger male members or of any female members. The family group was "joint" in the sense that every member of the family held a theoretical share of the property, but actual division and separate maintenance was another matter. The village panchayat was composed of elders. It was concerned not with the law as written but with the law as it suited the village and the panchayat. Separate inheritance was a matter of privy politics and intrigue, and this was a field of action which had been reserved for family heads—the class of persons least favorably disposed toward the partition of families.

The law courts recognized the right of any adult, married or not, to an equal share of the family property. For example, a bill formulated in 1928 and enforced in 1934 gave women the right to separate their property from that of the joint family and to adopt children. According to the law, women could not be excluded from inheritance on the grounds of sex or on the authority of religious texts. Any member of a joint family was given the right to bring about a division of the family on the basis of a unilateral declaration of intent to divide (Shama Rao 1936, II: 432). Judging by reports from Namhalli, the principles embodied in this bill had been in force at least as early as 1925. This change in the legal position of the joint family, combined with increased reliance by villagers upon the law courts, explains why all but one of the large families divided after 1920. By 1953 it had become almost customary for families to divide as soon as the children reached maturity.

Before World War I the large joint family had played a crucial role in the economic and social organization of the village. The castes had been interdependent and had been politically related to each other through family headmen sitting on the village panchayat. When all that was required for consensus was the agreement of five or six men, the panchayat had been comparatively effective. But the size of family groups dwindled until in 1953 only a few families contained as many as ten members. The population had increased from 300 in 1881, to 413 in 1901, and to 615 in 1953. The number of separate households reached one hundred in 1953. Because every family had its headman who considered himself a member of the panchayat agreement became more and more difficult to obtain. "In the old days," people say, "a few men used to run the entire village. Now there is a king in every house." This drift toward the decentralization of authority in the village might, in an earlier period, have been counteracted by the application of economic and social pressures such as outcasting and boycotting, which were the stock-in-trade of traditional village authorities. Between 1914 and 1953, however, these mechanisms had been rendered largely ineffective by law courts which forbade their use and by urban markets which provided goods and services regardless of boycotts.

Decrease in family size led to changes in agricultural methods as well. Most families, being small, could no longer afford to hire full-time agricultural laborers and began hiring day laborers instead. This began in 1915. As day laborers possessed no job security and were often transients, they could not be intrusted with responsibilities such as caring for gardens or livestock. At the same time, the average small family could not spare a family member for these tasks. This meant that garden and orchard produce was thoroughly consumed either by monkeys or by the hired help long before it could be harvested by the landowner. Toward the end of the twenties, the acreage devoted to valuable orchard and garden crops decreased progressively, while the area devoted to grain crops, which require less care and are harder to steal, increased.

Increasing population stimulated more intensive land use. Between 1934 and 1953 the acreage of pasture land in the village was reduced by more than fifty acres, the land being converted to raising grain crops. This required a reduction in the number of cattle in the village and resulted in a decrease in the quantity of fertilizer available. To some extent, then, decreasing family size and increasing population have reduced agricultural efficiency, although the net loss has been somewhat offset by the use of chemical manures on village ricelands after 1930.

Shrinking family size has led to the disappearance from the village of any unit of organization large enough to contain all essential economic operations within itself. The large family had a surplus accumulation of grain, capital, and labor sufficient to permit investment on the improvement of land. When this surplus must be distributed among six small families, there is little left over for emergencies or for investment.

Changing circumstances have produced numerous alterations in the social and economic position of different castes. The effect of the land settlement and the famine upon the position of the headman, who belonged to the *Jaṅgama* caste, has been mentioned. Increased trade between the village and the city had adverse effects upon several of the occupationally specialized castes. In 1900 the Weavers were a comparatively wealthy caste. As an old woman said in 1953, "The Weavers once had basketfuls of jewels. Now they have less than the *Mādiga*." Certain members of the weaving caste were the only people in Namhalli in 1953 who appeared to be on the verge of starvation.

Other artisan castes have fared somewhat better than the Weavers. The Blacksmith caste has been more helped than hindered by the introduction of urban products. Mold-board plows, for example, were introduced by a group of American missionaries in the twenties, and they are now made by the village blacksmith and sold for a profit. On the whole, urban manufactured goods appear destined to replace goods manufactured in the village. Village artisans are not masters of complicated arts. There is little made in the village which cannot be made better and more cheaply by machines. Increasing population and the loss of such specialized industries as weaving compelled an increasing proportion of village people to find employment in agriculture.

Another source of new occupations was the school system. Namhalli, like most villages in Mysore, has probably always had a "folk school" which was supported entirely by the villagers. After 1910 the government began paying part of the teachers' salaries. For some time after this, the school continued to provide instruction along traditional lines. After 1919, however, many schoolteachers were middle- and high-school graduates, and instruction deviated increasingly from the traditional pattern. In the years following 1920, the government began paying the total salary of schoolteachers and forbade them to accept contributions from villagers. As in other branches of the government service, there appears to have been a deliberate policy of transferring teachers as often as possible. Schoolteachers became less and less subject to traditional influences, and the content of their teaching became more and more subject to urbanized state policy.

In 1953, Namhalli had slightly more than thirty persons who were qualified as schoolteachers. Of these, about twelve were employed as teachers and four held other government jobs. Even when emigrants and village officials are omitted from the total, about one person in every six Namhalli families is a government employee. Other occupations which have increased in importance in the village include those of "blackmarketeer," storekeeper, betel-leaf and vegetable grower, tailor, and bus conductor.

These new occupations and the traditional one of agriculture may be followed by members of nearly all castes. Hence, occupational specialization by different castes has become progressively less capable of providing a basis for an economic and social hierarchy in Namhalli. From the time of the land settlement of the eighties, which divided most of the land in the village into small parcels, the economic hierarchy in Namhalli has become increasingly simplified. In terms of individual families, there are no families in the village in 1953 which could be considered to be exceptionally wealthy. More than sixty out of one hundred families own land, while only one family—a family of fifteen members, which includes five middle-aged brothers—owns as much as thirty acres of dry land. The major economic division in the village is between the 25 per cent of the population which barely supports itself on the subsistence level by performing agricultural labor and the 75 per cent of the population which possesses some land and can afford a few luxuries.

Changes in the over-all economic situation, the lessening of occupational specialization, the declining authority of the village panchayat and headman, and reductions in family size have occurred concurrently with a reduction of co-operative effort in the village. Namhalli has become more and more an aggregation of small and comparatively noninterdependent families.

Village-wide ceremonials continue to be performed, but on a reduced scale. Few wedding ceremonies last longer than a day or two, and, although members of most families in the village continue to participate in wedding ceremonies, the village elders no longer assist in selecting the bride. Dramas continue to be performed by groups of villagers, but they are no longer occasions for village-wide participation. Customary economic relationships with the blacksmith, the washerman, and a few other village artisans and servants continue, but a few families have ceased to maintain these relationships, and many of the artisans and servants were complaining in 1953 that it was difficult to collect their traditional dues.

Between 1914 and 1953, few additions were made to the social groupings in Namhalli, but there was a slow vitiation of traditional forms of organization. The only successful innovation appears to have been the introduction of a volleyball team in 1951. A government-organized co-operative and a government-sponsored village improvement society have had little influence despite their potential ability to fill the economic roles left vacant by the impoverishment of the headman and the disappearance of large joint families.

VI. SHIFTING RATES OF CHANGE: 1930–53

Described above are some of the changes in family structure and in social and economic relationships which occurred in Namhalli in the years following World War I. Although these changes have been described as if they occurred consistently over three or four decades, there was considerable variation in the rate of change during the decades beginning in 1930 and in 1940.

In the thirties, the village was affected by the world-wide depression. Grain became plentiful and money became increasingly scarce. The educational system suddenly ceased to be as rewarding as it had been in the past. Graduates from the middle school found themselves unemployed. They formed a gang and pillaged gardens belonging to neighboring villages. On several occasions they attended dramatic performances and started minor riots with gangs from other villages.

The restless behavior of Namhalli's young men was not a result of any lack of what old people in the village would have considered necessities of life. In the terms of traditional culture, there was no overpopulation in the village: there was plenty of food. The younger generation appears to have felt differently about this. They had gone to school in the hope of obtaining lucrative government positions; the depression years offered them nothing but a return to the land. The young people, bursting with new-felt needs, expressed their dissatisfaction by taking aggressive action against neighboring villages.

Except for this rowdyism, the thirties appear to have been an uneventful decade. There was little change in the membership of the village panchayat between 1920 and 1940, and it appears likely that the depression years enabled the aging panchayat members to reassert their traditional authority. Certainly, there was less ready resort to urban law courts than there had been in the twenties. In Namhalli time almost seemed to stand still during the thirties; in fact, the hands of the clock might almost have been seen moving backward. Against this background of peaceful immobility, population continued to increase, the middle school continued to turn out graduates who could not obtain jobs, and the felt needs of the younger generation of villagers continued to increase under the stimulation of motor-bus transportation and visits to the cinema.

The crisis which was presumably in the making at this point was resolved by another crisis—World War II. The depression period of the thirties was characterized by a fall in the price of *rāgi*. In 1914 the price of *rāgi* had been four times the 1900 price; in the thirties it had been only double the 1900 price. With the beginning of World

War II, the cash value of *rāgi* rose again to four times the 1900 price, and by 1953 it had risen to twenty times the 1900 price. Labor increased greatly in value during the war, with many men earning ten times the 1900 wage. After the war, the price of labor dropped, but the price of *rāgi* continued to rise. Land increased in value to more than four times the 1900 rate. The land tax remained virtually constant. The price of a gold sovereign in rupees doubled during the depression and more than doubled again following World War II.

The war period was a time of great prosperity in Namhalli. The environs of Bangalore were crowded with British, American, and Indian soldiers. Many villagers, both male and female, found jobs in military camps. For Namhalli's middle-school graduates there were highly paid jobs as clerks and factory laborers. There were opportunities for windfall profits from smuggling grain, misappropriating military property, or engaging in prostitution. The farmer also prospered. Officers in charge of procuring food for military establishments toured Mysore State in trucks offering high prices for "English" vegetables. Farmers began growing carrots, tomatoes, beets, cauliflower, and cabbages. Iron plows and improved livestock were purchased. New houses were built. Children were sent to high school riding on newly purchased bicycles. European-style haircuts became universal among the menfolk, and everyone who considered himself educated purchased a cotton, or in extreme cases a woolen, suit which could be worn on trips to Bangalore.

With the end of the war, wartime prosperity also came to an end. The familiar problems of ever increasing population and increasing numbers of educated, but unemployed, young men returned. By 1953, these problems had become more complicated than they were in the thirties. In the thirties, *rāgi* was cheap, and a laborer received sufficient money after one day's labor to purchase a supply of grain sufficient for several weeks. In 1953 a laborer received one meal and only enough money to cover the cost of a second meal. Partly this was the result of a series of poor harvests which forced food prices up and wages down, but it was also an expression of a change of attitude among Namhalli's landowning class.

As a result of wartime prosperity, the large landowning group in Namhalli, which includes most of the group previously referred to as the "middle-class" castes plus a few members of such "depressed" castes as the *Mādigas* and the Hunters, had become accustomed to urban luxuries. An ever increasing percentage of the grain, milk, and vegetables produced in Namhalli was sold in Bangalore. The money obtained in this way was used for new purposes such as paying doctor bills, betting on horse races, buying tailored clothing, paying electric bills, and attending motion pictures. Because the landowners outnumbered the landless laborers in Namhalli by roughly three to one and because there continued to be a labor surplus in the village, the wages of laborers did not increase.

Despite their success in keeping the wages of agricultural laborers at a low level, the members of the landowning group in Namhalli did not succeed in maintaining their own wartime level of living. Thus both of the principal economic classes in Namhalli appeared, in 1953, to be facing a peculiarly bleak future. Landless laborers, caught between rising food prices and inadequate employment, might attempt to solve their economic problems by emigrating to Bangalore, but the chances of finding urban employment would be no better than those of finding rural employment. In 1952, when harvests were particularly poor, many of Namhalli's landless laborers stole food and money from their wealthier neighbors. But robbery is a hazardous occupation in a region where the really poor are greatly outnumbered by the slightly less poor.

Namhalli's landowning group, while not threatened with starvation, has been faced, in recent years, with the problem of dividing a limited quantity of land among an ever increasing population. Within the village many solutions to this problem, ranging from abortion to the adoption of iron plows, have been tried. In almost every family in Namhalli at least one child has been groomed for urban employment. With the comparative absence of opportunities for employment as schoolteachers, factory laborers, or tradesmen, many a prospective emigrant has been forced to return to the crowded land.

Another possible solution to Namhalli's population problems would be the further modification of traditional agricultural techniques: fertilizer could be purchased for the *rāgi* crop, or electric irrigation pumps, already common in Mysore, could be installed. The major problem, here, is lack of capital. With the village divided into small family units which are often in conflict with each other and often in internal conflict as well, the co-operative efforts necessary for the accumulation of capital and the making of major changes in the agricultural technology of the village have not been forthcoming.

In 1953 the villagers of Namhalli had not successfully resolved the problem posed by increasing population, rising living costs, and a limited acreage of arable lands, but in this year, as in others, the course of change would appear to depend as much upon the interplay of external change-producing factors as upon any decisions which could be made by the villagers themselves.

VII. SUMMARY AND CONCLUSIONS

After the famine of 1876–78, the impact of external urban and governmental influences upon Namhalli was powerful enough to induce comparatively rapid cultural change. At the same time, the interplay of these external influences was such that many of the changes which might have been anticipated did not occur. After the famine the state government stimulated a situation in which arable land and marketable grain became surplus commodities. At the same time it attempted to introduce a European-style system of land tenure based on an assumption of high land values. Because of the contradiction between a land-tenure system based on high land values and an economic situation in which land values were low, many of the effects which might have been anticipated from the new system of land tenure did not occur until after 1914, when land values increased.

After 1914 many potential factors of change pressed strongly upon the village. Of these, the increasing cash value of land and of agricultural produce appears to have played a catalytic role. In the period following the famine of 1876–78, a fall in population appears to have been responsible for a reduction in the cash value of land and of agricultural produce. But when population again fell—although not quite as much—in the influenza epidemic of 1918–19, agricultural prices continued to be high. Evidently, agricultural prices had been freed from local limitations and had grown responsive to the rising demands of a world-wide market. The spurt of cultural change which occurred during the twenties may, to a considerable extent, be attributed to a superficially anomalous situation in which prices remained high while population declined. Population and prices, crucial variables in their effects upon cultural change, have had no consistent relationship to each other through the years. They have fluctuated almost independently, now reinforcing, now counteracting each other in their effect upon other potential factors of cultural change.

Namhalli's economic situation in the forties bore many resemblances to its situation during World War I; that is, after the doldrums of the thirties, the villagers once again were in a position to earn and spend cash. During World War I, however, the villagers earned cash through agriculture. In the forties, increasing population made this difficult. Unusual profits and opportunities for change came to villagers not so much from higher prices paid for grain as from temporary employment in factories and military camps. The village became almost a part of the city. Its inhabitants mingled with inhabitants of the city and adopted many forms of urban behavior. Suddenly, the war was over, and Namhalli became an agricultural village once more. Now, in the fifties, the interplay of external factors presents a set of problems quite different from those that faced the village previously. The wages of agricultural laborers have returned to prewar levels, while population and agricultural prices have continued to rise.

Although Namhalli has many unique or individual attributes, an examination of Namhalli's relationships with the outside world over a number of years leaves the impression that many of the changes which took place in Namhalli were dictated by happenings outside the village. Further, it would appear that the mere presence of urban influence has not been sufficient stimulus to guarantee change in Namhalli. It is rather in the interrelationships among external factors of change that the explanation for variations in the rate and direction of change in Namhalli is to be found. Change was thrust upon Namhalli by the interplay of change-producing factors in the external environment of the village.

This being the case, it is likely that other villages have been similarly influenced by the interplay of external factors of change, that they too have alternated between periods of comparatively rapid and comparatively slow change, and that they too have changed largely as a result of external pressures. Namhalli and other villages in the vicinity of Bangalore have changed far more rapidly and far more significantly than have other villages in India. This brings to mind the possibility that, as more remote villages are drawn increasingly under the influence of urban factors of change, they too may begin to follow a course of change resembling the one followed by Namhalli in the past.

REFERENCES CITED

Beals, Alan Robin

1953 "Change in the Leadership of a Mysore Village," *Economic Weekly* **5**:487–92. Bombay.

1954*a* "The Government and the Indian Village," *Economic Development and Cultural Change* **2**:397–407. Chicago.

1954*b* "Culture Change and Social Conflict in a South Indian Village." Unpublished Ph.D. dissertation, University of California, Berkeley.

BELL, Major EVANS
1885 *Memoir of General John Briggs*. London, Chatto & Windus.
BUCHANAN, FRANCIS HAMILTON
1807 *A Journey from Madras, through the Countries of Mysore, Canara, and Malabar*. 3 vols. London, T. Cadell & W. Davies.
RICE, LEWIS B.
1897 *Mysore: A Gazetteer*. Rev. ed., 2 vols. Westminster, Archibald Constable.
SHAMA RAO, M.
1936 *Modern Mysore*. 2 vols. Bangalore, Higginbothams.

NOTES ON AN APPROACH TO A STUDY OF PERSONALITY FORMATION IN A HINDU VILLAGE IN GUJARAT[1]

GITEL P. STEED

IN THIS PAPER I attempt to illustrate an approach to a study of personality formation in Kasandra, a Hindu village in Gujarat. I first state the approach theoretically, and then document it with evidence accumulated at two levels of field inquiry, sociological and ontogenetic. Part II describes those institutions that appear to have exerted pervasive socializing influences on the residents of Kasandra—especially on the *Rajpūt* residents—variously affecting individual behavior and roles in community life, and having consequences for the history of human relations in that village. Part III focuses on the personality, behavior, and roles of one of Kasandra's 850 residents, the *Vāghelā Rajpūt* landlord Indrasingh. It follows along his pathways of experience in the setting of Kasandra's social system, briefly exploring the possible effects of some idiosyncratic aspects of his personal development not disclosed by the discussion of general institutional factors in Part II.

Both the discussion of social structure in Part II and the portrait of Indrasingh in Part III aim principally to delineate sociological horizons in personality formation. They stop at an arbitrary point where psychological analysis becomes more appropriate.

I. SOME CONCEPTUAL AND METHODOLOGICAL HURDLES

A. THE APPROACH

At the beginning of the field undertaking, I wrote a communication to colleagues in cognate disciplines who would be collaborating with

1. The data on which this paper is based were gathered during twelve months of research in the village of Kasandra (a pseudonym) between November, 1949, and January, 1951. Research in Kasandra was part of a two-year inquiry on aspects of personality formation conducted in three villages of northern India (in this Hindu village in Gujarat, in a Hindu hamlet in Rajputana, and in a Muslim village in Uttar Pradesh) by members of the Columbia University Research in Contemporary India Field Project. The project was directed by Gitel P. Steed and was assisted for the entire period in Kasandra by James Silverberg, Bhagvati Masher, Kantilal Mehta, and Robert Steed. Assisting for briefer periods were Nandlal Dosajh, Cecil Massey, and Donna Crothers Silverberg.

me later on levels of research analysis not my own, especially psychoanalytic psychology (Steed 1949). In that communication I outlined a social anthropological approach to the study of personality in any society. This approach, while presupposing a universal human nature, incorporates the view that a functional and historical analysis of a particular people requires observing individuals in groups and discerning what happens to them under given social conditions. In the India village research, I would consequently be disposed to look into the social causes of the phenomena of individual personality and also into the more complex personal phenomena of individual differences which, by outward or manifest sign, appeared to be affecting the social order of the group. The field inquiry would thus be exploratory, aiming very broadly at discovering meaningful variables or determinants of "private" and "social" personality in the matrix of peasant society.

Two salient methods were planned to find the appropriate data: (1) clues to personality formation would be sought through aspects of village social structure, through its institutions in the context of village history, in the events and trends both local and national which help shape the villager's personal and social life, against the landscape of village demography, and in the basic conditions for settlement patterns and social organization; (2) to complement this broadly sociological approach, further clues would be sought at the deeper level of individual inquiry where unique, covert, and projective aspects of individual behavior are disclosed more readily, and where idiosyncratic as well as social factors of personality formation are to be apprehended. The villager's own views of his role in village affairs, his interpretations of his motivations and needs, his reflections upon his cycle of growth from infancy to adulthood, upon his relations to others, and upon his life-goals in general—these would provide insights concerning the private thoughts and feelings behind his public behavior and roles in village life (Steed 1949).

In accordance with the first of these methods, sociological documents were to be collected and, with the second, augmented life-history documents.[2] Data to be obtained from these documents

2. Although almost every person in Kasandra was interviewed for salient data about himself or others in the community, thirty persons, among whom Indrasingh was one, were selected for intensive individual inquiries. To elicit appropriate information about these individuals, a composite method designated as the "augmented life-history" was developed. The augmented life-history contains the following six elements, all of which were applied whenever feasible: (1) the individual's own narrative of his life as given in unstructured interviews up to a maximum of twenty-five sessions; (2) the individual's

were expected to help ascertain the villager's world views, his values and his way of dealing with drives, especially as conflicts arise between outer demands and the compelling demands of inner impulses and desires. These data would bring to light such individual acts and manifestations of personality traits as displacement, rationalization, projection to the outer world, identification, substitution or compensation—the constructs of Freud, as applied in contemporary psychoanalytic studies—and other inferences about processes of behavior which form a large part of what psychologists deal with as "personality."

B. THE CONCEPT "PERSONALITY"

Since connotations of "personality" are variable, and since this research was to focus on individual-society relationships, I was confronted inevitably with certain methodological hurdles concerning the concept "personality."

A given personality reflects a persistent pattern of behavior which is dictated by inner interests accommodating to institutional experiences. This pattern of behavior is frequently expressed through a number of "personality traits" which are presumed to represent an individual's persistent responses to inner interests.

But how are traits of behavior which reflect responses to inner interests to be distinguished from "traits" of behavior which reflect persistent responses to outer demands? "Traits" of the latter sort are not, strictly speaking, traits of personality at all, but are rather "modes of individual adaptation" (Merton 1949: 133) to pressures of social structure and cultural forms. When a person, for example, conforms to or retreats from certain roles or other functions in response to outer demands, he is manifesting "types of more or less enduring responses" (p. 133) which are not necessarily contingent upon his personality traits. The underlying assumption here is that social structure and cultural forms operate to exert pressure upon individuals, evoking one or another *alternative* mode of behavior. Such modes of individual adaptation are often ambiguously identified as personality traits; personality traits are often indistinguishable from modes of adaptation.

---

ideology, valuations and interpretations of institutional affairs obtained in structured and unstructured interviews with him; (3) biographical data—facts and opinions about the individual gathered in interviews with other persons; (4) observations of the individual's roles and behavior; (5) a battery of five projective tests—Rorschach, Thematic Apperception Test, Horn-Hellersberg, Color-Association, Draw-a-Man, Woman and Child; (6) spontaneous free drawings and water colors.

Now I expected this conceptual distinction about individual behavior to emerge in my reconstructions of the formation of given personalities in the changing society of Kasandra village, for I assumed that a person's modes of individual adaptation are largely contingent on the viability and durability of institutions. If village institutions are altered, modes of individual adaptation shift accordingly at varying rates, often with little effect on personality traits. Personality traits are not as flexible in response to external demands; they are more dependent on compelling inner interests and drives.

The years 1949–51, as it happened, were years of intense change in the social institutions of Kasandra. I hoped to use this situation of change, not only to distinguish personality traits from modes of individual adaptation, but also to make some tentative predictions concerning trends in the behavior of individual villagers. Predictions might be made either from a knowledge of personality traits or from a knowledge of individual modes of adaptation, or both. Predictions would depend on the disclosures of informants and on their life-histories, which spanned beyond the years of intense change, as well as on their behavior which could be observed during 1949–51.

C. THE PROBLEM OF GROUP PERSONALITY

If the distinction between personality traits and modes of adaptation could be made within the behavior of individuals, could it also be extended to all of the individual members of a cultural or subcultural group? Could one expect to find members of the same group sharing enough traits so that the modal personality structure (DuBois 1944: 2–5) of that group could be adduced? In other words, would the data enable one to draw up a typology of shared personality traits representing the personality or character of a family, lineage, caste, or village, and, by logical extension, a regional or national character?

Or, on the other hand, are the characteristics shared by members of cultural groups and subgroups really common modes of adaptation to the exigencies of the same institutions in the same society? Would a typology of shared modes of adaptation provide a more revealing interpretation of the data on shared group behavior?

Or would the attempt to draw up either kind of group typology—one of group personality traits or one of group modes of adaptation—have to give way to a negative finding that the group data are too difficult to comprehend within general types?

Although this paper does not attempt to provide a complete

answer to these problems of group personality, the data which it presents do illustrate some conclusions which seem to be supported by a larger sampling of personal histories from Kasandra. The data of Part II describe subcultural groups within the larger, heterogeneous village community which possess relatively homogeneous traditions and institutions; members of these subcultural groups generally share certain roles, functions, and modes of individual adaptation with each other.

But a complex of shared personality traits does not appear to characterize the members of any one of these groups. Similar personality types rather appear to be distributed across many groups, and to be found no more frequently in one group than in another. Furthermore, where a certain personality trait has been found in several members of a group, I have not been able to trace its origin solely to that group's shared institutional practices.

As illustrated by the example of the landlord Indrasingh (Part III), one can find within each subcommunity of Kasandra a heterogeneity of personalities. Like Indrasingh, all respond to subcultural standardizations of social tradition through modes of adaptation which are discernibly patterned, but which are by no means uniform. Indrasingh's career reminds us that, even in a strongly conformist society, each person varies greatly in the order of his institutional experience: the total experience of any individual, and therefore his unique personality, is a sum of many variables, the order of which can rarely match the order of the same variables in the total experience of any other individual.

D. THE VILLAGE AS AN AREA OF INQUIRY

The village appeared to me at the outset to be the most appropriate unit for an exploratory study of personality formation in peasant India, both because it would permit a preliminary delineation of the sociological horizons of personality formation and because it would represent much of the complexity of the region and nation.

Among those concerned with depth studies of individual character formation, the opinion is widely held that the family, and not the larger community, is the most fruitful area for inquiry. Such an opinion has been attributed to Freud (Bateson 1944: 726). But there were in 1949 no community studies in India against which this opinion or any other methodological hypothesis as to individual-society relationships could be tested. I therefore selected the village of Kasandra as one in which I might begin to delimit the sociological horizons of personality formation, in which I might try to ascertain the widest range or circumference of an individual's experiences (Steed 1950: viii). I soon learned that a measure of personal experience reaches out even "beyond the physical village" (Marriott 1954: 3) to extravillage associations of kin and caste, to markets, to religious centers, and to a greater cultural tradition (Redfield and Singer 1954: 63–68). But I soon found also that, while individuals move through several realms of interpersonal associations, each individual's personal history remains moored firmly within Kasandra's society of caste, kinship, and family.

Kasandra village was selected as representing caste, religion, systems of land tenure, and other institutions which are common in the region of Gujarat and in all of India. Such institutions were presumed and were found in fact to function in this one village as isolable determinants of social relationships and of individual behavior. But, in selecting one village rather than another, I could not avoid selecting a complex of interacting institutional variables which characterize and identify that particular village as distinct from all others. One village community may have a Muslim population attached to a feudatory system of land tenure with an enclave of Hindus working the land; another village nearby may have a population of Hindus cultivating the land under a system of freehold tenure with the aid of Muslims. The complex of institutional variables shifts in each village community, altering the order of individual social experiences and affecting the personal history of each individual (Steed 1949: 1–35).

Some villages possess a combination of widespread institutions which not only is unique but also is capable of insulating local social relations and of virtually closing the community against unwanted encroachments from the outside. Such insular villages have narrow traditions. They are more orthodox and conservative. In spite of existing channels of communication with the outside, the residents turn their interests, sentiments, and values inward, toward the inside community. Kasandra is such a village, in transition.

II. SOCIOLOGICAL HORIZONS OF PERSONALITY FORMATION

Kasandra village stands on the westernmost frontier of historic Gujarat in the Sanand Taluka of Ahmadabad District, Bombay State. Across the frontier lies Lakhtar, a tiny principality in the former native states territory of Kathiawar (now Saurashtra). Historically and culturally, Kasandra's affinities lie westward with the honeycomb of petty *Rajpūt* kingdoms and chieftainates across the frontier, but politically and economically the ties of the village at present lie eastward with Ahmadabad City, thirty-five miles distant. Ahmadabad City has a long history of British-urban penetration. It is India's second largest textile center and is the birthplace of Gandhi's political reforms.

Kasandra is one of thousands of villages which spread across the 34,000 square miles of Gujarat plain. Kasandra's 850 people give its village area an average density of 264 persons per square mile, which is about equal to the average densities of settlement in the region of Gujarat and in Bombay State as wholes. Anyone leaving Kasandra and crossing the plain in any direction will come upon a village every two or three miles. Kasandra itself can be spotted from a distance by the sudden appearance of a gently sloping elevation or ridge, shaded by a grove of trees. The trees appear to draw a curtain across a tightly packed cluster of mud houses and walled-in compounds.

Geographic isolation is not a feature of rural settlement in the region around Kasandra. Both the clustering of houses on the village site and the closeness of this site to the sites of other villages generate and sustain numerous arteries of communication across the plain. These arteries of communication are blocked only within the villages by barriers of ritualized social distance and by attitudes concerning proximity and privacy.

Kasandra village stands on rich alluvial soil at the southwest corner of the most productive part of Ahmadabad District. This productive area has until recent times drawn into itself a succession of population movements from the surrounding, more impoverished provinces on the north and west. Tribesmen from the outlying hills and *Koḷī* cultivators from the coast and from the desert plain have intersected the countryside around Kasandra. They have become part of the village caste complex, blending into the lower agrarian strata. High-caste *Rajpūts,* their ancestors having entered the area from Kathiawar, Kutch, and Rajputana as conquerors, are settled in these farming villages as self-styled "*Kṣatriyas.*"

The present ethnic composition of Kasandra village reflects the diversity of these past drifts of population, now stabilized by the agrarian structure of the village. The flow of population to and from the village is now limited for the most part to migrations of kinsmen and of affinal relatives.

Of great pertinence to the whole structure of social relationships in Kasandra is the influence of its *Rajpūt* rulers. *Rajpūts* are known for their secular, military ways, their practice of freebooting and dacoity, and their conservative family traditions. The inordinate control which *Rajpūts* exercise over other villagers in Kasandra is consolidated by their possession of overlord tenure estates. These estates were first acquired by their ancestors either through direct military seizure or through agreements with later governing powers. Kasandra and other villages of western Gujarat in which *Rajpūts* are numerous and powerful have thus come to be known as "*Rajpūt* villages."

A. OVERLORD TENURE IN TRADITION AND TRANSITION

1. *The legal system and its insular effects.*—Until they were liquidated in 1950 by national fiat and provincial legislation, eight or nine varieties of overlord land tenures flourished in nine-hundred-odd villages of Gujarat. The most widespread and ancient type of overlord tenure was *tālukdārī*, the type that prevailed in Kasandra. Two of the administrative districts of British Gujarat contained 557 *tālukdārī* villages. Within Ahmadabad District alone there were 393 *tālukdārī* villages, so that the district was officially recognized as the principal *tālukdārī* tract in Gujarat. In five administrative subdivisions of Ahmadabad District, *tālukdārī* villages encompassed more than half of all landholdings.

In Kasandra overlord tenure operated to insulate the social structure of the village and to inclose the lives of villagers. Kasandra's *Rajpūt* overlords were a class of absolute hereditary proprietors, owning their several estates and subject only to payment of government revenues. Until 1950, overlords rarely cultivated their own lands. They had the power to rent their lands and to mortgage them, but not the power to transfer their shares without government sanction. Overlords took rent from their tenants most frequently by a share-cropping levy (*bhāgbaṭāī*) of 50 or 60 per cent; less frequently they took a levy on cash crops (*vīgothī*) at a rate fixed by the acre. Kasandra's overlords used their control of the land to press tenants into whatever economic and political activities they desired. With most persons bound tightly to the land and to its overlords, orthodox Hindu traditions were emphasized in Kasandra, and barriers were erected against any penetration by British urban ways.

An impression of Kasandra's insularity under its overlords is reflected in rural stereotypes for all such villages of overlord tenure in the area. Both villagers and townspeople variously described Kasandra as "backward," "jungly," "unreformed," "orthodox," "traditional," "conservative," "inferior," and "thieving" (*dakait*), as well as calling the village or its people "royal" (*darbārī*) and "landholders" (*garāsiyos*)—as if villagers' personalities were congruent with the village's social structure or land-tenure system. Outsiders made frequent allusions to Kasandra and its inhabitants as "free" or "wild," referring in part to the fact that *Rajpūt* overlords with their *Koḷī* followers were subject to but slight restraint, politically and administratively, by the district and provincial governments.

Government officials, too, looked upon the inhabitants of all overlord villages as intractable and upon their village institutions as impenetrable. These villages were therefore scheduled as the last to be affected by land-reform legislation in Bombay State. The official point of view seemed to reflect local public opinion charged with prejudice, sentimentality, or pride, for it tended, like the opinions of laymen, to identify the mentality, outlook, and type of personality of certain villages with a particular caste, power group, system of land tenure, and place of origin.

Evaluating such opinions and other peripheral facts about the community, I inferred that the villagers of Kasandra were not readily accessible to change; I did not infer that as individuals or as a group they necessarily resisted change. The existence there of a land-tenure system which could bind the residents and bar political or economic encroachments from the outside gave sufficient presumptive evidence for the interpretation of inaccessibility to change. Opinions as to villagers' personal intractability and innate orthodoxy needed further inquiry for evaluation, however. Further inquiry was needed not only into villagers' public behavior but also into the less easily apprehended facts of their private careers. Villagers did, however, allude to themselves as "unreformed" and to the city people as "reformed" (*sudharel*).

2. *The impact of land reform.*—The year 1950, when field research was under way in Kasandra, was a period of radical transition for the village and its inhabitants. This period of radical transition had begun with independence in 1947, when the British transferred power to a government formed by the Indian National Congress party. Among major reforms contemplated by the Congress party was reform of the agrarian structure. The Congress program called for liquidation of a great variety of ancient and feudatory land tenures, including *tālukdārī*.

Kasandra villagers in 1950 were being exposed, therefore, to an abrupt shift of standards in interpersonal relations. The traditional subordinate status of all other castes under the authoritarian rule of a single landlord caste was now in flux. New *Gesellschaft*-like ideas of social reform, which heretofore had scarcely found expression, now came suddenly into the awareness of villagers. These ideas were being introduced from outside along with principles of social action by religious reformers, especially of Jain persuasion, by Congress members and by Gandhian uplift workers based in the strong Gandhian center of Ahmadabad City. As close as the residents of Kasandra had been to Ahmadabad through the years, they scarcely mentioned the names of Gandhi or Nehru—another demonstration of the village's previous insularity.

Tensions over agrarian relationships mounted during the course of 1950. Outright fractures of relationships between overlords and tenants occurred where they had rarely occurred before. These disturbances appeared to have their origins in a shift of individual goals. Litigation, which heretofore had been virtually nonexistent in Kasandra, now became an established device by which one villager could obtain redress against another villager. Disputes which previously would have been taken to the resident overlord elders, or to an intermediary selected by them, were now more frequently taken to the courts at Sanand and at Ahmadabad City. Taking any problem outside the village was a new and difficult experience for Kasandra's villagers.

During this year when plans for *tālukdārī* abolition were under way, shifts were discernible in economic relationships, in caste statuses, and in individual roles—in some of the village's so-called bedrock institutions. Actually for some time prior to the outright liquidation of *tālukdārī*, Kasandra's system of agrarian relations had been unable to preserve the full extent of its former insularity. The new market-place economy of the cities and the government's recent demands for greater food production had both made inroads. The new aim of increasing exportable crops was slowly breaking through old barriers set up by overlord tenure, was altering the patterns of land use, and was forcing a change in share-cropping labor relations. But the *Rajpūt* overlords of Kasandra rarely relaxed their absolute controls over the land. Their consistent indifference to the new demands, especially where farmers' interests were concerned, had the effect of checking individual initiative and incentive at almost every level of economic production.

Individual incentive and individual initiative were decidedly new approaches to self-preservation. They exemplify the new sentiments and values, the new goals for individual well-being which were being brought into the village by outsiders.

The force of these new ideas and the possible influence of the emergent institutional reforms required appraisal. Could they shape and perhaps even deeply take hold of individual thought and action in the village? Could they also affect the thought and behavior of groups in regular ways?

To appraise the influence of these new ideas and institutions, I attempted to record instances in which recent innovations had affected both individuals and groups. Although group regularities in the form and content of these new influences did not appear, I was able to note how new ideas and values were articulated in individual autobiographies, in dreams, and even in the materials resulting from projective tests (e.g., Steed 1950*b:* 10–15). Villagers themselves drew an imaginary line between the eras of "before" and "after" the abolition of overlordship, and I did not rule out the possibility that the dramatic attendant changes in institutional forms and thought might influence the direction of personality development and even alter established personality traits. The problem of judging this possibility was the problem of evaluating the strength and viability of recent innovations against lifetimes of exposure to traditional institutional situations. The personal history of Indrasingh given in Part III will illustrate the way in which many villagers absorbed into their personal worlds various social horizons in a time of historic change.

3. *Rulers and subjects.*—Although the foregoing changes were under way in 1950, Kasandra's villagers were still intricately linked with agrarian institutions of feudatory type under overlord rule, and among numerous hybrid traditions in the village, with *Rajpūt* traditions. Overlord rule locked the entire village population into an authoritarian and quasipolitical system of subject-ruler allegiances. The *Vāghelā Rajpūt* overlords, a minority of some 110 persons in the village, were the royal "rulers" (*darbārs*) under this old system. The remaining seven-eighths of the village population were known to the rulers and themselves as the "subjects" (*prajā*) of the overlords.

Members of the subject population of Kasandra were traditionally attached to particular lineages and branches of the ruling overlord group according to the rulers' genealogically determined shares in the village lands. Shares in the land, concomitantly shares in the subject population, were reckoned symbolically by the sixteen-anna parts of a rupee coin (*infra*, Fig. 1). But the number of "subjects" attached to respective "rulers" was approximate only, since the hereditary units of attachment were whole family and subcaste groups. Attachments of "subjects" to "rulers" were originally formed under various circumstances in Kasandra's long history of settlement. Until early 1950, the whole *Koḷī-Pagī* subcaste group of Kasandra was attached, for example, to the junior *Vāghelā* lineage. Such inherited and lifelong attachments have affected the development of the villager's self-image as a subject, as well as his attitudes and behavior toward the rulers and toward other subjects in the village population.

The subject population of Kasandra village had traditionally been governed by its rulers with interference from subdivisional and district authorities only in matters affecting government revenues or in cases of homicide. Unlike some neighboring "government" (*khālsā*) villages, Kasandra had no elected village panchayat. It had, in fact, no permanent councils capable of arbitrating disputes. Panchayats sprouted only as cases came up, and then disappeared. Rulers served as arbitrators in cases of disputes between subjects, and intermediaries, generally "big farmers" selected by the overlords, served in cases of disputes between overlords. The official village headman (*mukhī*), who was responsible in theory to the subdivisional administration, was an overlord and a ruler selected by his ruling peers.

Caste panchayats in Kasandra, though they were parts of larger intervillage caste associations, had never been strongly vocal under the dominant local rulers. In other nearby villages under the freer political administration fostered by direct individual land tenure (*rayatvārī*) caste panchayats were more effective; they could make decisions, and could serve as potential and actual interest groups for the local groups of caste members. No caste panchayats met in Kasandra during the year of field research. There were numerous reports, however, of efforts by these panchayats in the recent past to challenge, support, deflect, or cushion the political and economic power of Kasandra's rulers.

The quasipolitical statuses of rulers and subjects had never had legal value beyond the boundaries of the village, and after 1947 the relations of rulers and subjects became legally subject to checks by the subdivisional administration even within the village. As late as 1950, officials of Sanand Taluka still relied on Kasandra's overlord rulers for reports concerning the village's internal administration. Ultimately encouraged by Congress party backing in 1950, the subject population of Kasandra displayed an increased interest in pulling away from the authority of their *Rajpūt* rulers. The traditional extralegal government by the local overlords then acted as a stubborn, counterassertive force. The rulers continued to push their extralegal powers as far as they dared.

4. *The greater* Rajpūt *tradition.*—Kasandra's *Rajpūts* could be identified at once by an insistent, self-styled physical appearance and dress symbolically denoting strength—by the long moustaches most of them wore, by the nine-foot-long turbans which they wrapped around their heads, and by the swords or five- to six-foot-long spears which they carried with them everywhere. "Stoutness" was the desired physical build, though few achieved it.

Overlord rulers in Kasandra were members of a single subcaste (*jāti*), that of the *Vāghelā Rajpūts.* Reared and educated in the greater *Rajpūt* tradition, these *Vāghelās* of Kasandra were dedicated to goals of power and rule and to military standards of bravery. They held themselves to be descendants of the goddess *Vāgheśvarī,* a tigress manifestation of *Śakti,* herself a goddess of immense powers.

These rulers of Kasandra claimed earthly identity with recently deposed rulers of Kathiawar and Rajputana. They traced close ties of lineal kinship with younger sons of the former *Vāghelā-Solaṅkī* rulers of Gujarat. Younger sons of this dynasty had migrated into Gujarat to claim lands granted to them by their ruling senior kinsmen, to seize lands by military force, or to flee from fraternal disputes over the partitioning of joint-family territories elsewhere. Such disputes over the partitioning of joint-family holdings, called "brother separations,' continue prominently, especially among *Vāghelās,* in Kasandra today.

The landlord rulers of Kasandra had formal supralocal administrative ties with the subdivisional authorities at Sanand, and, through them, with the district collector of revenue at Ahmadabad. But the political, military, and emotional allegiances of the rulers of Kasandra were to a nominal liege, one of their *Vāghelā Rajpūt* kinsmen, the *Ṭhākor Sāheb* of Sanand. In him, one ruler of Kasandra told me, "We believe as in our God. He in Sanand is our King. If he calls ten thousand *Rajpūts,* we will go and give our heads to him."

Power, allegiance, sacrifice, and bravery were interchangeable and related ideals of a dominant *Rajpūt* theme. These same ideals were tangibly rooted in the long history of political, economic, and military power of the *Vāghelā Rajpūts.* Their *Rajpūt* heritage was felt and understood by Kasandra's village rulers. It was symbolized for them in a simple origin myth which they quoted frequently out of their subcaste history, the *Vṛttānt* (Anonymous 1914):

> *Brahmā* created the universe. The universe, surfeited with nonreligious persons, went to *Brahmā*. At *Brahmā*'s wish a *Kṣatriya*, or brave man, was created with ornaments, dress, and weapons. *Brahmājī* ordered the *Kṣatriya* to destroy the nonreligious persons in the universe, and then as a reward gave the *Kṣatriya* a kingdom.

Again quoting the *Vṛttānt*, *Vāghelās* drew their favorite portrait of *Rajpūts*, boasting of their ancestors as "proud, sinful people addicted to drinking who harassed other people and hated Brahmans and gods." And out of this much-valued *Vṛttānt* they also quoted a favorite stereotype of a *Rajpūt*'s destiny:

> A *Rajpūt* who bears an insult commits a thousand sins. He goes to a hell from which nobody can save him. It is the fate of a *Rajpūt* to complete his birth and rebirth by the help of his sword only.

Backed by these lively traditions, *Vāghelās* in the village were dedicated to the achievement of power with all of its attendant attributes. There were few individuals who, even though they possessed personality traits which appeared to go against this goal of power-seeking, could dissociate themselves from the social practices originating in this goal. Those *Vāghelās* in the village who could not live up to *Rajpūt* aspirations were carried along by other "strong" *Vāghelās*, by authoritarian personalities, by leaders of their lineages who were theoretically but not always the eldest males.

A *Vāghelā Rajpūt*'s authority in his kinship group and in the village depended in part on his age status as a mature elder, on his genealogical position in the lineage, on his landed wealth and on his prestige with superiors. Personal verbal skills and, above all, an ability to take action were also essential to individual authority.

An individual could achieve some of the role requirements for authority, as *Rajpūts* themselves admitted, by exercise of force and fraud. He could apply coercive "control" (*dāb*) or manipulate legal rights; he could employ guilt- and shame-producing mechanisms (*śaram*) resembling Chinese "face," impelling others to respond appropriately through their own efforts to save face; he could manipulate village-wide aspirations for prestige (*ijat*); he could demonstrate the personal skills noted above, as well as the generally esteemed skills of foresight, judgment, and capacity for self-control; and, last but not least, he could achieve some of the requirements for authority by manipulating alliances among rulers and allegiances of subjects to rulers in the overlord system.

5. *Seniority and authority among the rulers.*—Like members of a royal house, the *Vāghelā* rulers of Kasandra attempted to perpetuate their group's domination of the village through a system of hereditary chieftainship and through systematic stress on the authority of senior genealogical positions. The eldest son of the eldest branch of the senior lineage in the local *Vāghelā* group inherited through senior preference both the office of chief of the entire group (*ṭilāyat,* "he whose forehead is marked") and the largest share of the overlord lands and of the subject population in Kasandra village. Inheritance by senior preference in their chiefly lineages is a part of the caste law of *Vāghelās* as among other ruling *Rajpūts,* although it is not sanctioned by the normal Hindu law of inheritance.

The division of land shares and subjects among the rulers of Kasandra was reckoned according to the sixteen-anna parts of a rupee coin. The origin of this traditional reckoning was explained as follows by Partapsingh, a *Jhālā Rajpūt* "second-class" landlord of Kasandra:[3]

> This sixteen-anna system comes [down] from the past. According to our Hindu [calendric] system it is about five thousand years old, and it is found in the *Mahābhārat* also. The rupee was a coin even at that time. But that rupee was pure. This rupee today is not pure. Still the sixteen-annas-in-a-rupee system existed then. Shall I tell you where it is found in the *Mahābhārat?* (Yes.)[4]
>
> When there was a quarrel—I am talking about Delhi, which is our capital—between Karva [*Kaurava*] and Pandar [*Pāṇḍava*] brothers. At that time Karva told Pandar: "We won't give you anything." At that time, Dvarka's *Srī Kṛṣṇa* was in the panchayat. . . . [He explains panchayat as "when there is a dispute between two parties and the third person is between."] Pandar was the son of the older brother. Karva was the son of the younger brother. And the panchayat, through *Kṛṣṇa,* divided the whole thing into ten annas and six annas. This thing of the past five thousand years still exists. The same thing is still happening! . . .

The senior patrilineage, known as the "elder seat of power" (*moṭī delī*), owned a ten-anna portion of the Kasandra village estate. This portion was subsequently divided into three shares among three branches of the lineage in the proportion 6:2:2, the share of the eldest branch again being largest by the rule of senior preference. The junior *Vāghelā* patrilineage, the "younger seat of power" (*nānī delī*), owned a six-anna portion of the estate. Its portion was in turn divided equally into two three-anna shares between two branches, the rule of senior preference not applying among brothers of a

3. Throughout this paper all direct quotes from named informants, excepting those given in the opinion poll, are taken from the sections pertaining to those informants in Steed (1950*b*).

4. Words in parentheses are those of the interviewer, Gitel P. Steed.

junior lineage. In two hamlets nearby, the entire agnatic group of the rulers of Kasandra owned lands in common without subdivision, and managed these lands through a committee comprising the chief along with other representatives of each lineage.

An emphasis on seniority ran through the entire society of Kasandra's rulers, from the largest lineage grouping down to the single family. The chief, with his family, branch and lineage, maintained paramount authority at the top. Beneath him, the eldest member of each subgrouping inherited an established position of authority over his juniors—parents over children, elder brothers

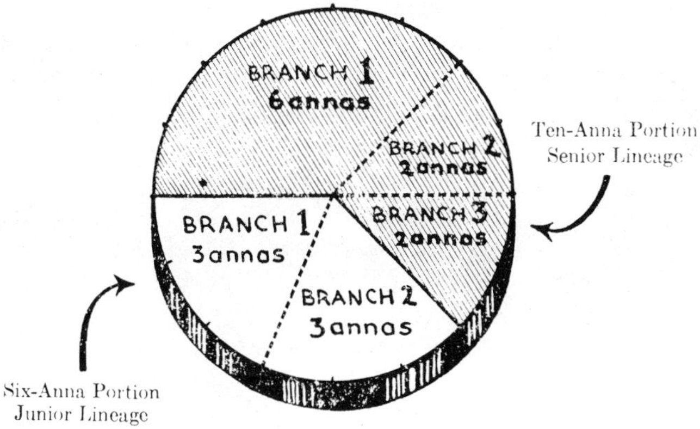

FIGURE 1. TRADITIONAL DIVISION OF LANDS AND SUBJECTS IN KASANDRA VILLAGE, 1950

Reckoned by the sixteen-anna parts of a rupee coin

over younger brothers, mothers-in-law over wives, and so on. This authoritarian structuring of social relationships among Kasandra's rulers was much in evidence in 1950–51.

Just as the *Vāghelā* rulers' authority over their subjects was governed by certain impersonal, *Gesellschaft*-like interests, so all *Vāghelās* among themselves were governed as much by impersonal interests as by more personal, intimate *Gemeinschaft*-like considerations. An authoritarian regime emerged among the *Vāghelās* from generations of attachments to landholdings and from their formal emphasis on seniority and oligarchic rule. The perpetuity of each family's position in this formal system of authority and the continuity of its economic interests in the future were insured by the group's genealogy, records of which were protected by a professional caste genealogist.

B. ECONOMIC STRATIFICATION

The population of Kasandra fell into four large and highly differentiated agrarian classes which reflected the vicissitudes of a land-tenure system in transition.

1. *Landlords and their pensioners.*—At the top stood an elite class of landlords and their immediate dependents, comprising nearly a third of the village population. The landlord class was further stratified into two grades which were described by the villagers as "first-class" and "second-class" landlords. The "first-class landlords" were the 110 *Vāghelā Rajpūt* overlords. These were the landed gentry of greatest wealth, power, and social position. The "second-class landlords" were the *Jhālā Rajpūts,* a group of peasant proprietors who had owned all of Kasandra village in 1607 but who possessed only one quarter (*vāṭṭo*) of it in 1950 under "gift" (*ināmī*) tenure. These "second-class" *Jhālā* landlords therefore owed traditional allegiances to the "first-class" *Vāghelā* rulers, yet they carried into the present an ancient enmity against the *Vāghelās* against whom they had not very long ago brought a legal suit for possession of Kasandra. The economic and political aspirations of the *Jhālās* had been severely thwarted, yet as *Rajpūts* they required power and status. "I care for my reputation twenty-four hours a day," was one *Jhālā Rajpūt*'s description of his reaction to his status of "second-class landlord."

Along with the landlords in the highest economic class must be placed the Brahmans of Kasandra who served and mingled with the landlords in return for high compensation, including charity landholdings.

2. *Middle class.*—A middle class of merchants, farmers, and artisans stood directly below the landlords in economic rank. Its members, like many other people of the village, held statuses which were partly inherited through the traditional agrarian system described above and partly acquired in the external market economy. The three divisions of this middle class may best be described separately.

a) The shopkeepers and land-management contractors (*kāmdārs*) were largely of Merchant (*Vāṇiyā*) caste. Villagers sometimes inconsistently placed Merchants as equals of the landlord elite, but the Merchants looked upon themselves as "subjects" of the rulers. Merchants held no land themselves and were not as wealthy or as powerful as the landlords. They acquired ties to the land as middlemen through exporting and marketing the village's agricultural products.

b) Cultivators (*kheḍuts*), members of seven different *Rajpūt* subcastes, stood next in rank to the Merchants within the middle class. All villagers considered these cultivators to be indispensable to agriculture. Cultivators in general formed an intermediate class between the landlords and the landless population. They enjoyed more independence than did other classes, although they were encumbered by their many bonds with the overlords.

Cultivators were of two sorts, permanent and temporary. The permanent cultivators, reared to customary rights over the use of their lands, had been secure economically even before the recent legal fortification of their rights. They were attached to overlords both through the share-cropping system and through the requirements of feudatory service (*salāmiyo*). As feudatory servants they could be pulled away from their fields at any time to serve as "protectors" and escorts of the rulers or rulers' wives on travels to or from the village, on pilgrimages, on visits to relatives, fairs, and on any other excursions. The hereditary standing of these permanent cultivators and their attachments to the *Vāghelā* overlords were both consequences of conquest. As *Rajpūts* under old allegiances they could be summoned to offer ritualized forms of consolation on demand, to bring "joy" (*ānand*) whenever their overlords were in mourning or were experiencing other sadness. Similarly, their wives could be pressed into service as singers of hymns (*bhajans*) for the overlords' wives.

In recent years, permanent cultivators opposed their landlords openly. Anticipating the liquidation of overlordship and their own rise to the status of peasant proprietorship, they repudiated their *Rajpūt* allegiances, refused to perform their traditional feudatory service, and forfeited the land grants and maintenance which they had once received in return for their services.

Temporary cultivators were a category of persons whose status shifted precariously from that of tenants to that of landless laborers, depending on the whim of the landlords. In 1950 they displayed confusion and insecurity. Lacking clear goals, they, like the untouchable farmers, were most easily intimidated by the rulers.

c) A dwindling enclave of artisans formed the third division of this agrarian middle class. These artisans—Goldsmith, Carpenter, Blacksmith, Potter, and Barber—often combined the functions of craftsmen, entrepreneurs, and farmers. Some who also occupied lower agrarian statuses were grouped ambiguously by villagers as members of the class of compulsory laborers described below.

3. *Landless laborers.*—Dependent on the overlords as subsistence workers and bound to them also as debtors were the landless laborers (*ubhardhis*). With more than three hundred members drawn from six lower subcastes, this class was the most numerous and most indigent economic class in the village. Its numbers were growing in 1950–51 in response to the recent increasing trend toward cash wages.

4. *Compulsory laborers.*—Less free than landless laborers, compulsory laborers (*vasvāyos, veṭhiyos*) were a serflike class of hereditary retainers and servants, members of many low subcastes, who had "belonged to" Kasandra's overlords under the old regime. Under the system of direct individual land tenure prevailing in most other villages of Gujarat, a similar class of indentured laborers was to be found. But under overlord tenure, as in Kasandra, such laborers also served as hereditary retainers and performed forced labor.

The class of compulsory laborers was decreasing almost in direct proportion to the increase of the class of landless laborers. Before 1947, when their status was legally abolished, they had been a large class in Kasandra. After 1947, overlords relinquished their traditional claims, but only when compulsory laborers became aware of their rights to freedom and began to resist those claims. Despite the laws against compulsory labor, there were in 1951 still twenty families in this class of compulsory laborers in Kasandra who had not yet thrown off the lifelong pressures of their overlords.

C. CASTE AND KINSHIP: THE MOST INSULAR TRADITIONS

1. *Hierarchy and segregation of the subcastes.*—The population of Kasandra, divisible first into "rulers" and "subjects" under the overlord tenure system, and divisible again economically into a number of interdependent classes, was still further differentiated into twenty-six corporate subcaste groups (*jātis*). Subcaste groups were the largest hereditary kinship divisions of village society, and through their kinship interests were deeply intrenched in the social structure of the village.

Its scope extended by the usual practice of village exogamy, each whole subcaste encompassed ties of consanguinity in many localities beyond Kasandra. The geographical frontiers of each subcaste were various and were not confined to any one set of territorial boundaries. For the smaller subcaste groups within Kasandra, the more extensive, supralocal subcaste groups functioned in effect both as kinship groups and as political associations.

The subcastes of Kasandra held to a traditional pattern of rank by which each was placed above or below every other subcaste in an order of economic, social, and ritual precedence. Each subcaste was also placed symbolically by villagers in one of the five ranks of the *varṇa* scale. The resulting social hierarchy of the subcastes was inconsistent, but was nonetheless a positive and self-conscious system.

The hierarchy of subcastes in Kasandra had two opposing tendencies. On the one hand, it tended to draw the entire population of the village into an intersubcaste network of ritually ranked economic exchanges, mutual obligations, festivals, and ceremonies. Virtually everyone in the village was bound by this network throughout his life. Thus *Jhālā Rajpūts* were bound as inferior landlords to their *Vāghelā* superiors. Brahmans were bound to perform religious services (*jajmānī*) for their customers in many subcastes, customers whom they either inherited or acquired through the grant of an overlord; Brahmans also received some of the most satisfying social and economic rewards (charity lands, food for maintenance, etc.). Below the Brahmans, some Merchants were bound to perform the services of land-management contracting (*kāmdārī*) for their hereditary overlords. Members of seven cultivating *Rajpūt* subcastes were required to perform feudatory service for their landlords; feudatory service was generally considered to be less respectable than contracting, but more respectable than compulsory labor (*veṭh*). Members of many lower subcastes (three *Koḷī* subcastes, *Koḷī-Pagī*, Potter, Barber, Herdsman, *Vāghrī*, *Rāvaḷ*) and untouchable subcastes (*Ḍheḍ*, *Śenmā*, *Bhaṅgī*) were bound to perform compulsory labor for their hereditary patrons. One effect of this strong local network of relationships among the subcastes was to insulate from the outside the social structure of the village as a whole.

On the other hand, and at the same time, the subcaste hierarchy gave ritual and economic sanction to a structure of social distance among the subcastes. Since subcastes were already familistic in nature, the effect of hierarchy was still further to segregate subcaste groups off from one another as islands within the village community. Each subcaste group preserved its partial segregation by inclosing itself within large compound walls, or by gathering its dwellings in rows on secluded streets.

But in 1950, as the freer economic classes of peasant proprietors and hired laborers grew in numbers, some of the old insularity of the subcaste groups showed signs of giving way. Subcaste groups remained important as holders of occupational monopolies, and sometimes continued to carry out managerial functions within themselves. But their members were tending to form new economic associations more often with members of other subcastes. Compulsory laborers of the lowest subcastes joined with free laborers of higher subcastes. Whole groups of members of the superior subcastes broke through some of their old barriers of ritual distance to form new and closer ties with members of three subcastes of *Koḷīs* and even, as never before, with certain untouchable *Śenmās* and *Ḍheḍs*.

2. *Consanguineal and affinal ties.*—Within his respective subcaste, each man and woman of Kasandra stood at the junction of three realms of lifelong familial attachments: paternal, maternal, and affinal. Each individual was reared and educated to a place in the adult world through his experiences in these three realms.

With varying degrees of emphasis, every man born in Kasandra was reared to have concern for the continuity of his patrilineal, patrilocal family line and to abhor the possibility of its extinction. More than others, every *Vāghelā Rajpūt* man was pulled into a nexus of involvements, especially those of property interests. Even a man who was enmeshed in such impersonal affairs still formed his most intimate, affectionate associations in his natal, paternal village.

Every woman born and generally reared in Kasandra, her paternal village, was educated with varying degrees of emphasis for the time when she would move out of her father's village (*piyar*) and into her father-in-law's village (*sasrā*). This conjugal village was a new and alien realm of family relationships which would form the bulk of her adult experiences. Her husband's kinsmen were an almost lifelong concern for every woman married into Kasandra, especially for a *Vāghelā Rajpūt* woman, even during the years before her coming to Kasandra, usually at about the age of fourteen.

Men did not share these concerns about their relatives in their father-in-law's village. *Vāghelā Rajpūt* men, as a rule, took wives from inferior *Rajpūt* subcastes in other villages, although they might marry a cross-cousin of such a subcaste within Kasandra. Consistent with the practice of female hypergamy, *Vāghelā* men commanded high dowries. Theirs was a position of superordination over their wives' relatives.

For both men and women, relatives in the mother's natal village (*mosāḷ*) were benevolent relatives. Just as a woman's paternal kinsmen continued to act as her surrogates and protectors after her marriage into Kasandra, so they acted as buffers or placators for the children whom she later bore.

3. *Stages of life: areas of individual achievement.*—Founded on ubiquitous Hindu ideals was a village-wide structuring of individual status according to age. As each individual grew older, he had the right to a shift of place in his family and subcaste.

Defining the four stages of life as most villagers defined them—childhood up to eighteen or twenty, youth from twenty to forty, maturity from forty to sixty, and old age as the later years of dependency and inability to work—Kasandra village could be called an abode of the young: in 1951 there were more than seven times as many children as old people (391 to 51) in the total village population. In the local *Vāghelā* subcaste group, there were twenty-nine children as against one old man.

One influential *Vāghelā Rajpūt* elder, Ravubha, interpreted the passage of age in the following way, stressing *Rajpūt* temperament along with the physical facts of age and along with the more general social values of Hindu tradition:

There are ideally four different phases of life, having to do with physical age, temperament, and social affairs. In order of growing up there are the stages of the child (*bāl*), the youth (*juvān*), the mature (*vṛddath*) man, and old age (*jhara*). The body undergoes physical changes, and the mind undergoes changes of intelligence. Ideas change.

In childhood, the child is small. As to physical matters, he knows everything about eating. But he knows less about social affairs. His thoughts are child's thoughts—all innocent thoughts: no cunningness, no deceitfulness, no shrewdness; absolutely pure. Playing, eating, drinking, joking and teasing are his activities. . . .

Youth [is the period of years from] fifteen to forty, sometimes forty-five: a man's body grows bigger, and he gains more strength. He slowly gets knowledge of worldly affairs. He has a feeling of ambition about earning, and he is ambitious about studying. . . .

Little by little a man finds all social matters and responsibilities resting upon him. He may have to flatter others to get wealth. He may have to serve others to get wealth. Thus he obtains knowledge about everything. If he has to acquire money through business, he obtains knowledge about that.

Anxiety about acquiring wealth predominates during youth. If a youth meets an obstacle in acquiring wealth, he may fall victim to anger. During childhood, his temperament is jolly, but during youth it changes to anger. The temperament is full of anger. In youth, if there is any instance of selfishness, then quarrels, fights, . . . cases, complaints in the courts—everything comes up. A child knows nothing about all this. During youth the body has tremendous strength.

During maturity, this anger and angry temperament change into a peaceful nature. A man has enough intelligence at this age to instruct two youths in fighting and in showing their anger. At this period, a man is able intelligently to coach his children and other youngsters. And physical strength has diminished a bit at this age. Social responsibilities also diminish a little now. The person's main attention is turned toward God—*slightly*. He engages in fights and mischief very much less. . . .

During . . . old age all the senses are less strong. Teeth are lost from the mouth and discharges pass through the nose, because there isn't much control of the senses. There is less strength to control urination and defecation as well. The ears hear less. Some men lose their eyesight during old age, and the body diminishes slowly.

And the temperament again changes to anger—quite hot. An old man doesn't like anybody else's speaking. Intelligence gets faster and faster.

He always has some disease, so the old man is full of disgust. He instructs people in the house and feels more disgust because no one listens. Old age is absolutely painful. Only a charitable soul can have peace during old age. . . .

My point of view is that individuals may differ—some may begin earlier, some later—but age is the main division.

4. *Summary.*—Up to this point, I have tried to delineate the principal horizons which frame the orbit of social relations for most residents of Kasandra village. Many of the social relations outlined are those of a feudatory structure in transition. In keeping with the major emphasis of the field approach, I have begun from the widest circumference of social relations within which villagers moved, and gradually narrowed the focus of observations upon the society of subcaste and family. Within these latter horizons of social relations are to be found the proximal and the deeper levels of socialization in given persons.

III. THE PRIVATE AND SOCIAL WORLD OF INDRASINGH

To illustrate this approach to personality formation at the individual level, I now enter upon the private and social world of a single villager in Kasandra, Indrasingh, a twenty-six-year-old resident overlord and person of local influence (Fig. 4). I explore his career through the familial society of his *Vāghelā Rajpūt* subcaste. Here I shift the axis of inquiry from that of the changing organization of the village society of Kasandra to that of a changing organization in the growing personality of one individual.[5] While illustration of the approach up to this point has been sociological and general, it is now ontogenetic and particular.

The psychological observations which are made in the following analysis are limited for the most part to those which can be made at cognitive, conscious levels of personal behavior. I make use of Indrasingh's fragmentary, screen memories of his past—his so-called

5. Cf. Redfield: "How do human individual personalities persist? The question of social change becomes one of the formation of human personality in a being becoming human. . . . Instead of looking for a frontier between two entities of societies or of cultures, we look at people with organized personalities entering into situations in which these organizations undergo some alterations. We find ourselves studying the same thing, but from an enriching viewpoint" (*in* Tax *et al.* 1953: 127).

anamnesic picture (Bateson 1944: 725)—and of his interpretations of his childhood self. But I use such materials solely in order to examine his modes of adaptation to the contingencies of community life—his values, his world views, his ethos, his externalized wishes and drives.

Little of the following data is interpreted here through the inferences and constructs of psychoanalysis, for these, as I have noted above, will be applied to the data by my colleagues of that discipline. I allude, however, to certain external points of reference—to certain ostensible, objective factors—which seem to invite probing of their implications for the formation of Indrasingh's personality. I assume that all the traits and complexes of Indrasingh's personality, even those fantasies and feelings which he holds back in the inner recesses of his private thought, are also linked to external points of reference. This is true, I assume, even if, by no contradiction at all, those points of reference have been deeply internalized.

The following is a picture, therefore, of the adult Indrasingh of 1950 placed against a background of family, kinship, and village. The picture is drawn from Indrasingh's earlier experiences, based on indirect evidence called up from the past, as interpreted by him in the present. It is a fusion of his earlier and of his later, more recent experiences.

A. INDRASINGH IN THE CONTEMPORARY SETTING

1. *Subcaste: the power of* Rajpūt *numbers.*—As one of the dominant subcaste group of *Vāghelā Rajpūts* in the "*Rajpūt* Village" of Kasandra, Indrasingh was reared in an aura of power. The power of the 110 *Vāghelās* was the power of numbers as well as the power of formal overlordship. In the *Rajpūt* tradition, numbers could win victories. Numbers of *Rajpūts* might sacrifice themselves for gods, for kings, or for profitable exploits. They might join armies or bands of outlaws, or might oppose one another in factions, or might upon urgent summons immediately close ranks against the outside. A *Rajpūt* derived a sense of safety and strength in numbers. The best *Rajpūt* was not the one who stood alone.

Indrasingh acknowledged that he found security in the traditional *Rajpūt* faith in the power and safety of numbers. For the ends they could achieve, he was willing to accept the premises of group manipulation and group exploitation. But he was unwilling to act upon these premises in a *Rajpūt* way. He shared neither *Rajpūt* aspirations for militant acquisition, nor the *Rajpūt* passion for consolidation of gains. Nor did he share *Rajpūt* zeal for physical prowess and for physical self-sacrifice. He valued nonviolent means for achieving desirable ends. He acceded, however, to the tradition of aggressive group action in a manner of ritual conformity.

Indrasingh's tendency to dissociate his private from his public attitudes appears in his responses during the interview reproduced below. The question of the interview was the form of group action which *Vāghelā Rajpūts* should take against the impending abolition of their overlordship.

(Yesterday you said you'd be happy to give up the management of your lands.)

I am glad internally, but still I feel the other way. We feel that to give up a little thing of ours is not easy to do, while this is our lifelong maintenance that we are losing. Suppose somebody comes and takes away this chair by force and we cannot do anything about it. We feel that [it must have happened] because we aren't strong enough, or because we haven't got enough power to prevent the other man from taking our chair away.

(And yet you are glad internally.)

I have two feelings. One way I feel is that we are surely going to be happy if we lose everything of ours. We'll be able to do something by ourselves. And the second way I feel is that not every man will become happy as soon as he loses everything. So both these ideas are always together in my mind.

(Are you trying to tell me that you personally will feel better but the others may not?)

Yes, something like that. . . . When the government takes away our land and properties in the land, we'll have to stand somewhere. Now we cannot stand in opposition and take our weapons out—that we cannot do. (Why not?) We don't have that much power. So simply to make our voice reach, we'll have to stand without weapons, with truth-seeking (*satyagraha*), that is, with passive resistance.

([Since this is virtually heresy for a *Rajpūt*, I ask him] Is that everyone's view or your view?)

No, it is *my* point of view. You see, they are taking Kasandra management in their hands as they said in the newspaper. Now we cannot oppose them with weapons. Passive resistance is the only method. We'll say, "Please don't do this. This is our life, our maintenance." Or if somebody comes to take our yield from the management, we can say "Yes" or "No" to that. And anyone who does anything against the government rules will be taken immediately to jail. . . .

(What will you do when you all meet [at an impending *Vāghelā Rajpūt* caste meeting]?)

At such times, the feeling of the crowd is always important. Naturally at that moment, I would not feel like telling them to give up everything of theirs. (So?) So in the meeting, every *Rajpūt* should have one and the same feeling—the feeling that we should try to hold down as much as we can. I personally should do the same thing. This is a matter of *Rajpūt* duty (*dharma*). (Should?) Ye-e-s. Yes. This second thought arises in my mind because the feeling of the mass arises in my mind. . . .

In spite of his personal attitudes and feelings to the contrary, Indrasingh's general mode of adaptation during 1950–51 was, as in this instance, one of conformity to *Rajpūt* standards.

2. *Kinship status: his place in the* Vāghelā Rajpūt *family cult.*—As a *Vāghelā Rajpūt*, Indrasingh inherited not only a general membership in a *Rajpūt* subcaste but also a particular place in a *Rajpūt* kinship group. Indrasingh's place in the *Vāghelā Rajpūt* kinship system affected both his inherited and acquired roles of power and responsibility in the family society. As a member of a particular family of a particular branch (*śākh*) of a particular lineage of the local *Vāghelā* subcaste, Indrasingh's destiny was anchored within one of twenty segregated kinship colonies of the village (Fig. 2). His private and social worlds, like those of most villagers, were centered within a seclusive colony whose members shared the same dwelling place for a lifetime. Traditionally the only members of these colonies who moved permanently out or in were women on the occasions of their marriages. Given the permanence and small size of each colony, its particular human composition could exert great influence on the career and personal development of each different member, as Indrasingh's did on him (*infra*).

As a male descendant of the eldest branch of the senior *Vāghelā* lineage, Indrasingh furthermore occupied a kinship place of special privilege in the scheme of senior preference. The lands controlled by his branch were the most extensive, and the number of subjects traditionally commanded by his branch was the greatest among all branches of the local *Vāghelā* ruling group. While Indrasingh's inherited place in the elder branch was a place of great potentiality, his own family was the third, or most junior, family of that branch. His attainment to the roles of "elder" and his effective leadership therefore depended importantly also upon the personal attributes which he acquired.

3. *Age status and leadership.*—By his absolute age, Indrasingh belonged to the class of "youths"—the twenty- to forty-year-olds. In his subcaste and lineage, however, as in the village as a whole, the classes of children and youths were large, while the class of elders was small. Of fifty-three males in the *Vāghelā* subcaste, thirty were children and seventeen were youths, while only six were elders of more than forty years of age. In Indrasingh's senior lineage group, there were eight youths, but only one man over forty.

The dearth of males over the age of forty in Indrasingh's kinship group meant that men of presumably suitable temperament and experience were not available to fill the roles of elders. Almost none were qualified by age to act as the authoritarian leaders and decision-makers who should form the core of Kasandra's ruling hierarchy. The existence in Indrasingh's lineage of only one man qualified by age as

Figure 2. The Place of Indrasingh in Space and Kinship

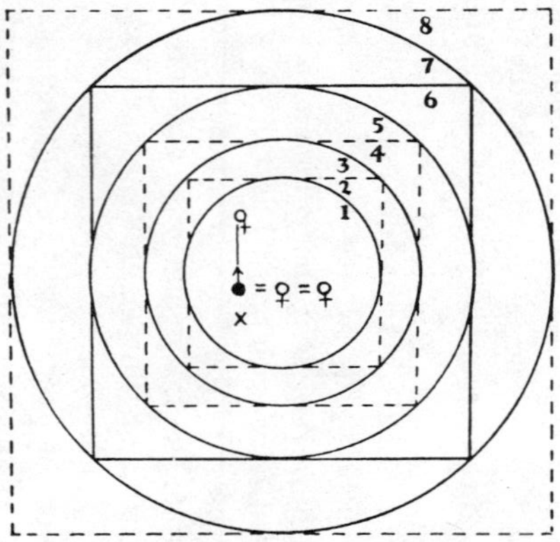

- [ ] Living space with potential mobility, e.g., exogamy
- □ Living space with barriers to mobility, e.g., women secluded within the compound, patrilocal residence
- ○ Kinship circles
- × Indrasingh and his immediate family circle

(1) Indrasingh (*X*) and his immediate family circle, including himself, his mother, and his two wives. They make up one of three commensal families living in

(2) One of three houses in the first wing of the senior lineage compound.

(3) The first, or elder branch, one of three branches of the senior lineage, occupying

(4) One of three courtyards or wings of the larger senior lineage compound.

(5) The whole senior lineage, whose members live within

(6) The walled compound of the whole senior lineage. This segregated residential colony is one of two patrilineal compounds whose two lineages together comprise

(7) The *Vāghelā Rajpūt* extended family group, which is identified both as a subcaste group and as an exogamous major lineage group, resident in

(8) Kasandra village. *Vāghelā Rajpūts* may marry with cross-cousins of other *Rajpūt* groups within the village, but generally marry with *Rajpūts* of other villages.

a potential elder exacerbated relationships between that one man and the eight youths of the lineage. The unity of the lineage group was fractured by their intralineage struggle for supremacy.

The younger men of the senior *Vāghelā* lineage fell prematurely into roles of authority, and were faced with new and intricate lineage responsibilities. As it happened, these responsibilities burgeoned most heavily upon the twenty-six-year-old Indrasingh himself, as he tells us, for example, in the following interview:

[At sixteen years of age,] because of my father's elder brother's presence, I didn't have to take part in any social affairs. After his death, I started taking interest, little by little.

For two or three years it was difficult for me to manage, but slowly it became all right. I had never done anything before. How to work? How to maintain social relations? How to manage?—I didn't know. . . . The first thing was to understand how do we stay so that our social relations are . . . how do we handle people?

(How do we "stay"?) When we are childish, we don't know anything about these affairs. Suddenly it comes to us how to manage giving and taking in this society, *with no internal feeling about it.* In the society, one always has to deal with many people, one has to give and take. . . . One has to learn how to behave and [in] what [way] to behave with whom. . . .

For some time, because I was new [to responsibilities], I had some difficulties. . . . I was aware of the social customs a bit. But I didn't have any knowledge of this: how to manage the land and how to manage to take the portions from the farmers.[?] I was eighteen years old then. (You were young.) [He smiles.] I was married at sixteen. After marriage I was separated [referring to the practice of joint family partition], and at the age of eighteen I had all the management in my hands. . . .

At this point, Indrasingh gives an account of his dispute with Jambha, the sole elder male of the middle branch of the *Vāghelā* senior lineage group. He reveals his own role in the guarded rivalry between youths and elders within the lineage group.

Problems can arise—many. I could manage the work here in this village with anyone's help, but I didn't work outside [on the *Vāghelā* properties in other villages]. All outside work would be done by Jambha. So there used to be problems at times. . . .

When my father's elder brother died, Jambha felt as if he were *the elderly person.* No one was cleverer than he was, and no one could tell him anything. Because of that, slowly, slowly our relations were cut off. . . . (How did you feel about this break with Jambha?) I felt it wasn't very nice to keep close relations with him when he felt very proud that he was the *eldest* and very clever.

(What did he want actually?) He wanted to use power. (How?) He wouldn't consider anyone else. (What did he do to you?) Nothing to me personally, but even from his talk, I felt that he had power in it.

(Did it worry you?) In worries there wasn't much, but I felt that he considered all of us to be children, and he himself the eldest, so that he could behave any way he liked or do whatever he pleased. So the worries were how to manage.

(How did you manage him?) In the outside villages I engaged contractors [to assist in the management of the lands] for me, and in this village I slowly took the management into my hands. (Did you have trouble about that?) No. What can he do afterwards? But whenever he went out to other villages, he raised objections of one sort or another.

(Is he the eldest in the whole extended family group?) Yes, at present he is. Until now my father's elder brother was the eldest, and that's why he had managed affairs for the whole group. . . . After his death, Jambha felt, "I'm the eldest, so I'll do as he did." One year he did and never showed anything to anyone.

Not only was there a dearth of older men in the *Vāghelā* subcaste group, but there was also a relative preponderance of females (sixty-three females to fifty-three males) and a great number of widows. Most of these widows were in Indrasingh's own lineage group. Since each widow held a lifetime lien on her husband's property, the many widows together held an edge of economic power over the men in this lineage. The power of the widows in Indrasingh's group was abetted by the traditional prerogatives held by widows, as respected elders, over younger persons in matters of discipline. The statistical accident of a preponderance of widows in Indrasingh's kinship group, like the fact of a dearth of older males, was not without effect on Indrasingh's unusual passage through the age statuses established in tradition.

When I encountered him in 1950, Indrasingh, though only twenty-six, was no fledgling youth but a ritually inducted, married householder who had achieved the status of a respected "elder" and leader both in his subcaste and in the greater community. Though lacking the absolute physical age expected in an elder, Indrasingh wore the ritual and social paraphernalia and the outward behavior of a man beyond his years. He associated as an equal mainly with more responsible leaders and elders of much greater age than himself, except on occasions when strong sanctions compelled him to give strict regard to the conventions of formal respect and subordination to those who were his superiors by age.

Not meeting the criterion of absolute age for his role as "elder," Indrasingh lacked as well the qualities of physical strength and stamina that were expected in a *Rajpūt* youth. Indrasingh was "delicate, didn't even have the strength to work a plow." Instead of going about armed, wearing an enormous turban and long moustaches, as was customary for young *Rajpūts*, Indrasingh cultivated a quiet, sophisticated appearance. He smoked English cigarettes rather than the pipe (*calam*) or the cheroots of the country-

FIGURE 3. *Rajpūt* WIDOWS

Widows of the ruling eldest branch of the senior lineage of *Vāghelā Rajpūt* overlords of village Kasandra in Gujarat. Indrasingh's mother, Nanaba, sits at the left, beside the widows of her husband's two elder brothers, one with her granddaughter.

FIGURE 4. SELF-PORTRAIT OF INDRASINGH

Water color by Indrasingh, *Vāghelā Rajpūt* landlord, Kasandra village, Gujarat

side. In keeping with his princely *Rajpūt* connections, he affected a green sherwani coat, worn over white jodhpurs or pajamas, with black oxfords of urban cut. He went about turbanless, except on ceremonial occasions when he donned the white turban of an elder rather than the brilliant turban of a youth. He wore a barely perceptible moustache, and carried no sword or spear as did the others.

4. *Public opinion of Indrasingh.*—Never wearing an aggressive *Rajpūt* manner and lacking the much-esteemed *Rajpūt* zeal for the wielding of brute force or threat, Indrasingh nonetheless appeared to fit other categories of eminence and influence which served *Vāghelā Rajpūt* ends, and appealed to other villagers as well. He manifested wisdom and moral prestige, qualities described by others as his "temperament."

The following opinions were expressed in a private poll of public opinion about Indrasingh (Steed 1950*c*):

KANTILAL (a Brahman): If farmers do anything against the rulers' wishes, they get a beating. . . . [The rulers] beat a farmer properly with a stick, with anything, even with a sword. . . . (Who beats?) Mulrajsingh and Bhavusingh—any one of the rulers will beat. (Indrasingh?) No, *he* won't! . . . He would tell them to *stop*, not to beat.

DEVGHAR (the sexton of *Śaṅkar*'s temple, *Bāvā* caste): Little Brother [Indrasingh] is the best one when it comes to paying in kind for compulsory service [*pasāyto*]. . . . I have trouble these days getting ghee. Jambha promised fifteen rupees, but he hasn't paid. When I went to him for [payment]—I went two times—he said, "Why don't you let me have my opium drink [*kasūmbo*] first?" Little Brother is the only one who gives. . . .

SHANTIBEN (a housewife of Merchant caste): Out of all the rulers, only Baby Brother is a nice person. But his mother is a very difficult woman.

MANILAL (a Carpenter): Of all the rulers, Little Brother and Babulal are the sweetest. They give royal food, fudge, etc. Babulal's father was a sweet, fine man and so was Little Brother's. These days they are having trouble, so they may not be as sweet. But they are the sweetest of them all.

MEGHA (a farmer of *Koḷī-Paṭel* caste): Elder Brother [Indrasingh] is a person who might help anyone.

PARTAPSINGH (a *Jhālā Rajpūt* second-class landlord): Little Brother [Indrasingh] . . . a very nice, innocent, simple man.

RAVUBHA (an elder of the *Vāghelā Rajpūt* junior lineage): Little Brother has no strength to work the plow. Addicter. Delicate.

NANGHUBHA (an elder of the same lineage): (Why did you offer the opium drink to Indrasingh first?) The one who is lovable gets it first.

NATIBA (a *Ḍheḍ* untouchable woman): Gentleman.

MAPABHAI (*Ḍheḍ* man): Gogalal and Little Brother are very nice people. . . . Very gentle. . . . But this one Jambha is the one who tried to fight for everyone else. . . . He's the wildest of all. He is very brave. He can kill the whole village.

When I asked Nanaba, Indrasingh's mother, what he was like as a child, she described him as

cold [meaning reticent, silent] and quiet from his childhood. Not very quarrelsome. . . . As he grew older, he became very mischievous. . . . When I went somewhere, he would never go with me. He was very nice—very wise—as a child. He would ask my mother, "Where is Ma?" and she would say, "She has gone out." Then he would keep quiet. He wouldn't follow me.

Indrasingh himself, discussing individual differences in behavior, judged his own behavior at my request as follows:

. . . I have never gotten work out of anybody by using my position as a *Rajpūt*. Any time I get my work done, I get it done by explanation.

Everyone's mind is different. An individual behaves according to his own [mind]. . . . According to custom, farmers get up from a cot when they see a ruler coming. If one [farmer] doesn't get up then those [rulers] who believe in power show it [then and] there. But if that has happened to me any time, I have never questioned anyone as to why he keeps sitting there.

(Why is that?) Because I don't have any objection. . . . (And why is that?) That is natural. Everyone has a different temperament. (How would you estimate yours?) Maybe as a slightly cold nature. (Cold?) Quiet. (In our country, "cold" means "indifferent.") I don't mean "cold" in that way, but [I mean that] I don't have the temperament to get angry if the opposite person does. I'm quiet.

(Are you ever inwardly angry?) Yes, sometimes I do become angry inside. I have anger in my mind because I have a particular reason for the other person to feel so, but I do not. (Why not?) I do not know how to.

[Smiles.] Some people can scold other people so well. I have to think how to scold a person; I don't know how to. (It's easy for some.) It is easier when it suits [an individual's] temperament; without that [temperament], even seeing one person scold another is difficult. It astonishes me—how can a person learn all this? (You had the tradition which should have given you the self-confidence.) That's true, but I don't know how. . . .

(Have you ever scolded anyone?) Seldom, but not nicely. I don't know how to. I may scold when I am angry, but instead of saying one thing, I say something else. (You think of the right thing to say too late?) [Laughs.] Ah! Yes.

5. *Public and private roles.*—In spite of his seeming personal disposition to the contrary, Indrasingh inherited a place in an authoritarian family world and a responsibility for aggressive "leadership" in the larger community. He also acquired social roles of responsibility and authority which began in the household of his small immediate family, ramified into a tangle of *Gesellschaft*-like involvements with kinsmen of his lineage group and subcaste, and ultimately through the greater *Vāghelā Rajpūt* caste association took him out beyond the village into the area of caste-controlled but class-oriented political action.

During the crisis of *tālukdārī* abolition, a crisis which formed one of the chief concerns of his kinsmen in 1950–51, Indrasingh was to be found in the following social roles, many of these roles reflecting a fusion of feudatory and recent urban activities.

At twenty-six, he was the head of a household and a husband. He lived with his mother, a forty-five-year-old widow, and his two wives. A third wife had died in childbirth. His first marriage had been at the age of sixteen. With the assistance of these women, he managed a household with an independent purse and kitchen.

He was the leading member of his elder branch of the senior *Vāghelā* lineage, and the manager of all the joint estates of that branch. These were the estates of his own family and of his father's two elder brothers' families. His role as manager required him to handle all farm-labor relations, share-cropping apportionments, tenancy agreements, and land-revenue payments. Indrasingh served further as a disciplinarian, though a mild one, of his father's older brother's sons, who were younger than he. He arranged rites of passage for members of all three families of his branch.

Indrasingh served in addition as acting chief of the *Vāghelā Rajpūt* corporation of Kasandra because his nephew, who was the proper heir to the chieftainship, though of age, was too immature for the role. As acting chief, Indrasingh helped to manage land revenues and share-cropping on the group's joint estates in two hamlets outside Kasandra. In the same capacity, he was consulted by the *Ṭhākor Sāheb* of Sanand, the paramount chief of all *Vāghelās*, on local affairs. Also as chief he frequently represented the views of Kasandra's *Vāghelā* leaders to government officials. Indrasingh did not participate, however, in *Vāghelā* subcaste councils, but deferred instead to elders of the prescribed absolute age. In Kasandra village he was one of two captains of the *Vāghelā* Volunteer Corps, a secret, supravillage military society of his subcaste set up to oppose the *tālukdārī* abolition program of the Congress government.

Socially in his local subcaste group Indrasingh also participated daily in gatherings for opium-drinking at the men's clubhouse, a place frequented principally by males of the senior lineage. He was one of the most devoted local worshipers of *Vāgheśvarī*, the *Vāghelā* clan-goddess. He was active with several others in arranging rituals and ceremonies of worship both for the local *Vāghelā* group and for other local *Rajpūt* subcaste groups.

Partly through his status and powers as an overlord and ruler and his prestige as chief, but also through villagers' deference to his fair-mindedness and ability, Indrasingh further acquired the chairmanship of the village co-operative society. This society was a farmers' organization which was open also to cultivating landlords. Because of his influence, Indrasingh was also chosen one of seventy-five members of a Congress party election committee in the area of Kasandra. He was prominent as one of two arrangers of village-wide ceremonies for the worship of *Śaṅkar*, of the goddess *Mātrīmā*, and of other deities. In this work he arranged for collection of religious taxes (*dharmādā*) to pay for libations, temple maintenance, etc.

Many of Indrasingh's social roles which have been mentioned so far appear to be reflexes of his structural positions—inevitable responses to the contingencies of *Vāghelā Rajpūt* life in a changing environment. But, even in the highly structured and conformist society into which Indrasingh was born, there is room for individual plasticity in modes of adaptation. I have already indicated how Indrasingh's public roles demonstrated his personal capacity for ritual conformity to *Rajpūt* standards and conventions and how, when certain practical ends were in view, he was capable of assertive, but not militant or aggressive, behavior.

A full review of data concerning him (Steed 1950*b*, I) demonstrates that Indrasingh tended to move between two extremes of behavior. He moved toward one extreme of public participation and even of public leadership; he moved also toward another extreme of intractable and almost oppositional private retreat. The private preferences and goals which he expressed disclose his predilection for isolation, for creative activity through cognitive pursuits, and for religious ideological thinking. Such predilections were essentially non-*Rajpūt*, if not anti-*Rajpūt*, in nature.

Indrasingh partially succeeded in reconciling his public and private natures. He internalized some of his private strivings in fantasy, or else consciously repressed them. Or, when he could achieve such a solution, he expressed his private predilections through public institutional practices—those of public religion, for example, or those of the characteristic *Vāghelā* opium addiction. When thwarted too painfully, however, Indrasingh responded with certain somatic symptoms—with vomiting and hysterical fits (*infra*). In the course of his conversations with me he recognized these symptoms as acts of rage, as "attacks against himself," and as mechanisms of self-punishment.

One alternative institutional role which Indrasingh did not attempt, but which he extolled in conversations with me and dreamed about (Steed 1950*b*, I: 93–102), was the practice of religious bachelorhood (*brahmacarya*). Ravubha, a *Vāghelā* of the junior lineage, had already chosen such bachelorhood as his way of life. Indrasingh esteemed this role for several reasons, of which two were important for him. First, it permitted withdrawal from domestic affairs; second, it offered access to powers which Indrasingh found himself incapable of acquiring through following *Rajpūt* norms. Indrasingh believed that sexual continence practiced as a technique of religious bachelorhood gives inordinate strength and success. According to Indrasingh, the monkey deity *Hanumānjī*, by containing his semen, gained the strength to overcome otherwise insuperable obstacles. *Rāma*'s brother *Lakṣmaṇ*, he also believed, practiced religious bachelorhood for twelve years and was therefore able to kill the demon *Rāvaṇ* who was invulnerable to attack by any other god. In spite of his esteem for the role of the religious bachelor, and in spite of his conceding that it was a role which suited his private "nature" best, Indrasingh when I knew him had not as yet considered making an actual choice of that role. His tendency to withdraw from domestic life into religious activities put him rather well on the way toward religious bachelorhood, however.

B. SOME EFFECTS OF A RADICALLY DIFFERENT UPBRINGING

Until now, through his various structural positions in Kasandra village society, we have glanced at those features of Indrasingh's role behavior which principally served *Gesellschaft*-like ends. But for insights into Indrasingh's polarity of behavior and for understanding the seeming incongruence between his public and private practices, we need to glance also at his socialization history, as interpreted in the present.

1. *Childhood residence in the maternal village.*—While the men in his local subcaste group were traditionally reared in Kasandra, their paternal village, Indrasingh in the opening lines of the first paragraph of his personal narrative began: "When I was a child my father was dead. So after [he died] I used to stay in my mother's father's place in Jhalia [a village and capital of a state in Kathiawar]."

From these immediate recollections, we learn at once about two radical differences between Indrasingh's childhood and the expected experiences of a *Vāghelā Rajpūt* boy: his loss of his father and his upbringing in his maternal village. The death of his father when Indrasingh was fifteen months old deprived him of the potentially most significant figure in his native village. Symbolically the father is the paramount chief of the family; he is "the lord [*ṭhākor*]" of controlling power and prestige for the son; he is "my father, the ruler";

he is the person before whom the son has learned to show the greatest formal respect and obedience, and with whom the son has the strictest ties of religious duty; he is the man who, until he dies, controls the son's economic, social, and political rights, claims, and privileges; he is the person whom the son is destined to replace in the patrilineal family line.

The death of his father resulted in a second radical difference in Indrasingh's upbringing: a shift in his status during his childhood from that of a son in his father's village to that of a sister's son (*bhāṇej*) in his mother's village. While Indrasingh's mother had economic liens on her husband's patrilineal holdings in Kasandra, she was nonetheless regarded as a stranger and an alien in her deceased husband's compound. Two years of marriage, nine months of these spent bearing her child in her own village, were not sufficient firmly to establish her social position in her husband's village. She returned to her own community, Indrasingh's maternal village, to be supported by her own patrilineal kinsmen. For Indrasingh this meant an upbringing as a sister's son until he was fifteen years of age.

Indrasingh's early years as a sister's son in his mother's village gave him comparative freedom from the kinds of social restraints experienced by his patrilineal cousins in his father's village. Traditionally a sister's son is loved and indulged by members of his mother's group. The position of "beloved sister's son" was especially bestowed upon Indrasingh because he made no claims against the vested interests of the sons of Jhalia village. He did not threaten their economic or political status, or the continuity of their family line, although he was a potential emotional rival.

Indrasingh's memories were replete with episodes concerning the freedom he enjoyed at his mother's village, but in his notion of this freedom he emphasized the chances it gave him for anti-authoritarian, rebellious activities—what he called his "mischief."

In Indrasingh's narrative of his childhood his mother emerged as the most significant disciplinarian among the beloved maternal relatives who surrounded him.

> Because I was an only son, my mother loved me very much. . . . [But she] kept a little control alongside her love so that her child might not get spoiled. . . .
>
> If I made any mischief or tried to struggle unnecessarily, she scolded. [But] if she went to sit at somebody's place, or to see someone, even then she carried me along with her. For that much love only, she nursed me for five years.

His mother, acting as his "paternal village" conscience, knowingly attempted to prepare Indrasingh for his future roles in Kasandra as a ruling overlord. But her efforts were continually curtailed by her indulgent kinsmen, who admonished her, according to Indrasingh, whenever she disciplined him. Thus in the first episode of his life-history narrative, Indrasingh recalled what happened when he had wanted to fast and rest on the eleventh day of the fortnight (*agiyāras*), a traditional day of worship.

My mother said, "You can't." . . . Then I said, "No, I do want to observe the eleventh day." Then she scolded me a lot. She told me, "Go to school."

Instead of going to school, I went straight to the railway road. I told my mother's brother's daughter, . . . "I am going to run away to Kasandra."

Then my mother's brother and my mother's father went to look for me. . . . They came toward the station thinking that I might be waiting there to catch a train to go to Kasandra. There I was, walking on the road. . . . They brought me home . . . and said, "Never run away from home like this. If you want to observe the eleventh day, you do it."

Indrasingh looked upon these maternal relatives as indulgent parental surrogates, which they were.

While Indrasingh's maternal relatives were those who said, "You can," his paternal kinsmen were those who said, "You can't." On one occasion when he visited Kasandra, Indrasingh recalled:

Once I and the other boys went to bathe in the lake. . . . My father's mother heard that the lake was full and that all the boys had gone to bathe there. Thinking we might be drowned, she sent my father's elder brother after us. He scolded me, got hold of me by my arm and brought me to the [main] porch. There was a . . . tree near the porch. He said, "Today I'm going to tie your hands and feet [smiles] and hang you on this . . . tree so that no bathing in the lake is possible."

There was another father's elder brother [the chief at that time] who said to this one, "I'm his bail. He won't go to bathe in the lake from now on. If he goes, I'll be responsible for bringing him back to you." [Then he said to me,] "Now you can go and do what you like," and I was released.

2. *Interference with education as a ruler.*—Indrasingh's upbringing in his mother's village varied considerably from the traditional education of a *Rajpūt* ruler. While Jhalia, like Kasandra, was a village of resident *Rajpūt* rulers, Indrasingh's status as a sister's son placed him in a passive role as a young ruler. He was not drawn into the kinds of superordinate-subordinate roles which he was later expected to fill in his father's place.

At his mother's village, Indrasingh was the passive recipient of privileges and favors. His recollection of his infancy and early childhood at his mother's village was virtually a catalogue of excessive feedings and sweetmeat indulgences given by the "beloved maternal" relatives to their "beloved sister's son." These indulgences went beyond the institutional pattern of feeding children upon demand which prevailed generally in these villages.

Since he was a sister's son rather than a son in Jhalia, Indrasingh participated with relative passivity in matters that required *Rajpūt* action. He was not trained as sons are to maintain and achieve power. His own conception of *Rajpūt* power did not stress domination over others.

From the beginning, my mind was quite different about power. I didn't feel the same way as the others. I did not behave in the manner in which other people who are fond of power behave. . . . For example, I did not think that everybody should do what we told them to do. If anybody refused to do something for me, I always accepted it. I behaved this way as soon as I started to understand. . . .

Even now when we [*Vāghelā Rajpūts*] are together I may express my opinion that this is the way to work such and such a thing. But if there is any other person, or elderly person, who says, "No, we don't want to," then I immediately forget my opinion and say, "All right, do as you please."

This description of his own behavior by Indrasingh seems fairly accurate, but I asked him if his attitude was noticed by others in his group. He replied:

Yes, many of those who are in touch with me should know [of my attitude]. All those who are fond of power show [their fondness]. . . . Everybody else reacts according to his mind, and I do what I myself believe. They [other *Vāghelās*] act according to their own minds. They have never said anything to me about [my attitude]. . . . That hasn't happened yet.

Indrasingh was educated to lofty ideas concerning rank and wealth through his royal connections at his mother's village. In recalling the power of his mother's group, he emphasized their landed wealth, elegant houses, automobiles, visits to Bombay, hunting parties, and their high status as princely junior kinsmen of the Jhalia State ruler. In his contemporary self-image as a ruler, Indrasingh emulated the ideal rulers of his maternal village. He perceived himself as a landed gentleman of elegance and wealth rather than as a man of power. His opinions concerning the impending loss of his status as a ruling overlord reflected these associations:

(Can you recall your immediate reaction to the news concerning *tālukdārī* abolition?)

It was painful, naturally, because we will not be able to live in the same manner as we have been living so far. So the feelings are hurt. . . . (To what extent?) These feelings are such that a man can never forget. (Can you describe them?) Ah! For example, if Kasandra management goes into the hands of others, we cannot have the same power over farmers and others which we had before. And also, the whole group will be unable to maintain the kind of living which we have had so far because of the decrease, the reduction in income. So I feel two things: loss of power and loss of income. . . .

(Which feeling is stronger?)
Income, because one doesn't care for power. [One doesn't care] if one has it or not. . . . [Power] is not important if you have the same income which you had before. The difference is only this much: the man over whom we had power before does not work for us in the same fashion as before.

In this opinion, Indrasingh differed greatly from most other *Vāghelā* overlords, who felt loss of power more acutely than they felt loss of income.

A factor, therefore, in Indrasingh's deviation from *Rajpūt* standards of behavior was his upbringing in his maternal village, away from his future patrilineal, *Gesellschaft*-like responsibilities.

3. *The factor of discontinuity: troubles at Kasandra.*—At fifteen, Indrasingh experienced a sharp break from his relatively free life at his mother's village. At that age he was recalled to Kasandra to participate in the arrangements for his marriage. His troubles began at once when he was introduced to his responsibilities in his patrilineal compound. These responsibilities pulled him immediately into factional disputes concerning the management of the estates owned by his branch of the senior *Vāghelā* lineage, and concerning his own marriage, perhaps his deepest personal crisis.

Arrangements for all three of Indrasingh's marriages were linked to the competitive interests of the three families which comprised his own branch of the *Vāghelā* group. Each family of the branch desired to retain economic and political control for itself. Further friction was generated by the pressures of their respective matrilateral relatives upon each of the families of Indrasingh's branch. The three local families were in bitter conflict over an issue which had begun twenty years ago: from which of the three sets of matrilateral relatives should a daughter be selected for marriage to Indrasingh?

When Indrasingh was ten years old, the former chief, who was childless, arranged Indrasingh's first betrothal to a daughter of his (the chief's) mother's brother's son. The chief's selection was frowned upon by both Indrasingh and his mother because of their stronger sympathies with the wishes of their relatives in Jhalia rather than with those of their kinsmen in Kasandra village. But they yielded to the chief's wishes because of the control (*dāb*) which he exercised over them, according to Indrasingh's mother.

(Who arranged the marriage?) This Gangaba's husband [the chief]. Nobody had selected [the girl]. . . . Is there anything like selection there? Because he said he wanted to do [it], we had to say, "Yes." Has anyone seen her or selected her? He was the eldest in our house, and we had to do as he wanted. (Why did he want that?) That [place] is after all his mother's place, and he didn't have any children. So he thought if he brought a girl from his mother's place it would be nice. Nobody could deny his wish. He left an obstacle for the whole of our life!

According to Indrasingh, the chief obliged him to yield by evoking guilt and shame (*śaram*):

Just at that time [when the marriage arrangement was being completed] I had informed my father's elder brother [the chief] not to make [arrangements] for me through other people. (How should he have made the arrangements?) Although they knew that an arrangement in father's elder brother's mother's place wasn't good for me, he made this [arrangement] in order to make them feel better. He didn't have children himself, and if we hadn't done as he suggested, he would have felt bad about it. . . . I was against this betrothal. My father's second elder brother, Gogalal's father, was also against it. . . . It was all [done so as] to please him [the chief].

Indrasingh married his first wife, the chief's choice, at sixteen, and not long after that his mother accused her of sorcery. Twelve months after the marriage, Indrasingh developed convulsions and fits of loss of consciousness, symptoms diagnosed by a German doctor at Jamnagar as hysterical epilepsy. Indrasingh connected this behavior with his marital difficulties. His doctor recommended a second marriage.

The second marriage, this time to a girl of his own mother's village, was arranged by his father's second elder brother when Indrasingh was eighteen. Following two unsuccessful deliveries, however, the second wife died, and the first wife was again accused of sorcery by Indrasingh's mother.

4. *Lack of heirs: the ancestral cult.*—Both wives had failed to bear Indrasingh a child. If the reason was not sorcery, according to his mother, it was harassment by the spirits of restless ancestors (*pitruṇs*) unable to achieve final release (*mokṣa*). These spirits might be affecting Indrasingh's potency powers and thus interfering with the perpetuity of the family line. There was also the curse of an ancestral *Vāghelā* woman which promised the ultimate extinction of all *Vāghelās*. The threat of extinction of his line created a series of domestic crises.

Both Indrasingh and his mother developed an obsessive interest in the cult of the restless ancestors. They believed that these ancestors needed to be placated through ceremonial offerings. They therefore hired *Nāgar* Brahmans from Ahmadabad, members of the highest Brahman subcaste in Gujarat, to conduct readings of the *Bhagavad Gītā*. Exalted and costly religious ceremonies were held, some lasting for seven days, and the entire local *Vāghelā* group as well as members of other local *Rajpūt* clans were invited. The goal was forcefully to placate the ancestors and the cursing *Vāghelā* woman so that Indrasingh could have an heir.

Accompanying these ceremonies, Indrasingh adhered to the strictest ordinances of fasting during certain months and days, while also worshiping *Vāgheśvarī*, his clan-goddess. His mother augmented these efforts of his by engaging in ceremonies of propitiation said to be effective even though they were proper to low and even untouchable castes. She kept vows (*bādhās*) to goddesses, although she was formally an adherent of *Viṣṇu*, and herself resorted to sorcery (*mūṭh-cūṭh*) to fight the threat of sorcery.

Indrasingh's mother's accusations of sorcery against the first wife appeared to stimulate Indrasingh's admitted fears of impotency and sterility. Further aggravations were created by her persistent pressures upon him, generated by tensions of her own, to father children and thus to secure lineage posterity. Her demands upon him increased when, following the death of his second wife, and again by arrangement with his maternal relatives, he took a third wife who was too old to bear children.

5. *Reaction formation: withdrawing behavior.*—Indrasingh's first signs of negative withdrawal were shown in the succession of hysterical epileptic fits which enveloped his first three years of domestic relations in his patrilineal compound. "Though other people were there, I felt as if I were alone. My attention wouldn't be on other people. I used to sleep. . . ."

Members of his family and others linked Indrasingh's hysterical behavior with the difficulties he was having with the women in his household. His third wife, Umiadevi, explained:

> She [the first wife] didn't get along with Mother or with *Sāheb*. After two years of his first marriage, he married another wife, but she died in fifteen months. The doctor advised [him] to marry again since he wasn't keeping well because of his first wife. She wouldn't behave according to his wishes. This would annoy him and make him unconscious. Thus he spoilt his health thoroughly. He used to vomit a lot, day and night, without stopping.

During his initial years of facing domestic dilemmas in his paternal compound, Indrasingh's mode of reaction thus took an idiosyncratic form: he withdrew through these somatic symptoms of hysterical epilepsy.

After three years, Indrasingh succeeded in abandoning these symptoms in favor of an institutionalized mode of retreating from domestic crises. He took instead to the *Rajpūt* overlords' collective habit of opium-drinking:

> My father's elder brother and others said, "Start taking opium little by little and let's see." I started taking it, and in four months everything [convulsions and vomiting] stopped. Since then I have never had any troubles.

In 1950–51 Indrasingh was showing a disposition to turn away from participation in opium-drinking with other *Vāghelā* overlords. Since he was not a "full addicter," he said, he was giving up opium in order to devote himself to those practices of goddess- (*Śakti*) worship which "will change a man's past, present, and future." When he was not absorbed in the affairs of the estate, in the duties of chieftainship, or in other pursuits, as his mother alternately complained and boasted, Indrasingh sought isolation "in the upper story with his worshiping."

Indrasingh principally worshiped three goddesses who, according to him, could be compared with human beings of three different temperaments: the hot-natured *Mahākāḷī*, the medium-natured *Vāgheśvarī*, and the quiet, peaceful-natured *Sarasvatī*. He first worshiped and appeased that goddess in whom he believed most—*Mahākāḷī*, the hot-natured one. With her he attempted intricate religious "experiments" which, he said, "helped to solve troubles." Indrasingh acknowledged that he altered his choice of religious practices according to his circumstances: when he was interested in learning, he gave most worship to *Sarasvatī;* during the recent upheavals over the liquidation of overlord tenure he worshiped *Lakṣmī* to help overcome the danger of losing his landed wealth. In Indrasingh's choice of religious practices, psychological elements were not inconsistent with sociological ones (cf. Robert Redfield *in* Cohn 1954: 3).

6. *Summary.*—For Indrasingh, his ten years as a married householder in his patrilineal family and village emerge as the most difficult period in his personal history. These years were marked by severe socialization anxiety with which he struggled valiantly. He underwent transformations from one pattern of retreating behavior to another in an effort to accommodate his inner demands and interests to an authoritarian and power-structured society for which, by earlier training, he was not fully prepared. Indrasingh first discovered a "cure" for his hysterical symptoms through opium addiction, and then discovered an ostensible "cure" for his opium addiction through religious ideational practices. And, throughout these

processes of transformation, his retreating behavior appears never to have drawn him out of his public roles.

By other members of Kasandra's village society Indrasingh's reactions were not regarded as socially deviant. The community's tolerance for his behavior may have been a factor helping him toward a new accommodation. His hysterical symptoms were deplored as harmful and painful, but to himself only. His opium addiction was looked upon as a collective affliction of *Rajpūt* overlords and not especially as his individual affliction; few other persons alluded to Indrasingh as an addicter. His recent preoccupation with religious practices was also well within a pattern of alternative choices that was common to the larger Hindu society. His preference for isolation did not offend his fellow *Vāghelās* in spite of his resulting nonconformity with an incomplete participation in their aggressive group action. His disposition seems in fact to have helped to take him out of a youthful status and place him among the elders of his *Vāghelā* group, as well as giving him a role of "welfare" leadership in the village.

Indrasingh's ostensible accommodation to group ends was not without consequence. His more positive goals, sentiments, interests, and values were not congruent either with his conciliatory and submissive public behavior or with his private retreats. Pressed irresistibly to conform, Indrasingh yielded at the expense of his own educated "nature," altering, as we have seen, the total integration of his personality.

REFERENCES CITED

ANONYMOUS

1914 *Vṛttānt.* (In Gujarati.) Ahmadabad, privately published. Translated by Bhagvati Masher.

BATESON, GREGORY

1944 "Cultural Determinants of Personality," in *Personality and the Behavior Disorders,* ed. J. McV. HUNT, Vol. 2, pp. 714–35. New York, Ronald Press.

COHN, BERNARD S.

1954 "The Changing Status of the Depressed Castes. Lecture II." (Comparison of Cultures: The Indian Village.) Chicago, Department of Anthropology, University of Chicago. (Hectographed.)

DUBOIS, CORA

1944 *The People of Alor.* Minneapolis, University of Minnesota Press.

MARRIOTT, MCKIM

1954 "Village, Region and Nation: Little Communities in an Indigenous Civilization. Lecture I." (Comparison of Cultures: The Indian Village.)

Chicago, Department of Anthropology, University of Chicago. (Hectographed.)

MERTON, ROBERT K.

1949 *Social Theory and Social Structure*. Glencoe, Ill., Free Press.

REDFIELD, ROBERT and MILTON B. SINGER

1954 "The Cultural Role of Cities," *Economic Development and Cultural Change* **3**:53–73. Chicago.

STEED, GITEL P.

1949 Personal communication to A. KARDINER, later to E. HELLERSBERG, A. COTTINGHAM, and M. NAUMBURG. (Typescript.)

1950*a* "Methods of Selecting Villages. Report." New York, Columbia University Research in Contemporary India Field Project. (Mimeographed.)

1950*b* "Life History Documents. I (Indrasingh), II (Ravubha), III (Partapsingh), IV (Umiadevi), and VII (Nanaba)." New York, Columbia University Research in Contemporary India Field Project. (Hectographed.)

1950*c* "Sociological Documents." New York, Columbia University Research in Contemporary India Field Project. (Typescript.)

TAX, SOL, LOREN C. EISELEY, IRVING ROUSE, and CARL F. VOEGELIN (eds.)

1953 *An Appraisal of Anthropology Today*. Chicago, University of Chicago Press.

PEASANT CULTURE IN INDIA AND MEXICO
A COMPARATIVE ANALYSIS[1]

OSCAR LEWIS

I. INTRODUCTION

ALTHOUGH peasantry still constitutes almost three-fourths of the world's people and makes up the bulk of the population in the underdeveloped countries, it has been relatively neglected by social scientists as a special field of study: anthropologists have specialized in primitive or tribal societies; sociologists, in urban societies; and rural sociologists, in modern rural societies. Thus, the great majority of mankind has had no discipline to claim it as its own. A comparative science of peasantry is only now beginning to take form.

In recent years, following the establishment of the Point Four program and other action programs dedicated to raising the standards of living in the underdeveloped countries, there has been an increasing recognition of the need for a better understanding of peasant societies. Anthropologists, in particular, have been giving more attention to peasant societies in contrast to their earlier almost exclusive concern with tribal societies. This new interest has been on both the practical and the theoretical level. Anthropologists have participated directly in action programs as administrators, consultants, and research workers, and have helped train specialized technical personnel for foreign assignments. At the same time they have begun to re-examine the concept "peasant society" and the typologies in which it appears, such as the folk-urban typology, in the light of more recent research experience. A series of articles on the nature of the folk and peasant society has appeared in professional journals within the past few years (Miner 1952; Foster 1953; Mintz 1953; Redfield 1953*b;* Lewis 1954).

1. The study of Rani Khera village in Delhi District was done between October, 1952, and June, 1953, under the auspices of the Evaluation Organization, National Planning Commission, Government of India, while I was acting as Consulting Anthropologist for the Ford Foundation. I am indebted to the Behavioral Sciences Division of the Ford Foundation, New York, for a grant-in-aid in 1952 which helped with the field work in India and with the preparation of this paper.

In this paper I want to compare, briefly but systematically, some of the similarities and differences between the North Indian village of *Rānī Kheṛā* and the Mexican village of Tepoztlan. The major purpose of this comparison is to contribute toward our general understanding of peasantry. It is recognized that there is something about being a peasant which makes peasantry seem so similar all over the world, even in the most different historical and cultural settings. On the other hand, it is also true that the cultural setting and the general nature of the larger society of which peasantry is a part must undoubtedly influence the forms of peasant life and the very nature of the people.

Since most discussions of peasantry have emphasized the common elements, I have chosen in this paper to elaborate more fully upon the differences in order to illustrate the wide range of cultural forms possible under the rubric of peasant society and thereby indicate the need for a typology of peasantry. At the same time, I recognize the crucial importance, especially for theoretical purposes, of discerning and documenting the similarity within diversity. Moreover, I suspect that this similarity will probably be greatest in the field of values, a field only touched upon in this report.[2]

Two additional and secondary aspects of this paper, bearing primarily upon methodological considerations, may now be mentioned. This study represents one of the relatively few examples of firsthand comparative field research by the same investigator in peasant society in the different parts of the world. It seems to me that this kind of research enables one to make more detailed and refined comparisons than is generally possible by the traditional library methods, since the investigator carries with him a common frame of reference, similar methods of work, and a similar sense of problem. From a more personal point of view this kind of research pays double dividends. Not only did it provide me with firsthand knowledge of a new culture but it also sharpened and somewhat altered my earlier understanding of Tepoztlan and of Mexico.

Second, this paper raises the question of the degree to which a single village, selected more or less at random in terms of our problem, can tell us something about the nation of which it is a part. It is my own belief that almost any village in a predominantly agricul-

2. I am grateful to Robert Redfield for his kind and stimulating discussion of this and other points in this paper. His paper "The Peasant's View of the Good Life" (mimeographed version of a lecture delivered at the University College, University of Chicago, May 14, 1954) is a pioneer effort toward getting at some of the common elements in peasant value systems.

tural nation reflects some distinctive aspects of the nation, its culture, and its problems. It is my hope that this paper will convey to the reader some feeling for the differences not only between Rani Khera and Tepoztlan but also between India and Mexico.

At the outset, I would like to point to a few difficulties in making comparisons between the two villages. In dealing with two villages in distant and contrasting culture areas of the world the question arises whether the village is a meaningful and proper unit for comparison, especially since the Indian village differs so markedly in its structure and functions from the Mexican village. Despite these differences, I believe that the two villages are sufficiently similar, isolable, and well-defined units for comparative study. However, to acknowledge that the village is an isolable unit does not mean that we should treat it as an isolate. To do so could lead only to a limited understanding. Neither Tepoztlan nor Rani Khera is an isolated entity. Each, in its own distinctive way, is part of a larger sociocultural system, a larger whole—the region and the nation—through which it must be understood.[3]

Comparison between a Mexican and an Indian village presents problems over and above those encountered in comparing villages within a single country or a single great tradition. Items which exist in one and not in the other are simply not comparable. For example, Tepoztlan has no caste system, and Rani Khera has no *compadre* system. In Tepoztlan the *municipio* is the landholding unit (for communal lands); in Rani Khera the village is the landholding unit. How are we to weight the influence of such items on the total culture pattern of the community? Both the caste system and the *compadre* system are cohesive forces in social life, but can we equate

3. The discussion of this point in my study of Tepoztlan applies with double force to the study of peasant villages in India: ". . . anthropological studies in Mexico . . . have been characterized by what might be called an ideological localism whereby each little community is treated as self-sufficient and isolated. Undoubtedly, this is a carry-over from an older anthropological tradition which was concerned with salvaging cultural data from rapidly disappearing primitive peoples. While such an approach might still have some justification in dealing with an isolated tribe in the jungles of New Guinea, it has little justification in studies of modern Mexico.

"In studying communities in Mexico [or India] it is important that the anthropologist become a student not merely of the single community but of the region and the nation as well. The anthropologist must be sufficiently versed in the more important historical, geographical, economic, and cultural characteristics of the region and nation to be able to place his community in relation to each of them, and to indicate just what the community is representative of in the larger scene. . . . the anthropologist must know what is unique to his community and what it shares with broader areas, what is new and what is old, what is primitive and what is modern" (Lewis 1951: xx, xxi).

them? The answer is probably "No," but the matter of weighting is not so easy.

The difference in size of communities may also be important. Tepoztlan is over three times as large as Rani Khera, and it may be that some of the matters to be discussed are related to size of population. Then there is the difference in topography and climate. Tepoztlan is in a hilly, mountainous area, while Rani Khera is on a level, almost treeless plain. However, this difference reflects national differences and to this extent our choice may inadvertently have been advantageous. We generally think of Mexico as a mountainous country and of India in terms of its vast plains.

In regard to climate, both are relatively dry areas. But the average annual rainfall in Tepoztlan is approximately sixty inches, while that of Rani Khera is less than thirty. This difference is less important than it seems, because in both cases the rains come within the four-month rainy season, and there is practically no rain for seven or eight months of the year. In both communities the greatest felt need is more water for irrigation.

Finally, there is the difference in the intensity with which each community was studied. I spent about two and a half years in five separate visits in Tepoztlan. I spent only seven months in Rani Khera and only a portion of this on a full-time basis, relying much more heavily upon my Indian research assistants. In short, I know Tepoztlan much better than Rani Khera, and what follows is subject to this limitation.

II. TEPOZTLAN AND RANI KHERA COMPARED

Tepoztlan is a Catholic village of about thirty-five hundred people, fifteen miles from Cuernavaca, the state capital, and sixty miles south of Mexico City. It is an ancient highland village which has been continuously inhabited since the Archaic period, or at least two thousand years. Two languages are spoken in Tepoztlan: Spanish and the indigenous Nahuatl. About half the population is bilingual, the other half speak only Spanish.

Rani Khera is a Hindu village of eleven hundred people, about fifteen miles from New Delhi, the national capital. It is only two miles from a major highway which runs to Delhi. It is an old village which was conquered about seven hundred and fifty years ago by the *Jāṭs,* an ethnic group which is now the dominant caste in the village. The language spoken is a local dialect of Hindi mixed with a sprinkling of Punjabi. Only a few people speak English.

Both villages may be designated as peasant societies in the sense that both are old and stable populations with a great love of the land, both depend upon agriculture, both are integrated into larger political units such as the state and the nation and are subject to their laws, both exist side by side with cities and have been exposed to urban influences for long periods of time, and both have borrowed from other rural areas as well as from urban centers but have managed to integrate the new traits into a relatively stable culture pattern. Moreover, both communities exist by a relatively primitive technology and depend upon hoe culture as well as plow and oxen in agriculture; both produce primarily for subsistence but also participate in a money economy and use of barter; both are relatively poor, have a high incidence of illiteracy, a high birth rate and a high death rate; and, finally, both communities have lived under foreign domination for long periods in their history and have developed that peculiar combination of dependence and hostility toward government which is so characteristic of colonial peoples.

A. SETTLEMENT PATTERN

So much for the broad similarities. Now let us examine some differences. One of the first things that impressed me about village Rani Khera and other Indian villages, as compared to Tepoztlan, was the village settlement pattern—or rather the absence of pattern—the greater density of population, the greater crowding, the housing shortage, the shortage of space for animals, and, in general, an atmosphere of much greater poverty.

Unlike Tepoztlan (and other Mexican highland villages), with its relatively well-ordered grid pattern of streets at right angles, its plaza and market place, its *palacio*, or government building, and its central church, in Rani Khera there is no orderly arrangement of streets, many of which are narrow dead-end alleys, there is no village center, no government or public building for the village as a whole.[4] The *paṭvārī*, or keeper of village land records, who is an official of the Revenue Department, lives with one of the better-to-do families and has no official residence as such. Were a new *paṭvārī* installed, he would have to make his own lodging arrangements.

4. That some of the elements here described may apply to India as a whole is suggested by the description by Spate, who writes of the settlement pattern as follows: "There is in general very little that looks like a 'plan,' other than that dictated by such site factors as alignment along bluffs or levees, grouping around a fort or a tank; but within the seemingly chaotic agglomeration there is, as a rule, a strong internal differentiation, that of the separate quarters for various castes" (1954: 172).

In Tepoztlan the houses are spread out, and most house sites have their own patio, corral, and orchard; in Rani Khera the houses are crowded together, and, unlike Tepoztlan, which has many vacant houses, there was not a single available house for our field workers in Rani Khera. With the increasing population and the scarcity of land the villagers are beginning to build two- and three-story houses, for the traditional village house-site area has been used up.

Another thing which stood out in Rani Khera because of its contrast with Tepoztlan was the much greater separation of the sexes. The preferred arrangement for family living is to have two residences, one for the women and children, another for the men and the cattle. There are also two *caupāls*, or men's houses, one for each division of the village, which are used for male smoking groups and other social gatherings.

B. LAND AND ECONOMY

I have said that agriculture is important in both villages. But here the similarity ends. In Rani Khera agriculture is much more intensive than in Tepoztlan. Of the 784 acres of Rani Khera, 721, or well over 90 per cent of the total area, is under cultivation, as compared with only 15 per cent in Tepoztlan. Moreover, Tepoztlan depends almost entirely on a single crop, namely, corn, with beans and squash of minor importance, whereas Rani Khera has a diversity of crops which include, in order of importance, wheat, millets (*juār* and *bājrā*), gram, sugar cane, and hemp. Unlike Tepoztlan, which has no irrigation and produces only one crop a year, Rani Khera grows two crops a year on about one-fifth of its lands which are under canal and well irrigation.

The apparently greater agricultural resources of Rani Khera are tempered by serious limiting factors. Rani Khera has practically no grazing lands and no forest resources. Indeed, the scarcity of trees was brought home to me by the fact that each of the thirty-seven trees in the village is listed in the village *paṭvārī* records. This makes for a crucial fuel shortage so that the valuable cowdung has to be used for fuel instead of fertilizer, and the cattle have to be stall-fed rather than pastured. By contrast, Tepoztlan has very rich forest resources (almost 50 per cent of the total area), and these provide ample firewood and charcoal both for domestic consumption and for sale.

Still other differences in the village economy need to be mentioned. In Tepoztlan over 90 per cent of the 853 families engage directly in agriculture as cultivators, and until recently even the shopkeepers and artisans would close shop to plant corn when the rains came. In Rani Khera only 53 per cent of its 150 families engage directly in agriculture, i.e., are cultivators, and most of these belong to a single caste, the *Jāṭs*.

The importance of this difference goes beyond the matter of the relative proportion in the community of what in the United States would be called the "farm" and "nonfarm" populations. It is related to a fundamental difference in the social and economic structure of the two villages. In Tepoztlan the family is much more of a self-sufficient unit, free to engage in a variety of activities and occupations, and it cherishes this self-sufficiency and independence from others. In Rani Khera the specialization of occupations along caste lines makes for a greater dependence of the villagers upon each other. But it is a dependence organized along hierarchical lines, institutionalized in the traditional, semifeudal *jajmānī* system of reciprocal obligations in economic and ceremonial affairs among the various castes. In the past the potential contradictions between the interests of the farm and nonfarm populations in the village were held in check by the power of the landholders and by the lack of alternatives for the untouchables and other low-caste people. Now that the system is weakening, primarily because of the increased opportunities for employment in munitions factories, the nonfarm population in the village is beginning to take on aspects of a rural proletariat with its own special problems and its own sense of growing power.

If, on the basis of other studies, one could generalize these differences on a national level, it would be possible to say that in India there is a much greater landless rural proletariat than in Mexico and that this may well have important implications in the respective political developments in the two countries. And I might add that the Five Year Plan of the Government of India, with its emphasis upon increased agricultural production, has relatively little to offer to the rural nonagricultural portions of the population.

Returning again to the agricultural economy, we find that in both villages there are privately owned and communally owned lands. The communal lands of Tepoztlan are truly communal in the sense that any member of the *municipio* of Tepoztlan has equal rights to their use. However, the communal lands of Rani Khera are held by the *Jāṭs* on a share basis, and the rights of the *Jāṭ* families in the communal, or *śāmilāt*, lands are proportionate to the size of their holdings of private land.

In Tepoztlan about 80 per cent of all the land is communally held either as municipal lands or, since the Mexican Revolution, as *ejidal* lands. In Rani Khera about 7 per cent of the lands are communally owned, and most of these consist of the village house sites, the village pond, roads, and some uncultivable areas. Traditionally, the communal lands in North India were intended to serve as pasture and woodland. In both Rani Khera and Tepoztlan the communal lands have been a source of constant strife, but for different reasons. In the former it was between families within the village who attempted to appropriate communal lands for themselves. In the latter it was between villages, concerning the rights of villages to the communal lands. It is important to note that in both cases the communal lands are not subject to taxation. In the case of Tepoztlan this means that about 80 per cent of its total area is tax-free.

Population pressure on the land is considerable in both communities. But whereas Tepoztlan has 1.5 acres of cultivable land per capita, Rani Khera has only three-quarters of an acre. The advantage for Tepoztlan is even greater than is indicated by these figures, for, whereas Rani Khera has practically no other land, Tepoztlan has an additional 8 acres per capita of forest and grazing lands, and about 10 per cent of this area can be used for growing corn by the primitive method of cutting and burning the forest to make temporary clearings.

In Tepoztlan only about 36 per cent of the families had private landholdings, as compared to 52 per cent of the families in Rani Khera.[5] But, while the landless families of Tepoztlan have access to the rich resources of the communal lands, the landless of Rani Khera have to depend primarily upon nonagricultural occupations. It may be noted that in both communities hoe culture is looked down upon as a last resort of the poor. In Rani Khera about fifteen low-caste families raise vegetables as a part-time occupation on land rented from the *Jāṭs*.

The size of private landholdings shows fundamental similarities in both communities. Holdings are very small. In both cases 50 per cent of the holdings are less than 5 acres, 70 per cent are less than 10 acres, and 90 per cent are less than 20 acres. The range in size of

5. Again the difference is somewhat offset because almost 20 per cent of Tepoztecan families have *ejido* holdings. During the course of the Spanish Conquest and domination of Mexico, from 1519 to 1810, Tepoztlan lost a portion of its best lands, which were converted into sugar plantations. After the Mexican Revolution of 1910–20 and as part of the national *ejido* program Tepoztlan recovered much of its lost lands, and these were divided among the landless villagers into small holdings.

holdings is also remarkably similar, i.e., from less than a half-acre, of which there are many, to 50 acres, of which there was one in each community. It is noteworthy that in both Tepoztlan and Rani Khera the peasants independently suggested the same figure of about 10 acres as a desirable minimum-size holding for a "decent" standard of living for a family of five. This figure is apparently based upon the acreage that can be worked economically with a single team of oxen.

As might be expected, there is a striking difference between the two communities in regard to the respective role of livestock in the economy and the attitude toward livestock. In India there is an ancient cattle complex, and most people are vegetarians. In Mexico domesticated cattle are relatively recent, dating back to the Spanish Conquest. The cattle industry was never very important and never became well integrated with the economy. In Tepoztlan there is relatively little livestock, and most of it is of poor quality. Investment in cattle is viewed as precarious. By contrast, the little village of Rani Khera supports a remarkably large number of livestock and this with practically no grazing resources. Whereas 85 per cent of the cultivators in plow agriculture owned at least one ox in Rani Khera, only 45 per cent owned oxen in Tepoztlan. The 78 *Jāṭ* landholding families in Rani Khera owned 103 oxen and bulls, 38 cows, 94 she-buffaloes, 270 calves, 7 goats, and 16 donkeys.

C. SOCIAL ORGANIZATION

It is in the field of social organization that we find the most remarkable differences between these two peasant societies. Indeed, they seem like separate worlds, and I might add that, by comparison with Rani Khera, Tepoztlan, in retrospect, seems much less complicated and much more familiar, very Western-like, and almost North American. Undoubtedly one of the reasons for this is the fact that the Spanish Conquest left its indelible mark on Mexican culture. Spain, for all its cultural idiosyncrasies in sixteenth-century Europe, was part of the Western European culture pattern.

The distinctive aspects of the social organization of village Rani Khera as compared to Tepoztlan can be discussed in terms of (1) the more pervasive role of kinship; (2) the presence of a caste system; (3) the existence of multiple factions based on kinship; and (4) the differences in the role of the village as a community.

1. *The role of kinship.*—In Rani Khera kinship plays a major role in the ordering of human relations and is the basis of most social and political groupings such as the *ṭolās* and *pannās,* the smoking groups,

the factions, the castes, the panchayats, or councils, and the intervillage networks. The extended family is strong and forms a basic unit for individual identification. The caste system acts as an integrating and cohesive factor in village life, primarily within the castes and to some extent between castes. Caste members are bound by kinship, by common traditions, interests, and social interaction. The castes in turn are bound by economic interdependence resulting from the specialization of occupations, and this is formalized by the *jajmānī* system of reciprocal obligations.

In Tepoztlan kinship is a much less pervasive force: the nuclear family predominates, the extended family is weak (the elaborate *compadre* system seems designed to make up for this), and social relations and social solidarity are organized around religious, political, and other nonkinship bases. The independence and individualism of the nuclear or biological family in Tepoztlan make for an atomistic quality in social relations. And while these discrete family units are organized into larger units such as the barrio, the village, and the *municipio*, these organizational forms are relatively impersonal and do not impinge as directly upon the lives of the individuals as does the extended family, the faction, and the caste in Rani Khera. In Rani Khera the extended family, the faction, and the caste are the units which demand one's loyalties and channelize most of one's life-activities. But by the same token they provide the individual with a much greater degree of psychological security than is present in Tepoztlan, and this in turn affects the quality of community life.

The role of kinship organization on the political level is also markedly different in the two villages. In Tepoztlan the connection between the village and the state and federal government is in terms of elected officials who vote as members of their *demarcación*, an arbitrary division of the village for secular purposes. The officials do not represent kinship units nor even the barrios. But in Rani Khera the political organization and the kinship organization are more closely intertwined. Each of the two headmen (*lambardārs*) of the village represents a *pannā*, which is essentially a kinship unit consisting of related patrilineal lineages.

Rani Khera, like other villages in North India, is fundamentally a part of a larger intervillage network based upon kinship ties. Other villagers are very often relatives, and entire villages are classified by the kinship terminology as mother's brother's village, grandfather villages, grandmother villages, etc. Village Rani Khera is a member of a four-village unit known as a "*caugāma*" and of a twenty-village unit known as a "*bīsagāma.*" These are known as "*Dabas*" villages, that is, they are descended from a common ancestor, Dabas. These twenty-village units in turn are members of larger intervillage networks which culminate in a 360-village unit, all of whose ancestors were related in the distant past. Within the four-village and twenty-village units there is a traditional division of labor for ceremonial and panchayat purposes. Some are known as "*caudhar,*" or leader villages, some are known as "*dādā,*" or grandfather villages, or "*dādī,*" grandmother villages, and some as "*vazīr,*" or minister villages. Each of these villages performs special functions at panchayat meetings.

These four- and twenty-village units are still active and functional in this area, though less so than in the past when they were strong enough to exile families and administer punishment and jail sentences. It is less than ten years since over a hundred thousand rupees was collected for the construction of the higher secondary school through the channels of these large intervillage organizations.

2. *The caste system.*—In Rani Khera the caste system organizes life in terms of hierarchical principles and plays up the status differences between groups. In Tepoztlan there is no caste system, and the society is much more democratically organized. In Rani Khera there are 150 households representing twelve castes as follows: seventy-eight *Jāṭ* families, fifteen Brahman, twenty *Camār* (Leatherworker), ten *Bhaṅgī* (Sweeper), seven *Kumhār* (Potter), five *Jhīnvar* (Water Carrier), four *Dhobī* (Washerman), four *Khātī* (Carpenter), three *Nāī* (Barber), two *Chīpī* (Calico Printer), one *Lohār* (Blacksmith), and one *Baniyā* (Merchant).

The *Jāṭs* are by tradition agriculturalists and own all the land of the village, including the house sites, i.e., the land upon which the houses of the other castes are built. In a sense, then, the other castes, even the Brahmans, are in the village at the sufferance of the *Jāṭs.* The village is officially known as a *Jāṭ* village, and clearly the *Jāṭs* dominate village life. Even the formal organization of the village into two *pannās,* each with its *lambardār,* or headman, is solely in terms of the *Jāṭs.* The lower castes tend to live on the outskirts of the village and are not part of this formal organization despite the fact that some of the lower-caste families are ancient inhabitants.

In Tepoztlan the picture is very different. No one group dominates the life of the village. Each family, whether rich or poor, owns its house site and house, has recognized status, and can proudly say,

"This is my village." The quality of interpersonal relations among Tepoztecans is comparable with what exists within the single caste of *Jāṭs*, that is, status differences are played down at least on a verbal level, and wealthy individuals are careful not to "pull rank."

In Rani Khera the caste system divides the village and weakens the sense of village solidarity. The caste generally represents a distinct ethnic group with its own history, traditions, and identifications, and each caste lives in more or less separate quarters of the village. There are separate wells for the *Harijans*, or untouchables; dining and smoking between higher and lower castes are still taboo; low-caste persons (this does not include *Baniyā*, *Khātī*, or *Nāī*) will not sit together on the same *cārpāī*, or cot, with a *Jāṭ* or Brahman; and when government officials come to the village and call meetings to explain the new community development projects, the *Harijans* may attend, but they stay off to one side in the audience and "know their place." In a sense, then, each caste, or at least those with larger representation in the village, forms a separate little community. The social structure of the village therefore has somewhat the quality of our urban communities with their variety of ethnic and minority groups and a high degree of division of labor.

In Tepoztlan the population and the tradition are much more homogeneous, and there is nothing comparable to the divisive effects of the caste system. Perhaps the nearest approximation to segmentation in the village results from the organization of separate barrios, each with its own chapel, patron saint, and *esprit de corps*. The barrios, like the castes, can be thought of as subcommunities within the village. This was truer thirty years ago, when barrio localism in Tepoztlan was stronger than it is today. But, of course, the barrio and the caste are very different in nature. The barrio is primarily a religious and social unit rather than a kinship unit. It does not control marriage, and there is no tradition that barrio members are of a common origin. And while the physical limits of the barrios have remained remarkably stable over the past few hundred years, barrio membership is changeable, and one can belong to two barrios at the same time, provided the barrio house-site tax is paid. Moreover, the barrio organization is strictly within the village and is unified on a village-wide basis by the central village church.[6] But the castes cut across villages and have their cross-village organizations.

6. For a detailed comparison of the role of religion and the ceremonial cycle in the life and organization of our two villages, the reader must await a later publication. It seems clear, however, that Catholicism and the Church, embracing the principle of hierarchy and centralization, play a much more decisive role in the formal organization

The caste system in Rani Khera is undergoing changes and in some ways may even be said to be breaking down. The proximity to Delhi, the Gandhian movement against untouchability, the preaching of the Arya Samaj (a reformed Hinduism movement), and increased off-farm employment opportunities as a result of the past two world wars have all had some effect.

Perhaps the greatest change in the caste system has occurred in relation to the occupational structure, i.e., caste and occupation are now less synonymous than formerly. Some of the *Jāṭ* families no longer cultivate their land, and their children have become schoolteachers or taken miscellaneous jobs in Delhi. The Brahmans no longer carry on their priestly functions. Most of them are occupancy tenants of the *Jāṭs,* but only four are cultivators; one family sells milk, another does tailoring, and the remainder are employed in jobs outside the village. Though the *Camārs* are Leatherworkers by caste, only two are now shoemakers, and they no longer skin the dead cattle. The substitution of Persian Wheels for the earlier system of drawing water with leather buckets threw some of the *Camārs* out of work; three families are weavers, four rent land from the *Jāṭs* for vegetable gardening, four are employed outside the village, and the remainder earn a living in the village by combining part-time agricultural labor with cattle raising. Of all the castes, the *Bhaṅgīs,* or Sweepers, seem to have shown the least change in occupation.

There have been other changes. Children of all castes now attend the village school, and there is no discrimination or segregation in the seating arrangements. And since 1949 a *Camār* has been elected to the newly constituted intervillage council consisting of four villages.

However, despite all these trends, the caste system is still very strong in the village.

3. *Factions.*—In both villages there are factions, but their structure, functions, and role in village life differ greatly. We will first consider factions in Rani Khera and then in Tepoztlan (for a fuller discussion see Lewis 1951, 1954).

In Rani Khera factions are an old, ingrained pattern in village life

---

of Tepoztlan and other Mexican villages than does Hinduism in Rani Khera and other North Indian villages. That the Mexican pattern applies over even wider areas is shown by Redfield and Tax (1953: 31), who write of Mesoamerican Indian society as follows: "The community consists of a village, a group of hamlets or a rural region, but in any case its residents look toward a common civic and religious center, where is housed the image of a saint that is patron to them all. The community tends to be endogamous. . . ."

and must be considered as a basic structural aspect of traditional village organization along with castes, *ṭolās, pannās, gotras,* and other groupings. Factions are locally known as "*dhaṛ,*" which means literally "the upper part of the body." The use of this term for groups of people carries out the idea of physical unity, i.e., members of the same *dhaṛ* are part of one body. The factions are generally referred to by the name of their leaders or by a nickname of the leading lineage represented in it.

Factions follow caste lines. However, factions from different castes may and do form blocs or alliances. In 1953 we found twelve factions in five of the twelve castes of the village. The distribution was as follows: six among the twenty-one *Camār* families; two among the ten *Bhaṅgī* families; and one for the seven *Kumhār* families. The *Jāṭ* factions were by far the most powerful and dominated village life.

The factions are relatively small and cohesive kinship groupings which act as units in defense of family interests. The major issues which lead to court litigations between factions and sometimes result in the development of new factions are quarrels over the inheritance of land and the adoption of sons, quarrels over house sites and irrigation rights, sexual offenses, murders, and quarrels between castes. The villagers sum it up by saying that factions quarrel over wealth, women, and land.

But factions also have positive, co-operative functions. All factions operate as more or less cohesive units on ceremonial occasions, particularly births, betrothals, and marriages; in the operation of caste panchayats; and in recent years in district board, state, and national elections. Moreover, all factions have one or more of their own hookah-smoking groups, which serve as informal social groups in which there is almost daily face-to-face contact.

Jāṭ factions have a few additional functions. They act as units in co-operative economic undertakings such as moneylending and the renting of land. In principle no faction will rent land to members of other factions if there is anyone in its own ranks that needs land. In the case of mortgaging, faction solidarity is even more striking, for there has not been a single case within the last five years of land mortgaged outside one's own faction.

Members of hostile factions will not attend each others' ceremonial celebrations, will not visit each others' homes, and, as a rule, will not smoke hookah together, except at the home of a member of a neutral faction. In panchayat meetings the representatives of hostile factions can be counted upon to marshal vicious gossip about rivals. However, direct attack in public is rare; indirection is developed to a fine art. Because members of hostile factions do not cease talking to each other and continue to be polite in formal greeting, there is always the possibility of improving relations or of joining temporarily with one hostile group against another.

There are some occasions when members of hostile factions unite for some common action. The major occasions are funerals, building of village wells, cleaning the village pond, repairing subcanals for irrigation, and participation in a few festivals such as *Tīj* and *Holī*. There is also a tradition of presenting an appearance of village unity to the outside. For example, if two men of hostile factions have married daughters in the same village, each, whenever he visits that village, must visit the daughter of the other and pay the customary rupee to symbolize the fact that she, like his own daughter, is a daughter of the village.

In Tepoztlan factions are political groupings rather than kinship groupings and reflect diverse social and economic interests. The factions are fewer in number, only two as a rule, and are larger and more loosely organized. Faction membership is less stable and faction loyalty more tenuous. In Tepoztlan, unlike Rani Khera, brothers may be members of hostile and opposed factions. In Rani Khera, first, second, and even third cousins are generally members of the same faction.

One of the major cleavages in Tepoztlan was between the *Bolsheviki* and the *Centrales*. These groups became clearly delineated in the early twenties when two socialistically oriented Tepoztecans from Mexico City, who were members of the Confederación Regional de Obreros Mexicanos, returned to the village to organize the peasants in defense of the communal lands against the sons of the ex-*caciques* who controlled the local government and allegedly were exploiting the forest resources of the *municipio* in their own interests. The *Bolsheviki* had their greatest strength in the smaller and poorer barrios of the upper part of the village, while the *Centrales* were strongest in the larger central barrios. To some extent this grouping corresponded to class distinctions, since, in the days before the Mexican Revolution of 1910–20, most of the *caciques* and well-to-do merchants lived in the center of the village.

In contrast to the predominantly private familial objectives of factions in Rani Khera, the objectives of the factions in Tepoztlan were broadly social and political. The aim was to dominate the local government and to appeal to the voters in terms of broad public issues. In the twenties the slogan was "Conserve the Communal Forests," and in the thirties the new organization known as the *Fraternales* had the slogan "Union, Justice and Civilization."

Since the middle thirties the factional groupings have more and more become political groupings which align themselves for or against the government in power. The establishment by Tepoztecans of two competing bus lines from Tepoztlan to Cuernavaca has led to bitter quarrels and violence and has again split the village into hostile groupings.

4. *The village as a community.*—The comparative consideration of the question, "Is the village a community?" is more complex than it seems, for there are numerous dimensions of "community," such as the ecological, physical, social, economic, political, religious, and psychological. To what extent do the physical limits of the village define the limits for these dimensions? Or to what extent do these aspects of community spill over into other villages so that the community might better be defined in terms of units larger than the single village? As we might expect, not all aspects of community have the same spatial distribution, so that a village may be a clearly self-contained unit for some purposes and not for others.

There is yet another aspect of the problem, namely, what is the quality of social relations, of mutual interdependence of persons or social groups within each village? We must be ready to deal with the possibility that, although Village A does not define the physical area of social, economic, and other relations as clearly as does Village B, yet the quality of such relations in A or subgroups within it may be so much more cohesive as to justify our saying that there is more community within A (as well as the villages into which this spills over) than there is in B. With these observations in mind, let us first consider those aspects of community which Rani Khera and Tepoztlan share and then go on to consider some of the more important differences.

Both Tepoztlan and Rani Khera are corporate bodies which enjoy legal status and can take suits to law courts. Both are units of taxation for the respective revenue departments. In both cases the greater part of the social, economic, and religious activities takes place within the village. The village is home and there is relatively little out-migration, but more in Tepoztlan than in Rani Khera. Of Tepoztlan it can be said that most villagers are born there, live and work there, and die there. This cannot be said of Rani Khera, for the married women were not born there, and the daughters of the village will not die there. Yet the very designation "daughter of the village" speaks eloquently for the sense of village consciousness.

In both villages, despite the existence of schisms and factions, there are occasions when the villagers act together as a unit for some common goal such as the building of a road or a school, drainage of a pond, or the defense of the village against attack from the outside. In the case of Tepoztlan the defense of the village last occurred in the twenties, when it was attacked by the *Cristeros*. In the case of Rani Khera one must go back almost a hundred years for a comparable occasion.

One of the important differences between our two villages is related to the contrast in settlement pattern between highland Mexico and the Indo-Gangetic Plain. The Mexican pattern is that of relatively self-contained nuclear groupings or pockets of a small number of villages centrally located within *municipios,* so that the density of population decreases almost to zero as one moves from the center or seat of the community to the periphery. In North India, on the other hand, there is an almost even and continuous scatter of large numbers of villages, so that no distinct pattern of groupings emerges. Thus in Mexico the physical groupings of villages practically define and encompass the social and political groupings, whereas in India the physical pattern gives much less of a clue, and one must trace out the specific kinship and other alignments which organize villages into units. This contrast between the centripetal settlement pattern of Mexican villages and the amorphous pattern of India applies also to the internal settlement pattern of the villages, so that the Mexican village stands out more clearly as a centrally organized unit.

From an economic point of view, the village of Rani Khera is a more clearly isolable and self-contained community than the village of Tepoztlan. Village boundaries are clearly fixed and contain within them the land resources upon which the villagers depend for their livelihood. In Tepoztlan the larger *municipio* is the functional resource unit. Village boundaries are ill-defined and are essentially moral boundaries, whereas the municipal boundaries are clearly demarcated. It is within the bounds of the *municipio* that the everyday world of the Tepoztecan exists. Here the farmers work the communal lands, cut and burn communal forests, graze their cattle, and hunt for medicinal herbs.

From the point of view of village government Tepoztlan stands out as a more clearly organized and centralized community. When I first studied Tepoztlan, local government seemed very weak indeed, but by comparison with Rani Khera and North India in general, it now seems extremely well developed, what with elected village presidents, councils, judges, the collection of taxes for public works, police powers, and the obligations of villagers to give twelve days a year for co-operative village works. The traditional local government in Rani Khera is much more informal and consists of caste panchayats which cut across village lines. Only recently has the government established a new statutory local panchayat with taxation powers, which, however, has not been effective so far.

Village-wide leadership in Tepoztlan is formally expressed by the local government. In Rani Khera it does not yet exist, and the idea of positive constructive leadership in the public interest is only now beginning, particularly in connection with the establishment of public schools. As yet, there are no village heroes or outstanding citizens who are popular for their contribution to village welfare as a whole.

In Rani Khera leadership is limited to faction leadership and is primarily of a protective and defensive nature in which each faction or combination of factions defends its family interests. The "leader" is essentially a spokesman for a family or a group of related families and has little authority to make independent decisions or to exercise power over the group.

In Tepoztlan there is more verbalization about village community spirit. Candidates for political office always speak in terms of "*mi pueblo*" and promise to improve their village. The fact that officials may in fact do very little and may even steal public funds is another matter. But at least the sense of village identification and loyalty exists as a potential ideological force. Village solidarity is also reflected, albeit in a negative sense, by Tepoztecan characterizations of the surrounding villages of the *municipio* as "assassins," "dullheads," "primitive," and "backward." Moreover, the bogeyman used to frighten children is often a man from a neighboring village. In Rani Khera there were no comparable designations of neighboring villages, most of which contain related lineages.

The difference in the role of the village as a community can also be appreciated if we examine marriage in both cases. In Tepoztlan over 90 per cent of the marriages take place within the village, and, lest this be thought a function of the larger size of the village, we can point out that 42 per cent of the marriages were within the same barrio within the village. The single important rule in marriage is not to marry close relatives, and this generally means eliminating first, second, and third cousins.

In Rani Khera the question of whom one can marry is much more complicated. Marriage is controlled by a combination of factors, namely, caste endogamy, village exogamy, limited territorial exogamy, and *gotra*, or sib, exogamy. Translated, this means: (1) you must marry a member of your own caste, i.e., a *Jāṭ* must marry a *Jāṭ*, a Brahman, a Brahman, etc.; (2) you must marry out of your village; (3) you must not marry into any village whose lands touch upon the lands of your own village; (4) if you are a *Jāṭ*, you cannot marry into any village known as a *Dabas* village, the *Dabas* being the predominant *gotra* in the village (this automatically eliminates twenty villages from marriage, for there are twenty villages which form a *Dabas* panchayat unit); (5) finally, you cannot marry into your father's *gotra*, your mother's *gotra*, your father's mother's *gotra*, or your mother's mother's *gotra* (this again eliminates a whole series of villages). As a result of all these prohibitions fathers or go-betweens must go long distances to find eligible mates for their daughters, and for months before the marriage season they literally scour the countryside for husbands. Remember that residence is of course patrilocal for males.

Our study of Rani Khera showed that the 266 married women living in the village came from about 200 separate villages at distances up to forty miles. We found also that the average distance between spouses' villages varied considerably by caste, with the lower castes, who are less numerous, having to go much longer distances. If we now examine the other side of the picture, that is, the daughters who marry out of the village, we find that over 220 daughters of Rani Khera married out into about 200 villages. Thus, this relatively small village of 150 households becomes the locus of affinal kinship ties with over 400 other villages. This makes for a kind of rural cosmopolitanism which is in sharpest contrast to the village isolationism in Mexico.

D. THE PEOPLE

Finally we come to a brief comparison of the people in both villages. I have noted elsewhere that Tepoztecans are a reserved, constricted people who tend to view other human beings as dangerous and the world in general as hostile. Children are required to be obedient, quiet, and unobtrusive, and parents play upon children's fears to maintain control. There is a certain pervading air of tension and fearfulness among Tepoztecans; the individual and the small biological family seem to stand alone against the world.

Despite the much smaller size of village Rani Khera, one has the impression that there are more people there. Crowds gather easily around the visitor and follow him down the narrow streets and in and out of houses. One rarely sees a solitary figure. Children play boisterously in large groups; men chat and smoke hookahs in groups. Women go to the well or collect cowdung together. The low value placed upon privacy in Rani Khera is in marked contrast with Tepoztlan, where privacy is so valued that one gets the feeling of an apartment-house psychology in this ancient village.

Faces are different in the two villages. In Tepoztlan, outside the home, faces are generally unsmiling, unrevealing masks. In Rani Khera faces seem more secure. Children are more open-faced and laughing, old men are bland and peaceful, young men restless but unrebellious, women straight and proud. Here too there is individual reserve and formalized behavior, but it does not seem to mask so much of an undercurrent of hostility and fear as in Tepoztlan.

The women of Rani Khera work even harder than the women of Tepoztlan, but they appear less drab and bemeaned. They seem strong, bold, gay, and sharp-tongued. Their skirts and head scarves are brilliantly colored and spangled with rhinestones and mirrors. Heavy silver jewelry on their ankles, wrists, and necks seems to validate their worth as women. Even with their faces modestly covered, the women of Rani Khera seem more independent than Tepoztecan women and have less of a martyr complex.

It must be remembered that these observations on the people of Rani Khera are highly impressionistic and deserve more careful study.

III. CONCLUSIONS

In conclusion, I believe our comparative data from these two villages demonstrate the wide range of culture that can exist in peasant societies. When I left for India in 1952, I expected to find many similarities between Indian and Mexican peasant communities, this despite my earlier critique of the folk-society concept. I did find similarities, but on the whole I was more impressed by the differences. The similarities are greatest in material culture, level of technology, and economics, and the differences are greatest in social organization, value systems, and personality. In terms of raising the standard of living the problems seem much the same, for the bulk of the population in both villages is poor, illiterate, landless, and lives so close to the survival margin that it cannot afford to experiment with new things and ideas. However, the poverty of the Indian people seems so much greater and the agrarian problems so overwhelming and complex as to defy any easy solution even on the theoretical level.

In making comparisons between Mexico and India, we must remember that they are in different stages of evolution in terms of nationhood. Mexico has had its political independence for almost one hundred and fifty years and has lived through the great Revolution of 1910–20, while India has only recently gained its freedom and has not had the equivalent of the Mexican agrarian revolution. These broad differences are reflected in many ways in our two villages.

In stressing the range of variation possible under the rubric of peasant society, I do not intend to suggest that the concept "peasant society" is not meaningful or useful as a classification for comparative research. However, it is not sufficiently predictive in regard to cultural content and structure to take the place of knowledge of concrete reality situations, especially in planning programs of culture change. For both applied and theoretical anthropology we need typologies of peasantry for the major culture areas of the world, such as Latin America, India, Africa, etc. Moreover, within each area we need more refined subclassifications. Only after such studies are available will we be in a position to formulate broad generalizations about the dynamics of peasant culture as a whole. The difficulties encountered in this paper suggest that a typology of peasant societies for Mexico or Latin America would hardly serve for North India. However, once we had adequate typologies for both areas, meaningful comparisons could more readily be made.

One of the most striking findings in our study of Rani Khera, especially when compared with the report of Beals (1953) on a South Indian village, is the remarkable stability of local village life and institutions, despite the proximity of Rani Khera to Delhi and the many urban influences to which it has been subject, such as Arya Samaj, the Congress and other political movements, and increased opportunities for education and jobs. The stability is particularly evident in the agricultural economy. The *Jāṭs* still love the land; in the last fifty years there have been only two families who sold their land and left the village. The land-tenure system continues as of old, with the *Jāṭs* still in control. The caste system still remains strong and dominates the thinking of the villagers, despite the many reformist movements and the coming of independence. But the *jajmānī* system has weakened, and this has increased intercaste tensions, particularly in the case of the *Camārs*.

Rani Khera and Tepoztlan face many common problems. In both villages population has increased rapidly in the last thirty years, means of communication have been improved, there is greater dependence upon a cash economy, education is increasingly valued, and the general aspiration level of the people is going up. But there have been no comparable changes in the agricultural production.

We have seen that both villages are meaningful units for comparative study. However, our analysis has shown the complexities involved in evaluating the extent to which each village is a community. From some points of view it would seem that Tepoztlan is more of an organized and centralized village community, that is, in terms of the internal settlement pattern, the greater ethnic homogeneity of the population, the formal organization of village government with elected and paid village officials, the religious organization with a central church, the village market and plaza, and the absence of multiple intervillage networks based on kinship.

From the point of view of ecology Rani Khera is a more clearly defined and self-contained community than Tepoztlan. Moreover, if we define community in terms of the degree and intensity of interaction and interdependence of people, then we might conclude that, despite the divisive effects of castes and multiple factions within castes, there is more community within Rani Khera than within Tepoztlan. Villagers in Rani Khera seem psychologically more secure and relate better to each other. There is a greater readiness to engage in co-operative activities within kinship and caste. The villager spends a greater proportion of his time in some group activity, in smoking groups, in the extended family, in co-operative economic undertakings, and in the caste councils. There is more frequent visiting and more sociability. It is tempting to view the greater verbalization about village identification and solidarity in Tepoztlan as a psychological compensation for the actual atomistic nature of social relations. And by the same token the absence of such verbalization in Rani Khera may reflect the greater cohesiveness of social relations.

Our data on social organization from North India call attention to aspects of village organization, both in its internal and in its external relations, which either have been neglected or have not been given sufficient weight in earlier considerations of peasantry and in the formulations of models for the peasant society. It will be recalled that in Redfield's model the peasant society is intermediate between the folk society and civilization. It differs from the folk society in that it has developed economic and political relations with the city, but in its relations with other villages it still retains a good deal of the folk quality of isolation and "looking in" (Redfield 1953*a:*33).

This formulation applies better to Tepoztlan and other Mexican villages than to Rani Khera and North Indian villages. It does not adequately provide for situations like Rani Khera, where the village is part of multiple intervillage networks and where a single village is related by affinal and lineage ties with over four hundred other villages, thereby making for a kind of rural cosmopolitanism.

The widespread affinal and lineage relationships of village Rani Khera find their closest parallel in reports of tribal societies rather than of peasant societies. And indeed there is a tribal flavor in *Jāṭ* social organization which recalls the description by Evans-Pritchard of the Nuer, a people of the Anglo-Egyptian Sudan numbering over 200,000 and consisting of many tribes, some of which have populations over 40,000. In both cases we find patrilineal clans, maximal and minimal lineages, the dominance of a single lineage within villages, and local exogamy (Evans-Pritchard 1947: 123–24; 1951: 1–48). Evans-Pritchard writes:

> . . . Nuer people see themselves as a unique community and their culture as a unique culture. . . . All Nuer live in a continuous stretch of country. There are no isolated sections. However, their feeling of community goes deeper than recognition of cultural identity. Between Nuer, wherever they hail from, and though they be strangers to one another, friendly relations are at once established when they meet outside their country, for a Nuer is never a foreigner to another as he is to a Dinka or Shilluk [1947: 123].
>
> Their members, individuals and families, move often and freely. . . . Wherever they go they are easily incorporated into the new community through one or more kinship links. . . . Nuer frequently visit all the villages in their neighborhood, and in all of them they have kinsfolk. . . . the different local communities of a whole tribe could be presented on a single genealogical chart. Given unlimited time and patience, the entire population of Nuerland could be so presented. *There are no closed communities* [Evans-Pritchard 1951: 29]. [My italics.]

The contrast is striking between the above and the picture of small localized hamlets of the mountainous areas of the Philippines in which groups in the next valley are fair game for headhunting.

Our data suggest that it may be helpful to re-examine a good deal of the literature on the social structure of folk and peasant societies in terms of our well-known and traditional concepts of endogamy and exogamy, but from a somewhat different point of view than in the past. I believe most discussions of exogamy and endogamy have been in terms of rules applying to some unit, generally a clan or lineage within a local community. But when the entire local group is exogamous or endogamous very important consequences follow—indeed so important that it might be useful to add endogamy and exogamy as crucial universal variables in our models of the folk society and peasant society. Moreover, these two variables seem to be quite independent of some of the other variables, such as size and homogeneity. The world view of a small, homogeneous, and endogamous village or local group will necessarily be more "isolationist" and "inward-looking" than that of a small, homogeneous, but exogamous village or local group. Furthermore, the difference between exogamy and endogamy sets up processes which in themselves accentuate localism or play it down. When half the total adult population (i.e., the women of the patrilocal exogamous village) goes out of the village generation after generation, and new women from other villages come in, there is the basis for a type of intervillage relations which differs considerably from that of endogamous villages or communities. In the former case there is a natural development of a "one-world" concept in terms of a region whose limits are determined by kinship bonds. Also, in the case of exogamic villages the children are reared by parents from different villages, so that in a sense village differences are bred out over the generations. Murdock has recently demonstrated this last point with American Indian data.

The difference between the "inward-looking" and the "outward-looking" peasant village is of course a relative matter. All tribal and peasant societies have some relations with the outside. It might therefore be more profitable to compare the nature, occasions, and quality of these relations. In the case of Tepoztlan and Rani Khera the differences are striking. In the former, trade is the primary bond between Tepoztlan and the outlying villages, with religious pilgrimages ranking second, and kinship ties a very low third. By contrast, in Rani Khera, intervillage relations result primarily from affinal and consanguineal ties, with religious pilgrimages ranking a low second, and trade a very low third. The type of impersonality in intervillage relations based on trade, reported by Redfield (1939: 53) for Guatemala and applicable also to Tepoztlan, would be unthinkable in the case of North Indian villages where relations are more intimate and personal because they are primarily familial relations and not trade relations.

While the distinction between relatively inward-looking and outward-looking communities may be one of the differentiating characteristics between a tribal society and a peasant society, the distinction also has meaning both *within* the tribal level and *within* the peasant level. It may be argued that kinship ties, no matter how far-flung, still represent an inward-looking orientation. We believe, however, that there is a significant social and psychological difference between relations confined within a small area and to relatively few people as over against relations which, though still based on kinship, are spread out over vast areas and encompass thousands of people who are personally unknown, yet are potentially accessible and part of the in-group.

A typology of peasant societies must also include as a variable the role of kinship, that is, the extent to which the society is organized on a kinship basis. Where the kinship basis is pervasive, as in Rani Khera, we can say that the society is more primitive or tribal. As Kroeber writes:

> It is generally accepted that among primitive peoples society is structured primarily on the basis of kinship and in more civilized nations largely in terms of economic and political factors. The function of kinship is relatively less in higher civilization, and may be absolutely less. But kinshio considerations always persist . . . [1952: 219].

On the basis of our comparative findings and in line with the generally accepted position as stated by Kroeber, we might go on to classify modern nations with predominantly peasant populations in terms of the role of kinship in the social organization of village life and intervillage relations. If our findings for Tepoztlan and Rani Khera could be generalized for Mexico and India as nations, and this is an empirical question, then we would have to conclude that, in so far as the role of kinship is concerned, India is much more "primitive" than Mexico and represents a different stage of sociocultural evolution.[7] However, in terms of other variables, such as ethnic composition of the population, we have seen that Tepoztlan is more homogeneous than Rani Khera. Similarly, the communal land system of Tepoztlan seems to be more primitive than that of Rani Khera.

One conclusion to be drawn from these facts is that separate institutions or aspects of culture develop at different rates, within limits, in accord with particular historical circumstance. It is this

7. The manifold implications of such a finding cannot be treated here. However, this finding suggests that the introduction of a modern Western democratic process, based upon voting, elections, and the spirit of individuality implicit in this system, is more foreign to contemporary Indian culture than to contemporary Mexican culture. Perhaps this is what Gandhi had in mind when he suggested many years ago that India would have to work out forms of representation which would be more in keeping with India's special tradition.

factor which creates serious difficulties in the construction of societal or cultural typologies which are not historically and regionally defined. This would also help explain how Tepoztlan and Rani Khera can be so similar in terms of economics and so different in terms of social organization.

REFERENCES CITED

BEALS, ALAN ROBIN

1953 "Change in the Leadership of a Mysore Village," *Economic Weekly* **5**:487–92. Bombay.

EVANS-PRITCHARD, E. E.

1947 *The Nuer*. Oxford, Clarendon Press.

1951 *Kinship and Marriage among the Nuer*. Oxford, Clarendon Press.

FOSTER, GEORGE M.

1953 "What Is Folk Culture?" *American Anthropologist* **55**:159–73. Menasha, Wisconsin.

KROEBER, ALFRED L.

1952 "The Societies of Primitive Man," in *The Nature of Culture*, by ALFRED L. KROEBER, pp. 219–25. Chicago, University of Chicago Press.

LEWIS, OSCAR

1951 *Life in a Mexican Village: Tepoztlan Restudied*. Urbana, University of Illinois Press.

1954 "Group Dynamics in a North-Indian Village: A Study in Factions," *Economic Weekly* **6**:423–25, 445–51, 477–82, 501–6. Bombay.

MINER, HORACE

1952 "The Folk-Urban Continuum," *American Sociological Review* **17**: 529–37. Menasha, Wisconsin.

MINTZ, SIDNEY W.

1953 "The Folk-Urban Continuum and the Rural Proletarian Community," *American Journal of Sociology* **55**:136–43. Chicago.

REDFIELD, ROBERT

1939 "Primitive Merchants of Guatemala," *Quarterly Journal of Inter-American Affairs* **1**:42–56. Washington, D.C.

1953*a* *The Primitive World and Its Transformations*. Ithaca, Cornell University Press.

1953*b* "The Natural History of the Folk Society," *Social Forces* **31**:224–28. Chapel Hill, North Carolina.

REDFIELD, ROBERT and SOL TAX

1953 "General Characteristics of Present Day Mesoamerican Indian Society," in *Heritage of Conquest*, ed. SOL TAX, pp. 31–39. Glencoe, Ill., Free Press.

SPATE, O. H. K.

1954 *India and Pakistan: A General and Regional Geography*. London, Methuen & Co.

LITTLE COMMUNITIES IN AN INDIGENOUS CIVILIZATION[1]

McKIM MARRIOTT

IF WE WOULD describe the small world of a village within the universe of Indian civilization, we must at some time consider two related questions of method: (1) can such a village be satisfactorily comprehended and conceived as a whole in itself, and (2) can understanding of one such village contribute to understanding of the greater culture and society in which the village is imbedded (Redfield and Singer 1954*a*)? In this paper I undertake to answer both questions of method by describing some ways in which the village of Kishan Garhi (*Kishan Gaḍhi*) in Uttar Pradesh is articulated with the Indian universe: first, through certain aspects of its social structure; and, second, through parts of its religious culture.

I. THE ISSUE OF THE ISOLATED WHOLE

The two questions are inversely related: if we say "Yes" to the first question, then we must say "No" to the second. Their inverse relationship is most apparent if we attempt to answer them, not for a village in India, but for urbanized little communities in an extreme situation—in the modern Western world. Here in the West we may answer, as sociologists often have done, with a strong "No" to the first question, but with a strong "Yes" to the second. Little communities of the modern West, having become increasingly parts and products of an urban civilization which is located mostly beyond themselves, cannot hope to be understood as wholes in separation from it. Not being conceivable in separation from that greater civilization, a single little community in the modern West can well serve to illuminate some of what is standard throughout its scope. "To study Jonesville is to study America . . ." (Warner 1949: xv).

1. This paper is based on field work in Aligarh District, U.P., from December, 1950, to April, 1952, and in the village here called "Kishan Garhi" from March, 1951, to April, 1952. Field work was supported through an Area Research Training Fellowship granted by the Social Science Research Council. Writing was made possible by the Indian Village Studies Project, Institute of East Asiatic Studies, University of California, Berkeley.

For their useful comments on this paper I am grateful to Alan R. Beals, E. Kathleen Gough, Oscar Lewis, David G. Mandelbaum, Jack M. Planalp, Robert Redfield, and Gitel P. Steed.

An inverse relationship between the same two questions is equally apparent if we attempt to answer them for little communities in an opposite extreme situation—in the most primitive world. If we say "Yes," as many anthropologists have done, "the most primitive little communities can be appropriately conceived as whole worlds in themselves," then we must recognize also that such primitive communities are too remote and distinct from any greater civilization for them to be able to contribute much to understanding of its particulars.

In India we are on middle ground. The relations there existing between little communities and civilization may be likened with some justification either to the primitive or to the modern Western extreme. Many anthropological students of social structure have insisted that traditional Indian villages, despite the great heterogeneity of their populations, may best be conceived by an extension of our models for conceiving primitive communities, as worlds in themselves. They have argued convincingly that up until the foreign or urban influences of thirty or fifty or one hundred and fifty years ago, little communities in Mysore, Kerala, Tanjore, and upland Orissa actually possessed clear structural definition, a high degree of economic self-sufficiency, political solidarity as against the outside world, and a sense of ritual integrity (Srinivas 1951: 1051–55; Miller 1952: 160, 163; Gough 1952: 534; Bailey 1953: 327–28). Beals tells us from Bangalore District that, "Until 1880 there was very little question as to the government's effect on the village . . ." (1954: 403). Srinivas characterizes the villages of pre-British India as having generally existed in a state of "isolation" from the rest of the world: each was a stable, self-subsistent whole, controlling its own affairs and yielding to the outside world only a land tax through cautious intermediaries (Srinivas 1951: 1051). Such a characterization is not without applicability to the village of Kishan Garhi, which I shall discuss below (cf. Marriott 1955).

If we accept such social structural characterizations of Indian villages as unified, though complex, wholes in themselves, then we may in answer to the second question logically emphasize the gulf between the life of the village, on the one hand, and the great tradition of Indian civilization, on the other hand. Newell expresses a feeling which is widespread among students of little communities when he writes that "small differences of [peasant] custom may reveal a new sociological theory much more clearly than a lifelong poring over the Vedas" (1952: 208). If each peasant community may best be conceived as a whole thing in itself, then it and the great literary tradition of Indian civilization are likely to have but little relevance for each other.

Opposite characterizations are also possible, depending in part upon the region of India in which little communities are studied. Holistic and isolated conceptions of Indian village communities have thus far seemed most appropriate to students of social life in southern India, where the ties of marriage and kinship are traditionally confined to the village and to a small surrounding area. But from northern India, where marriage and kinship generally reach to greater distances, there come evidences of different import. Thus from Delhi State in far northern India Lewis shows how the village of Rani Khera is vitally connected with the outside world by marriage, descent, and political alliances, while it is rent inside itself by factional divisions which recognize no more than a minimal common focus (Lewis 1954; cf. Marriott 1952). An attempt to conceive even the traditional village of Rani Khera as a whole in separation from the supralocal patterns which enmesh it evidently would require a strenuous mental effort. Marian Smith, writing of North Indian villages in Punjab, takes further note of ways in which traditional economic and religious organization run far beyond the village. She suggests that some structural unit larger than the single village might more appropriately be taken as a microcosm for holistic study (1953: 1298). Even in southern India, one devoted student of peasant life who has turned away for a moment from social structure to consider the content of religion finds that he cannot interpret the rituals and beliefs of Coorg villagers without tracing the same rituals and beliefs to literary levels in the much larger units of region and nation (Srinivas 1952, chap. VII). These facts brought forward by Lewis, Smith, and Srinivas take us far from any conception of the Indian little community as a world in itself. We return with difficulty to the view of Kishan Garhi as an isolated whole.

But now we seem to have contradicted ourselves. We cannot say both that an Indian village is comparable with a primitive isolate and also that it is dependent upon and part of a system that is outside itself. We cannot claim simultaneously that the great tradition of Indian civilization is relevant and that it is irrelevant to understanding of peasant life. To attempt to resolve these plausible but contradictory claims, I turn here to reconsider the social structure and the religion of one village, keeping the initial pair of questions in mind.

II. SOCIAL STRUCTURE

Kishan Garhi is an old Hindu village in an old cradle of Hindu civilization. Its ancient mound rises above the western plains of Uttar Pradesh in Aligarh District, between the Ganges and Jumna rivers, one hundred miles southeast of Delhi. Landlords of *Jāṭ* caste live in the crumbling mud fortress which tops the village mound, while the houses of farmers and specialists of twenty-three other castes huddle on the slopes below. Brahmans are the most numerous in the population of 857 persons. As tenants, farmers of Brahman caste in 1952 possessed about one-half of the village lands. Kishan Garhi is off the beaten track and far enough from newer urban influences for its people to feel conservative about much of their old culture.

A. KISHAN GARHI AS NOT AN ISOLATED WHOLE

First I consider how Kishan Garhi is *not* a world in itself by examining the outlines of its economy, its patterns of kinship and marriage, the social organization of its religion, and its political structure. In each of these aspects Kishan Garhi's society is cut deeply by internal divisions, and in each it also reaches out to form part of a wider system of relationships.

In Kishan Garhi there are internal divisions of economic interest among groups of landlords, tenants, share croppers, laborers, artisans, domestic servants, and shopkeepers. There are many external economic relationships, too. About one-third of the village crops, measuring them by their cash value, are sold every year outside the village. Approximately three-quarters of the three-hundred-odd animals now in Kishan Garhi were brought there from outside, just as were many other essentials, such as clothing. One-third of the credit which finances agriculture in the village was obtained from outside sources. The Brahman priests, Barbers, Potters, Carpenters, Watermen, and Sweepers who live in Kishan Garhi go out to serve hereditary patrons in some fifteen other villages and derive about one-half of their income from those outside patrons. Traders who live in Kishan Garhi regularly range over many miles of the countryside on their trading trips. Wage workers who maintain homes in Kishan Garhi during the present generation have gone out to work in at least twenty-five other places, including ten cities. During one period of three months I counted forty-four different specialists coming into Kishan Garhi from outside to provide goods and services; probably there were many more whom I did not count.

Internal divisions are apparent within Kishan Garhi's society also in matters of marriage and kinship. At least twenty-four caste groups are represented locally; each caste is perfectly exclusive in marriage. There are forty-six local lineage groups in Kishan Garhi, each wholly separate from every other in descent. There is no marriage inside the village within or among any of these groups. Daughters of the village move out and wives of the village move in at marriage, moving to and from more than three hundred other villages. Fifty-seven marriages currently connect Kishan Garhi with sixteen towns and cities. Half of the marriage ties of groups in Kishan Garhi connect them with places more than fourteen miles away, while 5 per cent connect them with places more than forty miles distant.

Social relationships concerned with religion in Kishan Garhi are fragmented to an extreme point. There is no temple of the whole village, no one cremation ground, no sacred tank or well. Instead, dozens of different trees and stones and tiny shrines are made objects of worship separately by members of the many caste and lineage groups. Four different priests divide the eligible families among them for domestic services; no priest serves families of the eight low and lowest castes. Most festivals are observed separately by each family, when particular family tradition does not forbid observance. Different families and sometimes even different individuals of the same family give their allegiance to many different religious preceptors and shrines outside the village. In the course of a few weeks of conversations, I found that I had recorded the names of more than fifty distant places to which villagers of Kishan Garhi had gone on pilgrimage.

Politically, also, Kishan Garhi is noncommunal and disunified in some obvious ways. Within the village there are factions whose members fight on the average a new court case each month. Usually there are three cases in progress at any one time, and many people become involved. Persons of other villages are frequently interested and involved in local disputes. And the organs of government—the bureaucracies of the police, the revenue system, etc.—are intimately intrusive within the village of Kishan Garhi.

These structural facts make Kishan Garhi seem very much less than an isolated whole in the primitive sense. Viewed as a society, as an economy, as a church, or as a polity, this little community has no close coherence or well-bounded physical locus. The very things which I must identify as parts of the little community reach beyond the physical village, while many parts of other communities and of the great community reach inside the village. This little community of Kishan Garhi cannot be very satisfactorily conceived of as an isolated structure or system.

B. KISHAN GARHI AS ISOLABLE

But still I am compelled to go on to say that the village of Kishan Garhi is like a living thing, has a definable structure, is conceptually a vivid entity, is a system—even if it is one of many subsystems within the larger socio-politico-religio-economic system in which it exists. Especially am I so compelled if I look at the concerns and emphases that the people of the village express, and if I try to evaluate the structural aspects of their lives as they evaluate them.

Economically, for instance, the village constitutes a vital nucleus of activity through its lands. Nine out of ten persons, despite their nominal caste specializations, depend in part directly upon the land for a living. Ninety-five per cent of the land on which they depend is contained within the village area.

Socially, the village of Kishan Garhi is a nexus of much informal activity among nonkinsmen and noncastemen. People come together casually, and sometimes convivially, because they are neighbors in their fields or houses, or because they use the same wells or adjacent threshing places. People of Kishan Garhi visit separately outside the village with their own respective relatives by marriage whenever they are called to a feast of birth, marriage, or death. But people of Kishan Garhi attend four times as many ceremonies and feasts inside the village, often with nonkinsmen, as they attend outside the village with relatives. Domestic ceremonies in all families above those of the lowest castes require that representatives of many other local caste groups and lineage groups participate.

Marriage ties outside the village are strong and compelling. But the quality of social relations that obtain among relatives by marriage is rarely one of much friendliness, or even reciprocity. Marital relationships are formally one-sided and unbalanced: the boy's side is the high and demanding side, while the girl's side is the low and giving side. At the wedding ceremony the groom proceeds to the bride's distant village in a procession of military style with as many guns and horses as he can muster. The groom's men demand and receive formal hospitality as their due by formal contract. When they ultimately carry off the bride to their own village, she weeps, clutches her brothers, and screams that she is dead.

To illustrate the quality of relations between marital relatives after the wedding, an anecdote which I heard told for entertainment at one wedding will serve. Villagers thought that this story was terribly funny, and it did touch on some sensitive points in their extralocal social organization.

A man comes to a village one evening and asks to be directed to the house from which a girl has been married out to a boy of Rampur village, a place twelve miles away. He is directed to that house, and there he demands the hookah to smoke. The girl's father, who of course cannot visit his daughter in her village of marriage, says to himself, "This must be someone from my daughter's father-in-law's house." He gives his hookah to the stranger and asks solicitously, "How is Ram Lal, my son-in-law?"

But the stranger just smokes and says, "Bring food!" He washes and sits on a cot. The girl's mother prepares a fine meal, and the girl's father brings it to the stranger on a brass tray. After the stranger has eaten, they ask him again, "Now tell us about our relatives. How are Ram Lal and his brothers?"

But the stranger just says, "I'll sleep now," and he goes to sleep. In the morning, as the stranger is ready to leave, the girl's father presses him hard, begging for news. "Say! How is everyone there in Rampur in your house?"

"My house in Rampur?" asks the stranger as he leaves. "How should I know? I'm from another village!"

This story makes two points about the supralocal organization of marriage. (1) A stranger may pass himself off as a relative by marriage. Relations between marital relatives are generally formal and distant, are sometimes even hostile, and may remain so throughout life. (2) To persons of the outside world a villager's primary identification must be with his own village. Hence the absurd twist of the story depends on the fact that the stranger had not been properly identified as a man of Rampur village before he was granted hospitality.

The first inquiry which is customarily made of anyone who is away from his home is, "What is your village, sir?"—not "What is your caste, clan, name, etc.?" A person's village must be known before anything else about him can become significant, before any other claim can be validated. Village identifications are not mere subjective matters; they are essential to the inclusive fictional kinship system by which everyone is placed in society.

Each village in the countryside around Kishan Garhi is regarded as a fictional agnatic group. People use agnatic terms for each other systematically, taking note of fictional generational standing throughout the village, ignoring all actual differences of caste and lineage. All villagers in Kishan Garhi tend accordingly to observe the same rules of intervillage hypergamy. They tend to classify the affinal villages of fellow-villagers consistently as high or low, thus recognizing the fiction of common local descent which binds the residents of each of those other affinal villages, as well. In the countryside around Kishan Garhi, village is as important a fact for identifying a person as is clan in aboriginal Australia. A man must be identified with his own natal village before his place can be established in the intervillage web of marriages. The wide range of exogamy, which seems to deny the local community and to diffuse social relations over a wide area beyond the village, serves in fact also to define what the village is and who its members are, and to give each village a distinctive position in rural society.

Politically, too, there is in some senses an isolable whole community in Kishan Garhi in spite of internal conflict and in spite of the weakness of formal local government. Factional groupings not only divide people but also unite people who would otherwise act together but rarely. In a sample of thirty-six groups of persons engaged in litigation, half the groups cut across caste lines and joined diverse persons together by allying them in common hostilities. The fact of intense factional struggle raises another question: If there were no compelling awareness of the village as a distinguishable world, then why would people fight inside one village so intensely as they do through litigation and through ceremonies? Indeed, there is a local stage on which relative dominance and relative prestige must be fought out in the village. Few fights within castes but outside the village can compare in intensity with these many local fights.

C. WAYS OF CONCEPTUALIZING THE SITUATION

Thus far I have admitted that a North Indian village society such as Kishan Garhi's is much less than an isolated whole. It has no neatly definable boundaries that are coextensive with its physical self. The social system of the village reaches beyond its central locus far into the outside world, while the outside world in turn reaches into the most central core of village society. In attempting to characterize Kishan Garhi as an isolable whole, I have had to call it a "stage," a "nexus of activity," a focal point of reference for individual prestige and identification. Although Kishan Garhi is a conservative and a relatively traditional village, I cannot say that it is a self-contained, complete little community comparable with primitive little communities. Nor, on the other hand, can I doubt that it is a community, and a very clearly isolable community for its residents. So how am I to conceive it within its larger universe?[2]

Steward and Manners, faced with the problem of characterizing contemporary Puerto Rico, report that they find the traditional holistic approach to community study inadequate (1953: 123). Steward (1951) invites me to sort out my observations instead into "levels of sociocultural integration." But in Kishan Garhi I have difficulty in distinguishing where the three general categories of "levels" begin and end socially and culturally—where, for instance, the national governmental level begins and ends in relation to the little community, so intimately does it penetrate into the village of Kishan Garhi itself (*infra*). I find difficulty also in deciding where to divide off the "horizontal segments" within the culture which Steward invites me to divide off. But in northern India just as in Puerto Rico there are surely "factors which have originated outside, yet strongly affected the way of life within each community and which have helped to create the sociocultural differences found within and among the communities" (Steward and Manners 1953: 124). Not only do such factors exist also in Kishan Garhi, but they seem to have existed there for a very long time. Outside factors have been there so prominently and for so long that they can hardly be characterized as "segments" or as "levels" in the present.

Hanssen (1953) invites me to view Kishan Garhi in another way as a collection of "activity fields" linking parts of town and village society, the fields overlapping with each other in varied ways. His invitation is attractive, since it permits direct statement of the incongruence of the multiple extracommunity and intracommunity relationships which exist. But the delineation of activity fields is a technique rather than a conception of the whole. While Hanssen's techniques of mapping might satisfactorily depict the structural and some of the systematic aspects of Kishan Garhi's position in relation to the outside world, the results of the mapping would be very complex, and the problems of interpretation from such maps would be immense. I am still in need of a positive and constructive way of conceptualizing Kishan Garhi's intermediate position in its universe.

The folk-urban continuum offers one constructive way of conceiving intermediate states of society. Betty Starr (1954), building on the concepts of that continuum, invites me to view Kishan Garhi as a

2. Some of these alternative ways of conceptualizing peasant communities were suggested to me by a reading of the manuscript of *The Little Community* (Redfield 1955).

step in a series of "levels of communal relations" like those which intervene between little communities and great cities of Western type in modern Mexico. Structurally, Starr's levels of communal relations comprise a hierarchy of inclosing greater communities, each community having its discrete nucleus. At the level of each successively wider community, social relations tend to become less frequent, less personal, and more affected by the principle of superordination and subordination.

But the concept of levels of communal relations contrasts with much that is most characteristic of Kishan Garhi. A series of inclosing, nucleated greater communities is not evident; instead, social relations of each different kind spread out in widely different patterns. Thus Kishan Garhi's most frequently exercised ties—its ties with its principal market—place it within the sphere of one small town five miles to the east, while its administrative ties join it with a center of government seven miles to the west. Its hundreds of marital ties recognize no inclosing boundary, but are dispersed over tens of thousands of square miles of the countryside. The village's dozens of ties with places of pilgrimage are limited only by the boundaries of the whole nation, one of the most popular pilgrimages requiring a round trip of six hundred miles. The spatial patterns of Kishan Garhi's livestock trade may be taken as another illustration of the complexity of that village's situation: cows are bred and obtained mainly in the village or from low affinal relatives in the south, following the web of marriage; bulls and bullocks are obtained largely by purchase at markets or from traveling traders, often from the far north and west. Inside the village, neighborhoods are indistinct and lack discrete nuclei; families are inclosed within lineage groups, and lineage groups are inclosed within caste groups, but, because of the small size of each of these groupings, social relations are almost inevitably more frequent outside than inside them. Finally, social relations within the village of Kishan Garhi are already maximally affected by the principle of superordination-subordination; further movement toward the urban pole cannot increase but can only decrease the effects of that principle.

The concept of levels of communal relations traces the passage of the folk community toward a type of civilization which is its opposite—the type of civilization which is familiar to us in the urbanism of the modern West. To distinguish it from an older, indigenous kind of civilization, Redfield designates this newer type of civilization as "secondary" (1953: 41–42 and chap. III). Urban communities and urban culture in such secondary civilizations are necessarily different from the society and culture of the indigenous folk. Secondary civilizations are heterogenetic in origin and in manner of growth; in content they continue to include much that is foreign and to recognize it as such. Urban ways in secondary civilizations are often seen as foreign to folk ways, and are also often regarded as superior to folk ways in authority. The same urban ways, since they oppose folk ways, may simultaneously be regarded by the folk as morally corrupt.

Differing from the concept of secondary civilization and emphasizing continuity rather than discontinuity is the type of "primary civilization," illustrated with Indic urban materials by Redfield and Singer (1954*b*). This concept of a primary civilizational type and process is one of the most inviting of available models for conceptualizing Kishan Garhi's relations with its universe. A primary or "indigenous" civilization is one which grows out of its own folk culture by an orthogenetic process—by a straight line of indigenous development. The "great tradition" which is characteristically developed by such a primary civilization is a carrying-forward of cultural materials, norms, and values that were already contained in local little traditions. If the great tradition absorbs foreign materials, it subjects them to syncretism. An indigenous great tradition remains in constant communication with its own little traditions through a sacred literature, a class of literati, a sacred geography, and the rites and ceremonies associated with each of these. One effect of the development of an indigenous great tradition is to universalize the cultural consciousness of persons within it as they become aware of a greater sphere of common culture.

Given such a primary continuity of culture and society, little communities would almost seem to cease to exist as isolated, distinctive wholes. Redfield and Singer have described the development of an urban community in a primary civilization as "one of a series of concentrations and nucleations within a common field" (1954*b*: 71). The same description would appear also to suit the little communities of a primary civilization. It seems to fit the facts of Kishan Garhi most aptly.

The remainder of this paper is an attempt to extend the concept of an indigenous or primary civilization by examining its implications for one little community. I have outlined above the general situation of the village of Kishan Garhi in its larger context. I turn now to a more detailed examination of village data on two aspects of social structure which particularly relate the village to the outside—governmental land administration and the organization of caste—and then to an examination of data on village religion.

D. LITTLE COMMUNITIES AND THE STATE

"In government and administration," write Redfield and Singer in describing the indigenous type, "the orthogenesis of urban civilization is represented by chiefs, rulers and laws that express and are closely controlled by the norms of the local culture . . . " (1954*b*: 63). Such orthogenesis was evident in the administration of many villages around Kishan Garhi in 1951–52. The revenue-collecting headmen (*nambardārs*), appointees of the state government, are descendants of the same *Jāṭ* chieftains who seized control of the region some three hundred years ago. They are the heads of the leading families of their localized lineages, the principal proprietors of the village lands, and, by the same token, quasi-officials of the state. Ancestors of the present *Jāṭ* headmen, being in *de facto* control of hundreds of villages, had secured rights of revenue collection under provincial officials of Shah Jehan and Aurangzeb (Nevill 1909: 92–93). Before the *Jāṭs*, chieftains of a *Rājpūt* clan had held the same villages and lived in the same mud fortresses in much the same manner, according to local tradition.

Such an orthogenetic relationship, by which government grows upward, as it were, from village to state, is evident in North India generally (Baden-Powell 1892, II). Studies of other single villages convey detailed views of the indigenous administrative forms. In Senapur village in Jaunpur District, U.P., a division of the village lands and administration first into halves, then of each half into thirds, reflects a genealogical division within the local ruling *Rājpūt* family (Opler and Singh 1948: 468–69). In village Rani Khera in Delhi State, the two *pannās*, subdivided into four *ṭolās*, are both segments of the lineage group of the *Jāṭ* proprietors and basic units of state land administration (Lewis 1954: 424). Land administration representing three or more levels of kinship segmentation is not uncommon elsewhere: thus one village next to Kishan Garhi was held in 1952 by local proprietors under the superior proprietorship of a *Rāja* who is the living heir of the senior lineage of their own *Jāṭ* clan. The clan corporation of these proprietors had grown to be in effect a part of the state government. All these villages of northern India have in common a kind of administrative connection with the state by which parts of local kinship organization and parts of state government mutually interpenetrate one another to the point of becoming indistinguishable.

Village land administration in other parts of modern India, especially in southern India, presents a contrast with the highly orthogenetic structures of the north (Baden-Powell 1892, III: 1–320). The headman of village Kodagahalli in Mysore District, for example, is regarded in his official capacity as a salaried agent of the state, not as the commissioned agent of a local corporation of owning kinsmen (Srinivas 1952: 1052). In another village near Bangalore, state intervention in the village through direct individual taxation played an important part in disrupting traditional family organization and indigenous leadership. Such disruptive intervention by the state appears to have been stimulated in part by heterogenetic, specifically British administrative conceptions (Beals 1953; 1954: 403). Recent land reform in northern India, too—reform which has affected such villages as Kishan Garhi deeply (Marriott 1952)—has substituted direct, individual land administration through state officials for feudal land administration through landlords and dominant local groups of kinsmen.

The contrasts and changes that are evident in the relations of village and state in modern India raise the suspicion that even older "orthogenetic" land administration in northern India may have been a result of deliberate governmental policy coming down from the top as much as it was a result of indigenous growth upward from little communities. Statements of early British administrators in northern India confirm this suspicion for the nineteenth century. Lieutenant-Governor James Thomason's *Directions for Revenue Officers* in what is now Uttar Pradesh and a part of Punjab, a manual first published between 1844 and 1848, crystallized an orthogenetic British policy toward village social organization (Thomason 1858; cf. Misra 1942: 75–77). Previously, during the first two or three decades of the nineteenth century, British administrators had tried a variety of devices for collecting the land revenue. They had made settlements for the revenue sometimes directly with cultivating proprietors, sometimes with the highest bidder at auction regardless of the absence of previous right, and sometimes with existing petty rulers, among whom some had arisen only during the time of troubles immediately preceding British entry. The early rates of taxation were often so high as to drive out many of the most ancient proprietors along with those of most recent origin (Hutchinson 1856: 28–42; Nevill 1909: 125–28; Misra 1942: 54–60).

By the 1820's, however, a different policy had begun to evolve—that of the *mahālvāri* system of land tenure. Many elements of this different policy were in fact traditional, and those elements that were in fact new were justified as being traditional. "The system," writes Thomason, ". . . professes to alter nothing, but only to place on record what it finds to exist" (1858: 9). A first and somewhat novel requirement of the system was to divide up the whole countryside into village units for administration (p. 2); previous Mughal policy had often been to recognize estates as units, even when they cut across several villages. Thomason directed further that, wherever possible, the whole body of proprietors in each village should be made individually and collectively responsible for paying the land tax. Where the proprietors were in fact members of several different lineage groups, their lands were to be divided only into the largest possible lineage group units within the village; where they were members of one lineage group, their proportional rights in the corporate estate were to be measured according to ancestral shares (pp. 2, 7–9, 49–54). Every effort was to be made to preserve the collective financial responsibility and legal solidarity of these lineage groups where they existed among the proprietors, as they did very generally (pp. 8–9, 195–96). Tax rates were to be lowered so as to give these lineage groups a common proprietary interest that would be worth maintaining and worth improving (pp. 3–4, 40–41). In general, this system for the handling of land revenue by lineage group units may be characterized sociologically as the disposition to treat each village as if it were a great family.

Beyond these principles of revenue settlement summarized by Thomason, other regulations and laws concerning record-keeping, maintenance of local police, and transfer of holdings were enacted by British administrators with the same purpose in mind—to preserve strong authority in the dominant proprietary lineage or lineages of each village. Within the village, then, the British began and continued during most of the nineteenth century in northern India to pursue a land-revenue policy which was orthogenetic in conception. They did so for reasons of efficiency, just as previous rulers had pursued similar policies before them, in spite of their being themselves aliens to India.

Beyond the village, however, certain British innovations were contradictory in effect, being heterogenetic in conception. The new courts of law to which anyone was entitled to appeal tended to undermine traditional norms and traditional forms of dominance and submission, as Thomason himself noticed as early as 1837 (1838: 115). Also, the very fact that each holding—indeed, each field—was now written down itself became a disruptive fact: absentee proprietorship was thereby protected and increased, while fractional shares too small to maintain themselves in a less formal system were multiplied. In spite of minute recording, in spite of the possibility of appeal to outside courts, and in spite of other opposing, secondary civilizational factors, the general trend of British land policy favored the maintenance of lineage properties in many villages. In the village of Kishan Garhi, over the first sixty-eight years of British rule, only one-fifth of the village lands had passed out of the hands of the original *Jāṭ* landlord lineage; between 1871 and 1952 a further change of only 9 per cent occurred.

The broader effects of the *mahālvāri* system of land tenure on village social organization seem to have been great. At least three effects may be listed.

1. Lineage groups of proprietors were encouraged to keep together. Their lands were recorded as parts of one estate (*mahāl*) or village unit, under one formal revenue headman, who was chosen from among their own ranks. This headman was externally appointed, but often he became strong as a result, if he was not already the first power among his kinsmen. Petty dynasties of much local power thereby arose, or were maintained, in Senapur (Opler and Singh 1948), in Rani Khera (Lewis 1954), and in Kishan Garhi, as quite generally in North Indian areas under *mahālvāri* administration. In Kishan Garhi the lineage group of the *Jāṭ* proprietors possesses a genealogy known to be seven generations deep from base to apex—a known depth greater than that of any other lineage group of the village and twice as great as the average known depth of lineage groups. The existence of a single lineage group estate through many years also acted as a deterrent to the immigration of nonlineal relatives: the *Jāṭ* landlord lineage group, although it now includes nine separate commensal families, is still perfectly agnatic in composition. At the same time tenant and landless lineage groups of the village, lacking corporate legal definition, have absorbed large numbers of immigrant affinal families.

2. A second effect of *mahālvāri* land-tenure administration is evident in the residential patterns of many North Indian villages. The major quarters of Rani Khera (Lewis 1954: 424–25) and the six wards of the village of Senapur reflect governmental recognition of kinship segmentation among the village owners.

3. Finally, political opposition and conflict within villages under *mahālvāri* tenure tends characteristically to occur at points of cleavage within and among proprietary lineages (Baden-Powell 1908: 142–43; cf. Thomason 1838: 102, 104–5, 107–8). The "moieties" of Senapur once served to give a peaceable channeling to competition among large kinship segments of the proprietors, each with their followings, it seems (Opler and Singh 1948). The "factions" of Rani Khera are composed basically of large lineage groups of landed *Jāṭs;* Lewis tells us that such factions require for their existence a long corporate history, agnatic homogeneity, and economic power (1954: 445–50)—precisely the requirements whose fulfilment is encouraged by *mahālvāri* tenure. In Kishan Garhi similarly, all major court cases and many other quarrels which came to my attention involved persons on opposite sides of cleavages or incipient cleavages within the landlord lineage group. Sharers, ex-sharers, and would-be sharers in a *mahālvāri* estate have ample reason for rivalry over the allegiance of tenants, or over legal and genealogical inequities in their shares of the corporate lands.

What I wish to suggest about these little communities of northern India is that much of what seems most typically "little" about them—certain features of their kinship structure, of their village layout, and of typical modes of conflict—turn out to be not merely isolated indigenous developments but also reflexes of general state policy. Little communities even in their "traditional" forms here cannot be imagined as existing in isolation from intimate effects of the state. While village structures grow upward toward the state, state policy may determine what village structure shall be.

Up to this point I have indicated only some very recent evidences for the interaction of village structure and state government, evidences drawn entirely from the nineteenth and twentieth centuries. Yet if such interaction is evident in 1952, in 1882, or in 1822, it may also have been occurring for centuries, even for millenniums, in the past. Redfield and Singer (1954*b:* 53–54) point out that a "middle-run perspective" of history somewhat longer than the "short-run perspective" that typically comes within the anthropologist's view must be attempted in order to comprehend the workings of large civilizations. Short-run perspectives of thirty or fifty or one hundred and fifty years can be appropriately used to examine recent external influences on the social structures of little communities, as they often have been used in village India (Srinivas 1951; Miller 1952; Gough 1952; Marriott 1952; Carstairs 1952; Mandelbaum 1952; Bailey

1953; Beals 1953, 1954). But exclusive use of such short-run perspectives is likely to carry with it the misleading implication that before the heterogenetic influences of recent times villages were somehow isolated and free from the effects of state policy.

We have only to put this implication as a question in order to realize that the answer is otherwise. As far back as we are able to look, the social structures of little communities in the area of Indian civilization must have been profoundly affected by state land policy. And we know that past policy was not uniform but was most various from time to time and from place to place. There was at one pole the policy of recognizing clan monarchies, under which familistic controls could reach from the dominant lineage group of the village all the way to the king himself (Ghoshal 1929: 234–36, 241, 259–60, 288). At another pole was the policy, evident in ancient Hindu times, of a direct approach by agents of the state to the village cultivators (Ghoshal 1929: 46–57, 142–52). And in between were a great variety of feudal, semifeudal, and theocratic arrangements (Ghoshal 1929: 137–39, 187; Moreland 1937: 451–55; Peter 1952: 44). Lest it be supposed that these older land policies of the state were less effective in shaping the past social structures of little communities, Baden-Powell cites examples to show how certain governmental policies in pre-British times actually created lineage group estates in villages of whole regions where no such estates had previously existed (1900; 1908: 107–9).

Even if we knew nothing of the history of intimate and mutually interpenetrating relationships of village and indigenous state in the India of earlier times, we might easily be led to suspect their existence when we listen to the personal names current among villagers today. For example, I came across such principal personal name elements as—translating them—"Overseer" (*Karoṛī*), "Minister" (*Muṉśi*), "Clerk" (*Bābū*), "Baron" (*Navāb*), "Law" (*Hukam*), "Treasury" (*Ḳhazān*), "Paymaster General" (*Baḳhśī*), "Collector" (*Kalektaṛ*), and "Deputy [Collector]" (*Dipṭī*), not to mention such ancient and common affixes of given names as "King" (*Rāj*), "Protector" (*Pāl*), "Lord" (*Nāth*), etc.

E. LITTLE COMMUNITIES AND CASTE

If integration and continuity between little communities and civilization are evident in the structural relations of village and state in India, they are evident even more plainly in the organization of caste. The existence of an extensive system of castes, present in all villages and cutting across many villages, perhaps provides the ultimate in proofs of the ancient inseparability of the little communities of India from the greater community which they collectively constitute. Three aspects of caste organization in particular demonstrate the mutual influence of little and great communities: (1) its complex ethnic composition; (2) its partial correlation with and determination by differential allocation of wealth and power; and (3) its maintenance by elaborate ritual usages.

1. Villagers in Kishan Garhi today refer to the twenty-four caste groups of the village by the terms *zāt* (birth, race) and *kaum* (tribe, people)—in other words, as representatives of different ethnic groups. Each caste group in each village is one of many dozens or hundreds or thousands of local caste groups which make up the whole membership of any endogamous caste. As villagers see the situation today, the village is a local association of representatives of many ethnic groups, some being early settlers, some later immigrants, and others conquerors. One conventional metaphor for the "whole" of any large village in the region of Kishan Garhi is "all the seven peoples (castes)." While some of the groups which are now ethnically separate may have originated by fission within formerly united populations, many are likely once to have existed in something like actual spatial separation. Taking the middle-run perspective of India's civilizational career, we know that the development of local and regional caste systems could have occurred only by such local accommodations among once separate peoples as a large-scale political order can make possible. There is some evidence that such has been the history of certain present castes and of the caste system (e.g., Majumdar and Pusalker 1951: 356, 386–87). The present highly differentiated and extensive caste system may be regarded thus in part as a living monument to a primary adjustment among tribal peoples emerging into a civilization of greater organized range and scope.

2. A second kind of interaction of greater and lesser communities is evident in the differential allocation of wealth and power to the ethnic groups which are presently higher and lower castes. In the region around Kishan Garhi today, as in the village itself, the two highest castes—Brahmans and *Jāṭs,* by local opinion—are the two castes whose members possess the greatest amount of landed wealth. In part, such correlations of wealth with the caste order may represent a recognition in the general caste order of indigenous *de facto* stratification. From remote Coorg we have the relevant example of a

people, the Coorgs, who follow a number of habits that are repugnant to Brahmanical custom: they drink liquor, eat domestic pork, and permit the remarriage of their widows. They could by these tokens be counted as a very low caste, possibly untouchable. But, since they also control the lands of an entire district, they are more conveniently admitted to the caste hierarchy as "*Ugras*" or "*Kṣatriyas*" (Srinivas 1952: 33–34). The Coorgs' high position may be considered as an instance of orthogenetic addition to the general system of castes, an addition which has passed directly from the little communities of a region into the great categories of the wider civilization. More complicated sequences of interaction, many of them originating immediately in the orthogenetic state, may be found to have brought about the correlations of caste rank and power now existing in many other little communities. The Brahmans of the Tanjore village of Kumbapettai, for example, appear to owe their wealth, their secular power, and much of their effective ritual authority to a royal land grant (Gough 1952: 531). Whatever the hieratic, feudal, bureaucratic, or indigenous origins of unequal wealth and power as between higher and lower castes, some formality and fixity of lands and offices through the devices of a greater state seems everywhere to underlie the order of caste ranking.

3. A third kind of link between the caste hierarchies of little communities and the great tradition of the greater community can be described only speculatively: this is the body of ritual usages by which the ranking of castes is managed in each place. The castes of Kishan Garhi place each other in positions of relative rank according to an elaborate order of ritual usages, especially usages concerned with the giving and receiving of food, water, and services on ceremonial occasions in each household. It is difficult to imagine how such elaborate ritual usages capable of ranking so large a number of different castes could have come into being without something like deliberate contrivance, without some context in centers more sophisticated than those of the village households. Even within such a village as Kishan Garhi, a stratification of these ritual usages is already evident, for the number of services and the rules of handling food and water are more elaborate in the highly literate landlord's household than in the tenants' and are more elaborate in the higher castes than in the lower.

Beyond the village and far back beyond the present we can have glimpses of the processes of filtering down between great and little communities which may have given rise to present village usages, but glimpses only. In later vedic times there were two classes of sacrifices: simpler ones which could be conducted by householders themselves, or with the assistance of kinsmen, and more elaborate ones which could be conducted only by kings with the help of professional ritual specialists. Royal sacrifices grew more elaborate in time, their ritualists more specialized (Renou and Filliozat 1947: 348–49; Majumdar and Pusalker 1951: 386–87). By comparison with their Aryan forefathers, villagers in Kishan Garhi probably now practice more elaborate household sacrifices, too, and employ a larger number of specialists.

Hocart points out that many of the kinds of ritual relationships which exist among Indian village castes today may be regarded as results of a "degradation of the royal style" (1950: 155). If the king has a royal chaplain or a royal barber in his retinue, then no peasant home can afford to be without one. Even a poor householder in Kishan Garhi today retains six or seven servants of different castes mainly to serve him in ceremonial ways demonstrative of his own caste rank. Householders and their servants formally address each other by courtly titles. Thus the Brahman priest is called "Great King" (*Mahārāj*) or "Learned Man" (*Paṇḍitjī*), the Potter is called "Ruler of the People" (*Prajāpat*), the Barber "Lord Barber" (*Nāū Ṭhākur*), the Carpenter "Master Craftsman" (*Mistrī*), the Sweeper "Headman" (*Mehtar*) or "Sergeant" (*Jamādār*), etc. About half of the twenty-four castes of Kishan Garhi also identify themselves with one or another of the three higher *varṇa*, thus symbolizing their claims to certain ritual statuses in relation to the sacrifice or the sacrificer of Sanskrit literary form. "Thus the apparent degradation of the royal style becomes a step in social evolution" (Hocart 1950: 155).

If communication with the great tradition of the greater community has had much to do with the development of a ritual hierarchy of castes in the village, then the village has also provided a social unit whose small scale of relationships among its members is essential to the flourishing of such a ritual hierarchy. The village and the royal court have this small scale in common. Villagers are able to maintain their many ritual ranks precisely because they are able to recognize each other individually as a Brahman, a Barber, a Potter, or a Sweeper. A villager of one place cannot move to a village far from his own or to any town without loss of caste recognition and without confusion as to caste ranks, for both individuals and intercaste usages of rank vary from place to place. Whether a *Jāṭ* Farmer may accept a hookah handed him by a certain Barber may depend on whether the local Brahmans accept food handled by that Barber. The intricacies of the Hindu system of caste ranking cannot be imagined as existing in any but small packages.

F. SUMMARY

Viewed from the perspective of Kishan Garhi, the villages which are the little communities of India today may be conceived as relative structural nexuses, as subsystems within greater systems, and as foci of individual identification within a greater field. They cannot be conceived as things in themselves in their organization of marriage and kinship, residence patterns, modes of conflict, or caste organization. Nor are they ever likely to have been conceivable as isolates since Indian civilization began. The traditional social structure of the greater community of India similarly cannot be understood as apart from its continuing existence in relation to hundreds of thousands of little communities. Both little communities and greater communities are mutually necessary conditions of each other's existence in their present forms. One must consider both in order thoroughly to understand either.

III. FESTIVALS AND DEITIES

To add another dimension to the answers given above from social structural materials alone, I turn at this point to examine some cultural contents of the religion of the people of Kishan Garhi. If I would describe the religion of these people as it exists within the universe of Indian religion in general, I must consider as a matter of method (1) the extent to which the religion of the little community can be conceived as a whole apart from the religious great tradition of Indian civilization and (2) the extent to which the religious great tradition of Indian civilization is understandable through study of the religion of one little community. Fortunately, I can take as my guides in answering these questions both the concept of a primary or indigenous civilizational process (Redfield and Singer 1954*b*) and that set of hypotheses concerning the spread and effects of Sanskritization which has been drawn up by Srinivas (1952, chap. VII).

A. FESTIVALS AS PRODUCTS OF GREAT AND LITTLE TRADITIONS

Table 1 gives immediate proof of the existence of the great tradition of Hinduism within Kishan Garhi, if that tradition is understood to be the literate religious tradition, embodied in or derived from Sanskrit works which have a universal spread in all parts of India.

At least fifteen of the nineteen village festivals are sanctioned by one or more universal Sanskrit texts. The festivals of Tenth and of Lights, for example, are sanctioned as celebrations of climactic events in the *Rāmāyaṇa* epic, while most of the other festivals are connected with stories in one or several *Purāṇas*.

Nearly half the festivals in Table 1 not only have connections with great-traditional texts but are themselves observed very widely, if

TABLE 1

PRINCIPAL ANNUAL FESTIVALS IN KISHAN GARHI

Month	Fortnight and Day	Local Name	Translation [or Implication]
Cait (March–April)	1:11	1. *Ekādaśi*	"Eleventh"
	2:1–9	2. *Patthvārī Pūjā* or *Durgā Naumī*	"Stony One Worship" or "*Durgā* Ninth"
Baisākh (April–May)	Varies	3. *Bāsor Pūjā* or *Devī-Devatā kī Pūjā*	"Leftover Food Worship" or "Goddess-Godling Worship"
	Varies	4. *Kue kā Devatā kā Melā*	"Fair of the Well Godling"
	2:1–15	5. *Pitar kī Pūjā*	"Ancestor Worship"
Sāvan (July–Aug.)	2:3	6. *Tīj*	"Third"
	2:15	7. *Salūno* and *Rākhī Bandhan*	"Beautiful"(?) and "Charm Tying"
Bhādoṉ (Aug.–Sept.)	1:8	8. *Kṛṣṇa Janam Aṣṭamī*	"*Kṛṣṇa*'s Birthday Eighth"
Kuār (Sept.–Oct.)	1:1–15	9. *Kanāgat*	[Ancestor Remembrance]
	2:1–9	10. *Naurthā* or *Nau Durgā*	"Ninenights" or "Nine *Durgās*"
	2:10	11. *Daśahrā*	"Tenth"
Kātik (Oct.–Nov.)	1:3	12. *Karvā Cauth*	"Pitcher Fourth"
	1:15	13. *Divālī*	"Lights"
	2:1–2	14. *Gobardhan Pūjā*	"Cow-Nourisher Worship"
	2:11	15. *Devuṭhān*	"Awakening of the Gods"
Pūs (Dec.–Jan.)	Varies	16. *Būṛho Bābū kī Pūjā*	"Old Clerk's Worship"
Māgh (Jan.–Feb.)	1:1–2	17. *Sakaṭ*	....
Phāgun (Feb.–March)	1:13–14	18. *Śiv Rātrī*	"*Śiva* Night"
	2:13–15	19. *Holī*	[Saturnalia]

not universally, in India. Eight of these festivals of Kishan Garhi may be listed as probably universal, at least in name. The eight are *Durgā* Ninth, Eleventh, Charm Tying, Nine *Durgās*, Tenth, Lights, *Śiva* Night, and *Holī*. Possibly parallels of two or three others among the festivals of Table 1, such as *Kṛṣṇa*'s Birthday Eighth, *Kanāgat*, and Awakening of the Gods, might also be found in the annual cycles of villages in most regions of India.

The remaining half of the festivals observed in Kishan Garhi have more limited regional or local distributions. Regional festivals include Cow-Nourisher Worship, Pitcher Fourth, Old Clerk's Worship, and probably others. The Fair of the Well Godling and Leftover Food Worship must probably be counted as local festivals, although they are not without resemblances to festivals elsewhere in the region. Only for the last four festivals mentioned have I been unable to find any trace of great-traditional sanction, however.

The great tradition of Hinduism is not merely present as a part of most festivals of Kishan Garhi, but it has achieved, through the festivals, an integrated position in village life. Great festivals of Sanskritic rationale and nomenclature provide, along with domestic ceremonies, the principal occasions on which most villagers may engage in concerted symbolic activities. Most of the festivals in Table 1 are observed by most of the castes, lineage groups, and families of Kishan Garhi, and many festival observances cut significantly across the routine barriers of social structure.

From such a simple listing of the names and distributions of principal festivals in Kishan Garhi one might presume that there is not much in the festivals of this little community which conceptually could be set apart from the predominant Sanskritic great tradition. One might well expect to find the great tradition predominant in a village which, like Kishan Garhi, lies in the heartland of Aryan settlement. One might with reason imagine even that Kishan Garhi once knew a purely Aryan religion, and that the process of Sanskritization first began to operate there between Aryan and non-Aryan religious traditions (Hutton 1946: 192–201). In any event, the religion of Kishan Garhi must have been subjected to constant Sanskritization over a period of about three thousand years. If time and geographic location have important effects upon the degree of Sanskritization—on the spread of the great tradition—then one might expect to find that the religion of Kishan Garhi is notably closer to the religion of the great tradition than is, for example, the religion of the Coorgs in remote mountains of southern India.

But the presumption that the festivals of Kishan Garhi are approximately identical with those of the great tradition needs to be qualified in at least four ways. These four qualifications bring us to confront the little tradition of Kishan Garhi.

First, there are four festivals which have no evident Sanskritic rationales: Leftover Food Worship, Fair of the Well Godling, Pitcher Fourth, and Old Clerk's Worship.

Second, those festivals of Kishan Garhi which do have Sanskritic rationales represent only a small selection out of the total annual cycle of festivals which finds sanction in the great tradition. Of the 13 major Hindu festivals recently listed by a group of Hindu scholars (Morgan 1953: 423), only 7 are observed in Kishan Garhi. Of the 35 presumably all-Indian Hindu festivals listed by Swami Sivananda (1947: 1–57), only 9 occur in Kishan Garhi. Of the 270 festivals of the Hindu religious year in the list compiled by Underhill (1921: 136–59), only 11 are observed in Kishan Garhi, and then on somewhat variant dates. Even lists of festivals drawn up especially for the state of Uttar Pradesh or its districts rarely include as many as half of the festivals which are observed in Kishan Garhi and listed in Table 1; conversely, all the festivals observed in Kishan Garhi are rarely equal to more than a small fraction of even regional compendia (e.g., Growse 1880: 246–49).

Third, between the festivals of Kishan Garhi and those sanctioned by the great tradition, connections are often loosened, confused, or mistaken because of a multiplicity of competing meanings for each special day within the great tradition itself. Each festival of Kishan Garhi is likely to have at least two or three Sanskritic stories available to explain it. To explain *Holī*, for instance, a villager in Kishan Garhi may choose between or combine the puranic story of *Prahlād* and *Holikā* and that of *Kṛṣṇa* and *Rādhā* or the *Gopīs*. Particularly auspicious dates of the calendar tend to accumulate layer upon layer of mythical events—birthdays of deities, victories of gods over demons, etc.

When I went with villagers of Kishan Garhi to witness the Car Festival (*Ratha Yātrā*) in a town nearby, I found that different villagers held very diverse explanations of the festival. When they saw the focal idol being towed through the streets on a great car, with swordplay, hymn-singing, and roll of drums, some said it represented the Goddess (*Devī*), others that it represented *Ṭhakurjī* riding triumphant after a victory, others that it represented the divine epic couple *Sītā-Rām*, and still others that it represented *Kṛṣṇa* celebrating his birthday. Accustomed to an interminable variety of overlapping Sanskritic mythology, villagers have ceased to be much concerned with distinguishing the "right" great-traditional explanation of a festival from such Sanskritic-sounding and possibly newly invented ones as may be convenient.

Fourth, behind their Sanskritic names and multiple great-traditional rationales, the festivals of Kishan Garhi contain much ritual which has no evident connection with the great tradition. The festival of Lights, for example, as it is celebrated in Kishan Garhi, contains many elements which are not connected either with a celebration of *Rām*'s triumphal return from *Lankā* or with a celebration of *Lakṣmī*'s wedding. To be sure, villagers do set out oil lamps in the evening and say that they do so in order to celebrate either or both of these great-traditional events; many do also worship *Hanumānjī* by name the next morning to celebrate his part in *Rām*'s triumph.

But on these same dates of the festival of Lights villagers also perform the following other rituals. (*a*) Small incendiary sacrifices are made by each householder in the name of each of his personal gods

FIGURE 1. *Saurtī*
A parochial *Lakṣmī*

and godlings and ancestors, as well as in the name of *Hanumānjī*. (*b*) A crude figure of a goddess called "*Saurtī*" is drawn in each household, usually on the wall (Fig. 1), and is variously worshiped, then implored to grant prosperity and preservation to the family and its animals. A few villagers identify *Saurtī* with *Lakṣmī*, but most do not, because, as several men said, "*Lakṣmī* is a goddess only of rich people." (*c*) Another female deity called "Lampblack" (*Siyāho*), represented by a mound of dung with a straw stuck on top, is worshiped with songs by some women of the higher castes at 4:00 A.M. Actual lampblack is manufactured while the songs are being sung, and this lampblack is applied to the eyes of children during the ensuing year to protect them from evil eye. Most people in Kishan Garhi do not know about the worship of *Siyāho;* I could find no one who was willing to connect *Siyāho* with any other deity or story (but cf. Rose 1919, I: 915). (*d*) An old winnowing fan is beaten through the rooms of each house, also at about 4:00 A.M., the owner crying as he beats, "Get out, Poverty!" (*e*) Some of these old winnowing fans are immediately burned by small boys, and some are burned along with the straw image of an old man. This image is called "Flag Grandfather" (*Jhaṇḍī Bābā*), possibly to commemorate a garrulous man of that name who actually resided in Kishan Garhi a generation ago. Here, then, contained within what seems from its name to be a major festival, sanctioned in the great tradition of Hinduism, are many elements having precedents only in lesser traditions without literary form.

Like the festival of Lights, the contents of most other festivals in Kishan Garhi also show a combination of some great-traditional elements with many other distinctive, non-Sanskritic elements. Although we cannot conceive of all the contents of religious festivals in Kishan Garhi as existing apart from a great tradition which is both within and beyond the village, we can nevertheless distinguish a substantial body of festival contents which are partly unique to the region and to the village and which partake, therefore, of lesser traditions. A part of village religion thus remains conceptually separable, both for the people who live in Kishan Garhi and for the outside analyst.

If we consider this same combination of great- and little-traditional rites as representing the extent of "the spread of Sanskritic rites, and the increasing Sanskritization of non-Sanskritic rites" (Srinivas 1952: 208), then we must conclude that spread and Sanskritization in Kishan Garhi have scarcely begun, despite their having continued there for some three thousand years. While elements of the great tradition have become parts of local festivals, they do not appear to have entered village festival custom "at the expense of" (p. 208) much that is or was the little tradition. Instead, we see evidence of accretion and of transmutation in form without apparent replacement and without rationalization of the accumulated and transformed elements.

Whatever the processes that lie behind the present combination of great and little traditions in the religion of Kishan Garhi, villagers now regard both traditions as old and indigenous. When I asked for explanations of the diversity of the seemingly unconnected rituals which were being observed at the festival of Lights, villagers replied that the dark-moon day of the month of *Kātik* is a very auspicious day for many gods and for themselves, hence that all these rituals naturally fall together.

Since the great tradition derives its authority from faith in its native belongingness, hardly anyone thinks of replacing elements of the little tradition with elements of the great. Bright lithographed pictures of *Lakṣmī* and *Hanumānjī* in Sanskritic regalia are available in the shops at Kishan Garhi's market town, and have long been used by villagers as household decorations. But only one young man of lower caste, a critic of his father and of the social order, put one of these printed pictures on his wall for worship at the festival of Lights in place of the little-traditional *Saurtī*, rudely drawn with rice flour or ghee (Fig. 1).

1. *Universalization.*—For understanding why Sanskritization has gone so short a way in so long a time in the festivals of Kishan Garhi, and for understanding why Sanskritic rites are often added onto non-Sanskritic rites without replacing them, the concept of a primary or indigenous process of civilization again offers useful guidance. By definition, an indigenous civilization is one whose great tradition originates by a "universalization," or a carrying-forward of materials which are already present in the little traditions which it encompasses (cf. Redfield and Singer 1954*b:* 68).[3] Such an indigenous great tradition has authority in so far as it constitutes a more articulate and refined restatement or systematization of what is already there (pp. 6–7). Without subsequent secondary transformation of its contents and without heterogenetic criticism of the little tradition, the indigenous great tradition lacks authority to supplant the hoary prototypes that are the sources of its own sacredness.

I am not able from having visited Kishan Garhi in 1951–52 to report that I have witnessed the whole process of universalization upward from festivals of a little tradition into sacred events of the great tradition of Hinduism. "Time to simmer is an essential part of this concept . . ." just as it is of the concept of filtering down—"time to integrate . . . to rework" (Foster 1953: 164). Such a festival as the festival of Lights nevertheless suggests and allows me to speculate upon the course which such processes might have taken in middle-run perspective. The Sanskritic goddess *Lakṣmī*, for example, appears to be a credible literary apotheosis of such local figures as the unlettered *Saurtī* and the inchoate *Siyāho;* she is the antithesis of poverty and old things, and is an object appropriate for worship on a day already held sacred in the little tradition for renewing one's reverence to the multitudes of gods and spirits. And what better day than this auspicious dark of the moon could have been chosen by

3. Redfield and Singer in the paper cited use the term "universalization" only in the phrase "universalization of cultural consciousness." From this point onward, I use the term in the broader sense indicated here to designate the carrying forward and upward, not only of cultural awareness, but also of cultural contents.

the puranic poet for staging the marriage of *Lakṣmī*, or by the epic poet for staging the curtain scene of *Rām*'s adventures (cf. Crooke 1896*b*, II: 295–96)?

Materials suggestive of such ancient processes of upward universalization are ready at hand in many other festivals of Kishan Garhi. The festival of Charm Tying can supply one further example here. This all-Indian festival coincides and blends in Kishan Garhi with the festival known regionally as *Salūno* ("Beautiful"[?]), a festival which marks the end of that annual fortnight during which most young wives return for a visit with their parents and siblings. On *Salūno* day, many husbands arrive at their wives' villages, ready to carry them off again to their villages of marriage. But, before going off with their husbands, the wives as well as their unmarried village sisters express their concern for and devotion to their brothers by placing young shoots of barley, the locally sacred grain, on the heads and ears of their brothers. Since brothers should accept nothing from their sisters as a free gift, they reciprocate with small coins. Brothers and brothers-in-law then join in sports contests.

On the same day, along with the ceremonies of *Salūno*, and according to the literary precedent of *Bhaviṣyottara Purāṇa*, among other Sanskrit works, the ceremonies of Charm Tying (*Rākhī Bandhan* or *Rakṣa Bandhan*) are also held. The Brahman domestic priests of Kishan Garhi go to each patron and tie upon his wrist a charm in the form of a polychrome thread, bearing tassel "plums." Each priest utters a vernacular blessing and is rewarded by his patron with cash, for it is thought impious to accept anything as a free gift from a priest. Parallels between the familial festival of *Salūno* and the specialized Brahmanical festival of Charm Tying—between the role of the sister and the role of the priest—are obvious. The likelihood that Charm Tying has its roots in some such little-traditional festival as *Salūno* tempts speculation. The ceremonies of both now exist side by side, as if they were two ends of a process of primary transformation.

A further, secondary transformation of the festival of Charm Tying is also beginning to be evident in Kishan Garhi, for the thread charms of the priests are now factory-made in more attractive form and are hawked in the village by a local caste group of *Jogīs*. A few sisters in Kishan Garhi have taken to tying these heterogenetic charms of priestly type onto their brothers' wrists. The new string charms are also more convenient for mailing in letters to distant, city-dwelling brothers whom sisters cannot visit on the auspicious day. Beals reports,[4] furthermore, that brothers in the electrified village of Namhalli near Bangalore tuned in to All India Radio in order to receive a time signal at the astrologically exact moment, and then tied such charms to their own wrists, with an accompaniment of broadcast Sanskrit *mantras*.

2. *Parochialization.*—If the indigenous origins and connections of the great tradition limit its authority to uproot any little tradition, the essentially unlearned and nonliterate nature of the little tradition also obstructs the direct transmission or spread of elements downward from great to little. Downward spread, like universalization, is likely to be characterized by transformations.[5]

The festival of Cow-Nourisher Worship as it is celebrated in Kishan Garhi exemplifies some of the kinds of limits upon, and changes that take place during, the course of a downward transmission of cultural contents from great to little traditions. Villagers today know at least two stories to explain this festival, both of them evidently derived from Book X of the *Bhāgavata Purāṇa*, a Sanskrit work of the tenth century A.D. (Renou and Filliozat 1947: 418). The contents of this Sanskrit book, which comprise a biography of *Kṛṣṇa*, have been popularized among villagers by a succession of vernacular renderings, among which one of the latest is the nineteenth-century Hindi version entitled *Prem Sāgara* (Lallū Lāl 1897: 1–2). The story from this great-traditional book which is most generally taken to explain the Cow-Nourisher Worship concerns *Kṛṣṇa*'s adventures with his cowherd companions at a hill named *Gobardhan* ("Cow Nourisher"), which is actually located about forty miles distant from Kishan Garhi. In this story, *Kṛṣṇa* directs the cowherds of Braj to worship the hill that is near at hand rather than such great but distant gods as *Indra*. The cowherds comply with *Kṛṣṇa*'s directions. In anger over the resulting defection of his worshipers, *Indra* sends violent rainstorms to destroy the cowherds and their kine. *Kṛṣṇa*, however, lifts up the hill to provide them shelter, and all are saved (Lallū Lāl 1897: 65–72). At the actual hill of Gobardhan in Mathura District, an annual ceremony of circumambulation and worship is still enacted (cf. Growse 1880: 280).

By the time that this great-traditional story has reached ritual enactment in a festival of Kishan Garhi it has taken on a cruder form and accumulated a number of homely details which have no evident justification in the Sanskritic myth. Villagers, indeed, seem to have

4. In a personal communication, April, 1954.

5. My attention was first called to this process by Morris E. Opler.

taken the story's parochial moral to heart. "Cow Nourisher" (*Go + vardhana*) has become by a village etymology "Cowdung Wealth" (*Gobar + dhan*) (cf. Grierson 1880; Temple 1883: 38).[6] The sacred hill of the *Purāṇa* has become in each household yard a literal pile of cowdung, shaped into a rough homunculus with four embracing walls appended to its neck, and decorated on top with "trees" of straw and cotton. Within these walls are crowded rude loaves representing all the cows, bullocks, and buffaloes that the family owns or would like to own. To secure any possible benefit to the family's milk and fodder supply, feeding troughs, milking vessels, churns, etc., are also represented in fecal model. The family cowboy is there, too, modeled in dung—the real family cowboy gets a rupee on this day—and so is a model tank to which the cowboy can take the animals for water. The women and children of each family finish this dung construction by day; in the evening all the agnates of each family worship it jointly by placing a lamp on its navel, winding a thread around its trees, and shouting in solemn procession, "Long live Grandfather Cowdung Wealth!" Members of the Weaver caste of Kishan Garhi add their bit, too, for on the next morning they must be paid to sing a Cowdung Wealth awakening song before the dung images can be broken up for use as daily fuel. But a portion of the cowdung remaining from the celebration must be set aside: this portion is reshaped and scored into the form of an enormous cracker; the cracker is dried and preserved as sacred until it can be contributed to the great annual all-village bonfire at the *Holī* festival six months later.

To refer to the kind of transformation of cultural contents which is apparent in the festival of Cow-Nourisher Worship—the downward devolution of great-traditional elements and their integration with little-traditional elements—a term is needed. For this movement, which is the reverse of "universalization," I suggest the term "parochialization." Parochialization is a process of localization, of limitation upon the scope of intelligibility, of deprivation of literary form, of reduction to less systematic and less reflective dimensions. The process of parochialization constitutes the characteristic creative work of little communities within India's indigenous civilization.

The festival of Nine *Durgās* in Kishan Garhi presents another specimen of parochialization. This festival has innumerable precedents in Sanskrit literature of the great tradition. The nine days on

6. Thanks are due to Murray B. Emeneau and to Norvin Hein for pointing out this etymological shift.

which it takes place are sanctioned in myth for the worship of *Durgā*, *Kālī*, *Pārvatī*, *Śakti*, and all other names and aspects of the great Goddess (*Devī*) and the spouses of *Śiva*. During this festival in Kishan Garhi, bas-relief idols representing a feminine deity called "*Naurthā*" are constructed of mud in some variety in about every tenth household of the village (Fig. 3). Each morning and evening during the nine days, small groups of women and girls worship *Naurthā* by bathing, by singing songs before their respective idols, and by making mudballs or figurines, which are piled below each idol in a little mud hut. On the ninth day of the festival, each worshiping group carries its accumulated mudballs or figurines and deposits them on top of the mound of another deity called the "Stony One" (*Paṭṭhvārī*), which is located at the west end of the village's residential area.

In dozens of houses and from dozens of worshipers I inquired who or what *Naurthā* represents. Eventually, from those few persons who were willing to hazard an identification, I received a variety of somewhat contradictory answers including "*Durgā*," "*Śiva Śaṅkar*," and "*Sītā*." But most worshipers told me firmly that *Naurthā* is herself one of the "Nine *Durgās*," is another one of the many aspects of the Big Goddess (*Baṛī Devī*). No one whom I asked in the village was able to tell me what seems obvious from comparison with the Sanskritic name of the festival—that the word "*Naurthā*," considered in the region around Kishan Garhi to be the name of an indigenous goddess, is nothing more than an old dialectic variant of *nava rātra*, which means "nine nights."

The festival of Nine *Durgās* in Kishan Garhi thus exemplifies the continual fertility and creativity of little communities within Indian civilization: by sheer linguistic confusion and loss of meaning in the contact between great and little traditions, a new minor goddess has been created. But no sooner has the parochial goddess *Naurthā* been born into the villages of Aligarh than she is reabsorbed by peasant conception as a new manifestation of the great Goddess principle.

3. *Residual categories.*—The processes of upward universalization and downward parochialization, if we could in every instance trace their courses, might serve to conceptualize some of the characteristic relations between little and great traditions and might account for the present distributions of many religious elements between great and little communities in India. In practice, however, since universalization and parochialization have both proceeded for a very

long time, we are ordinarily unable to trace the course of either process with certainty, or to decide whether a given present configuration of religious contents is the result of one, and not also the result of the other, of these two processes. Thus in the festival of Lights and in the festival of Charm Tying, which have been described above, certain apparent homologues between little and great traditions suggest that a process of universalization has occurred. But some of the same pairs of apparent homologues may equally well be imagined to have originated as precipitates of the process of parochialization. *Lakṣmī* may be a universalized *Saurtī*, or *Saurtī* may be a parochialized *Lakṣmī;* the priestly charms of the Charm Tying festival may be universalizations of sisterly barley shoots, or the barley shoots may be parochializations of the priestly charms. Thus also in the festivals of Cow-Nourisher Worship and Nine *Durgās* we have no guarantee that the movement of cultural contents has been wholly parochial in direction. The Sanskrit tale of *Kṛṣṇa*'s adventure with the cowherds' hill may have arisen out of still more ancient peasant rituals of animal prosperity in which dung had played a part. As for parochialization in the festival of Nine *Durgās*, the worship of goddesses, even by techniques like those in use today, is attested to be far older in India than the verbal manufacture of the goddess *Naurthā* could possibly be (Wheeler 1953: 68, 83): the great Goddess, who seems to be *Naurthā*'s mother, may herself be a village goddess grown great by devouring her little sisters.

In dealing with so ancient a phenomenon as the festival of Nine *Durgās* in Kishan Garhi, if we choose between universalization and parochialization as *the* explanation for similarities and differences between great and little traditions, then we are stopping arbitrarily in mid-cycle what must in fact be a circular flow. Circular flow is familiar to European folklorists (e.g., Foster 1953: 169 and 172, n. 12). Describing the culture of Switzerland, Weiss writes that the little tradition "can well be considered as a catch-basin, as an ocean in which the springs, brooks and rivers of the creative cultural processes of the millennia collect and to some extent remain. However, this ocean is no stagnant swamp in spite of the continuity dictated by tradition. Instead, the entering flows are transformed and mingled upon their entrance. And as the water of the ocean rises afresh to the clouds, so also does the folk culture return once more to its own sources. As in the eternal cyclical course of the waters, so in the giving and receiving of cultural contents a continual exchange takes place between the two levels of culture" (1946: 42).[7] Further research—literary, ethnographic, distributional, and historical—may diminish our present ignorance and assist in answering some of these questions as to opposite processes and possible cycles of exchange between great and little traditions in the festivals of village India.[8]

Apart from our ignorance of past processes, however, residual categories seem likely to remain necessary for conceiving the distribution of cultural contents within either the great or the little tradition. These residual categories of cultural contents represent neither the results of upward movement, nor the results of downward movement, but rather the stability of contents, created and retained within either tradition. Created within the great tradition and by necessity remaining there in their details are the hundreds of Sanskrit works of literary invention and of philosophic subtlety which have been woven about the legendary histories of *Śiva* and *Viṣṇu*, of *Rāma* and *Kṛṣṇa*. Such works can rarely be translated for peasant understanding without some loss of their distinctive refinement. Unintelligible but more Sanskritic and therefore more authoritative versions of literary works are often retained in village use along with their vernacular renderings (cf. Hein 1950).

The little tradition also has its residuum of festival contents which appear neither to have arisen out of nor to have descended into it. Parts of the festival of Lights as it is celebrated in Kishan Garhi have already brought us to confront the little tradition as a residuum of religious elements which are separable from the great tradition. Almost all the contents of the festival of Pitcher Fourth appear to belong to the residual category of the little tradition, *sui generis*.

The little-traditional festival of Pitcher Fourth is in essence a celebration of wifely devotion for the sake of the welfare and long

7. I am indebted to Mr. Per Gräslund of Stockholm for directing me to this parallel analysis by Weiss.

8. Prof. W. Norman Brown (1919) finds himself at a similar threshold of ignorance in his efforts to discover the extent of borrowing into oral Indic folklore from literary sources. After reaching an estimate that at least half of all known oral Indic folk tales are derived from Sanskrit or Persian literature, Brown cautions the reader that his estimate of the borrowed proportion grows constantly larger as his own knowledge of the written literature grows (p. 11). The same caution may be applied to the problem of estimating the little- and great-traditional proportions in the deities and festivals of Kishan Garhi. This caution may be applied not only to the problem of estimating the borrowed portion of the little tradition, however, but also to the problem of estimating the borrowed portion of the great tradition. The more one knows of either tradition, the more one becomes able to find evidence suggestive of communication and borrowing from it to the other.

life of the husband. Wives of all castes but the *Jāṭ* caste fast by abstaining from bread during the day. While they are fasting, each wife completes a mural picture showing two "moons" and depicting the events of the Pitcher Fourth story (Fig. 2). The story is told before each picture by one of several elderly ladies, mostly Brahmans, who make a specialty of storytelling. Wives gather in small groups to hear the story, and then all sing any devotional song which they may know. Their fast continues until the real moon rises in the evening. Then each wife goes to where she can see the moon, sketches a sacred crossroads at her feet, and pours water onto the crossroads out of a spouted earthenware pitcher as an offering to the moon. She next worships the moons of her mural picture by pressing food against their "mouths"—a few wives also make mud figurines of a goddess at this point—and then breaks her fast after serving food to the men of the family. The moon is here often spoken of as having masculine gender rather than as the "Moon Mother" of usual speech.

From one storyteller I heard the story of Pitcher Fourth in the following version. There were seven married brothers living together. They had a younger sister, who was also married. Once, on Pitcher Fourth day, the younger sister kept fast at her brothers' house along with the wives of the seven. The youngest brother, feeling pity for his sister in her hunger, climbed a tree and showed a lamp behind a sieve, saying, "Sister! The moon is already up!" The sister offered water, then broke her fast. Her husband at once died. But she sat by her husband's cot for a whole year, not allowing ants or worms to come near, and not allowing his corpse to decay. The next year, when the festival of Pitcher Fourth came again, she once more kept fast. Her brothers' wives said, "You can't keep fast with us, because you are a widow." But the younger sister said, "I'll keep fast anyway!" When the moon rose, all the seven wives went to offer water. The sister took hold of her youngest brother and said, "Give me back my husband! Revive him!" Then she split open her finger and let the blood flow into the mouth of her dead husband. He came back to life, chanting the names of God.

In a second version of the Pitcher Fourth story, the sister avoids being deceived at all. In a third version, the brothers are five rather than seven. In several other versions, one of the wives, strangely called "maid servant" (*dūtī* or *mantharā*), is herself said to be involved in the plot to deceive her husband's sister; she is represented in some of the mural pictures as undergoing punishment by hanging from her heels.

FIGURE 2. PAINTING FOR THE FESTIVAL OF PITCHER FOURTH

This design, made as a wall painting for worship by one housewife of Kishan Garhi, shows some events in the festival story of a wife's ritual devotion to her husband (pp 203–6). Also shown are the painter's own combs and necklaces, together with peacocks. elephants, favorite trees, magical signs for birth and good luck, and a Potter woman bringing a headload of spouted pitchers for use in the festival. The original painting is executed in bleached rice paste on a ground of red ocher mixed with cowdung plaster and measures three feet in height.

Even this essentially little-traditional story of Pitcher Fourth is not without minor echoes of Sanskrit literature, however. The story's theme of wifely devotion bears an over-all resemblance to the theme of the *Sāvitrī* legend—a legend which occurs both in *Mahābhārata* (*Vana Parva*, 293–99) and in *Matsyapurāṇa* (208–14). The detail of the intriguing wife or servant seems clearly to have been borrowed from the episode of the intriguing Queen Kaikeyi and her servant in the *Rāmāyaṇa*. And the variant which begins with five brothers cannot but hint at the *Pāṇḍava* brothers of the *Mahābhārata*.

The Pitcher Fourth ritual of worshiping the moon seems furthermore to derive by direct descent, as it were, from an even older upanishadic cosmology in which the moon was the transitory abode of dead spirits awaiting rebirth, and the heavenly form of the life-giving *soma*. The wife's pouring of water from a spouted pitcher held before the moon with the aim of preserving or reviving the husband suggests a magical enactment of the prayer that moon-dwelling spirits descend through rain, then through the husband's semen to enter the wife's womb for rebirth (cf. *Chāndogya Upaniṣad* 5. 10. 3–7; *Bṛhadāranyaka Upaniṣad* 6. 2. 16).[9] But, in speculating on the possible Sanskritic cosmology which underlies the mute ritual of Pitcher Fourth, I am going beyond what is conscious or relevant to villagers today.

Whatever their ultimate origins, most of the ritual contents of the festival of Pitcher Fourth appear now to refer not to any greater tradition but rather to the residual little tradition. The story of the younger sister and her devotion to her husband, which provides the manifest rationale of the festival, is unmistakably built up out of the objects and life of the village. As far as I have been able to determine, and as far as villagers in Kishan Garhi were aware, neither the story nor the ritual of Pitcher Fourth has resulted from the devolution of any Sanskritic myth. As for universalization, the *Purāṇa* of the younger sister's fast has yet to be written. In this festival, which seems to be distributed at least as far as Hardoi (Crooke 1896*a*, I: 172) and Mainpuri districts (Wiser 1936: 89) on the southeast and Muzaffarnagar District on the north,[10] we seem to have isolated an original, if not pristine, contribution of the regional little tradition in its creative aspect.

9. I owe the second part of this interpretation of the ritual of Pitcher Fourth to a suggestion made to me by Dr. Norvin Hein.

10. For evidence from Muzaffarnagar, thanks are due to the personal recollections of Urmila (Mrs. Satya P.) Agarwal, originally of that city.

B. DEITIES, GREATER AND LESSER

An examination of the deities of Kishan Garhi may serve to review the questions and answers which have been suggested above through analysis of more complicated materials concerning festivals. The deities lend themselves to finer discriminations, even to some rough statistical statements, and to further understanding of social processes which are involved in the relations of great and little traditions.

These deities may be examined through a collection of information concerning ninety gods, goddesses, and godlings made between March and October, 1951, in Kishan Garhi. About half of these ninety deities were mentioned to me spontaneously in various contexts over a period of five months; the other half of these deities came to my notice for the first time during the festival of Lights, when I consulted forty-six persons throughout the village as to the deities which they were themselves worshiping on that sacred day. The list of ninety does not exhaust information about deities in Kishan Garhi; it does seem, however, to represent an approximation to the total list of deities whose cults are actively practiced in the village today.

To what extent can the religion of the little community be conceived as a whole apart from the religious great tradition of Hinduism? For the deities, as for the festivals, the answer must be "to a very limited extent only." About thirty of the total list of ninety deities, or one-third of the whole list, are recognizably gods of the great pantheon. Among these gods of the great tradition are *Viṣṇu*, *Lakṣmī*, *Hanumān*, *Rām*, *Kṛṣṇa*, *Śiva* or *Mahādev*, etc.

These gods of the great tradition not only are in the villager's range of knowledge but are found within the common core of objects worshiped by castes of all ranks (cf. Srinivas' "vertical spread" [1952: 218]). Fifteen deities may be specified within the common core of objects worshiped by members of at least three out of the four major blocs of castes in Kishan Garhi (Brahmans, high castes, low castes, lowest castes). Of these fifteen core deities whose cults are actively practiced, seven or eight deities may be identified as gods of the great tradition. Just as in the festivals, great-traditional elements thus play a part of central importance among the gods of this little community of Kishan Garhi.

But there is yet another substantial portion of the list of ninety deities—about sixty deities, or two-thirds of the total list—which does not seem to require us to take much notice of the great tradition of Hinduism. In this portion of the list we meet once more a part of village religion which approaches separability.

The less-than-great-traditional portion of the list of deities may be subdivided into shorter lists, descending from more widely known, regional deities with vernacular literatures, temples, and professional devotees down to purely local ghosts and spirits. People of Kishan Garhi worship at least twelve deities which have elaborate cults and which are known over areas of from several districts to several states. Such regional gods include the "Saint Apparent" (*Zāhir Pīr*), the "Goddess of Nagarkot" (*Nagarkoṭvālī Devī*), the "One of Agra" (*Āgrevālā*), the "One of the Well" (*Kuāṉvālā*), "Auspicious" (*Kalyāṇī*), the "Old Gentleman" (*Miyāṉ Sāhab*), *et altera*. Among these regional gods, as also among local gods, are included several of Muslim name or origin, notably the Saint Apparent (cf. Temple 1884–1900, II: 121, III: 264; Rose 1919, I: 172–92), the One of Agra, and "Saint Adam" (*Ādham Pīr*). Sectarian or other differences of origin are of slight concern in a civilization used to adopting and syncretizing any material that meets the criteria of interest and local availability.

The remainder of the list from Kishan Garhi, about one-half of the whole collection, consists of deities whose names are foreign even to any vernacular literary tradition, and whose cults have but little professional elaboration. Among these minor deities are "They of the Garden" (*Bāgvāle*), "They of the Twelfth Day" (*Doādśīvāle*), a goddess named "*Laṅgubir*," "She of the Tray" (*Thālvālī*), etc. Here are found some forty-five names in all. In this list are the names of many mother-goddesses: "Mother of Jalesar" (*Jalesarvālī Mātā*), "Mother of Gurgaon," "New Spaghetti Mother" (*Nayī Semarīvālī Mātā*), etc. Although some of these nonliterate deities are known to the little traditions of other districts—four of the forty-five are found in Wiser's list for a village seventy miles away in Mainpuri (1933: 262–63), while one occurs in Griffiths' list from Rewa three hundred miles away (1946: 133–34)—all lack felt connection with any thing or place far away from the villages where they are worshiped, and may therefore be counted as local deities. Only a handful of these deities have sufficient spread or fame to have made their ways into even so large a compendium of Uttar Pradesh village religion as Crooke's (1896*b*). A few of these local deities appear to be known only to the people of Kishan Garhi village, and then not to all of them. Partly because of the wide range of country from which wives of the village are drawn, there is nevertheless great diversity in adherence to such local and regional deities from family to family and from individual to individual. The village list from Kishan Garhi appears to contain a sampling of the local theological diversity of a large area.

In the common core of objects of worship—that is, among the fifteen deities which are worshiped by members of most blocs of castes in Kishan Garhi—these little-traditional deities play a large part. While Sanskritic deities make up seven members of the common core, or nearly half of the total, regional deities account for four members and local deities for another four members. This little-traditional core component is subjectively important to villagers in Kishan Garhi, for next to the worship of their own respective ancestral spirits of the last two generations, villagers are most attached, I would estimate, to the worship of four local godlings of no refinement whatsoever: *Cāmaṛ*, *Alop*, "Earthy" (*Bhūmiyā*), and the "Stony One" (*Patthvārī*). In these little-traditional deities, as in festivals, in caste rituals, and in kinship organization, we again come upon an area in which the little community feels itself to be and can be conceived as a partly distinctive and partly isolable nexus within greater communities. Here again we come upon the paradox of isolability within nonisolability, for the theological great and little traditions, like the great and little communities which bear them, are continuous with each other.

1. *Stratification of deities and their slowness of spread.*—The distribution of deities through the caste hierarchy of Kishan Garhi helps to explain why great-traditional religious elements are unable to achieve exclusive dominance in the little community, despite the many continuities between great and little traditions.

Adherence to deities of the great and little traditions is distributed through the hierarchy of castes in Kishan Garhi in the relative proportions which have been stated hypothetically by Srinivas (1952: 218). Sanskritic deities of the great tradition play a larger part in the devotions of members of the Brahman caste and generally in the bloc of the high castes of Kishan Garhi than they do in the devotions of the lower castes. Forty-five per cent of the deities worshiped by Brahmans are Sanskritic; 35 per cent of the deities worshiped by members of ten high castes below the Brahmans are Sanskritic; but only 15 and 19 per cent, respectively, of the deities worshiped by members of the low and lowest castes are Sanskritic deities.

That so small a proportion as 45 per cent of the deities worshiped even by Brahmans are Sanskritic may occasion some surprise, considering that Kishan Garhi stands in an ancient area of Brahman settlement and characterization (cf. O'Malley 1935: 129). The lands between the Ganges and the Jumna appear to have been a region of Aryan settlement in the time of the *Brāhmaṇas* (Majumdar and Pusalker 1951: 251–52); they appear as the *Brahmarṣideśa,* as the *Madhyadeśa,* and again as the domain of the ancient *Pañcālas.* Brahmans still hold a quarter of the lands of the district as hereditary cultivators and still form more than 10 per cent of its population. In each village of the countryside around Kishan Garhi a Brahman lineage group controls the hereditary office of priesthood of the village site (*kheṛāpatī*). The *Sanādh* Brahmans of Kishan Garhi are thus people of the soil rather than people of the book. They are vernacular Brahmans: excepting the four individuals who are professional priests, the Brahmans of Kishan Garhi address their deities with familiar prayers in the local dialect of Braj Bhasha, not with vedic *mantras.* In spite of the ancient habitation of Brahmans in this original area of orthodoxy—perhaps, considering the conservatism of local custom which is inherent in an indigenous civilization, one should say *because* of their ancient habitation in this area—more than half of their deities in Kishan Garhi are non-Sanskritic and still un-Sanskritized.

The relatively slight Sanskritization of the Brahmans in this area contains a clue to the general slowness of Sanskritization and to the relatively small proportion of great-traditional contents in the religion of the rest of the castes in Kishan Garhi. Brahmans are, by their position in the caste hierarchy and by their association with priesthood, the best potential local agents of the great tradition. Since their religious forms are in large part little-traditional, what filters down from the Brahmans to lower castes in Kishan Garhi must also be in large part little-traditional. Thus the festival of Pitcher Fourth, whose lack of Sanskritic reference is described above, is explicitly identified in Kishan Garhi as a festival of Brahman wives, who may not remarry if they are widowed; this festival is said to have been taken up in recent generations by the lower castes of Kishan Garhi. So, too, the priesthood of the village site, which descends in the most influential Brahman lineage of Kishan Garhi, is the priesthood of the non-Sanskritic mother-godling called by the untranslatable name of "*Cāmaṛ*"; when persons of lower caste would propitiate this powerful mother-godling of the Brahmans, they must take their offerings, not to any temple of the great tradition, but to *Cāmaṛ*'s rude mound of stones and mud.

No doubt there has been through the millenniums some spread of Sanskritic deities from higher to lower castes in Kishan Garhi, as posited by Srinivas for Hindus in general (1953: 218, 226). But those few persons and groups of Kishan Garhi who have demonstrably in recent times taken on more Sanskritic, great-traditional forms of religion seem in every instance to have obtained them, not from the local higher castes, but from itinerant teachers of exotic cults, from urban-centered associations of recent growth, from new state schools, or from the market place. A newly standardized great tradition is thus externally available to the people of Kishan Garhi as a transformed, now heterogenetic criticism of the indigenous religious order of the village (cf. Hutton 1946: 204–5).

2. *Civilizational processes: parochialization and universalization.*—We may learn more of the processes of growth in Hindu civilization from the careers of these deities of Kishan Garhi if we conceive of civilizational growth not only as a process of Sanskritization which proceeds from high caste to low caste, or from place to place, or as a process of the distribution of literate elements to nonliterate people, but more broadly as all those processes by which many little traditions come to be related to a more universal great tradition. The processes of universalization and parochialization move along a vertical axis of Sanskritization and de-Sanskritization, but their range of play extends somewhat below its nether pole.

Parochialization—the downward movement and transformation of contents between great and little traditions—is evident among deities as it is among festivals in Kishan Garhi. In the festival of Nine *Durgās* described above, the local female godling *Naurthā* thus seems to have descended into the little tradition through linguistic change and loss of the meaning of a Sanskritic *tadbhava*.

The career of the Sanskritic divine sage, "Master of the Sperm" (*Śukrācārya*) (Renou and Filliozat 1947: 491), in Kishan Garhi further exemplifies the process of parochial devolution. "Master of the Sperm" is said by some Brahmans of Kishan Garhi to be the same as the planet Venus, the star which governs marriage and acts as a special patron of Brahmans. Possibly in pursuance of some one of these beliefs, ancestors of the leading lineage of Brahmans in Kishan Garhi at some time now forgotten seem to have erected a stone for the worship of "Master of the Sperm" beside a tree in a disused cremation ground. Every new bride brought into that Brahman lineage is still taken out with her groom a few days after her first arrival in order to worship at that stone. But only two or three old men of the lineage now recall the former Sanskritic significance of the stone. As far as women of that lineage are concerned, as far as anyone else in the village knows, including the Barber woman who must serve at every ceremony of worshiping the stone, that stone in the old cremation ground is no Sanskritic planetary deity, but simply the abode of the ancestral spirits of the Brahman lineage whose members placed it there. Such instances of downward movement and eventual severance from the great tradition may be compared with the downward growth and eventual fall of a stalactite.

The beginnings of universalization, like the precipitates of parochialization, are apparent far below the level of Sanskritization among the deities of Kishan Garhi. Universalization among these deities appears to begin especially through the deification of spirits of ancestors or of famous other local residents of the village who are now deceased. Thus the "Lord" (*Ṭhākur*), the "Lady" (*Ṭhākurānī*), and "They of the Garden" in Kishan Garhi, who are the spirits of powerful landlords of two or more generations ago, have become public ghosts; for the most part, they operate within the area of Kishan Garhi itself, but occasionally they seize people of other villages who pass through. So I was told by one professional exorcist of Kishan Garhi.

Building upward from the littlest tradition toward a slightly greater tradition is the spirit of one late villager named "Happy Eyes" (*Nain Sukha*). In life, Happy Eyes was a famous curer of scabies, of the seven-year itch. Since his death, he has gained a public shrine, which consists of two dung-plastered bricks, located at the base of a tree in front of a Sweeper's house. Happy Eyes' shrine is now worshiped along with the local shrines of many mother-godlings of skin diseases by all women of the village on the day of Leftover Food Worship, or Goddess-Godling Worship. The Sweeper, who receives all offerings to Happy Eyes' monument, is naturally interested in promoting Happy Eyes' cult, since he thereby gains leftover food with which to feed his pigs. Happy Eyes is still called a "[male] godling" (*devatā*), but change of sex or the status of consort seems to be destined for him sooner or later, considering his many feminine companions.

Further along toward a more universal deification is the deity who is worshiped in Kishan Garhi under the name of "Auspicious" (*Kalyāṇī*). Auspicious is the deification of a famous Hindu ascetic who actually resided long ago in the next district of Etah (Crooke

1896*b*, I: 220). Auspicious is now worshiped not merely at a pair of bricks by the people of one village, as is Happy Eyes, but at a temple shrine in Etah which is attended annually by thousands of persons coming from several districts.

Still more widely known and more broadly intelligible among the deities worshiped in Kishan Garhi is the "Old Gentleman" (*Miyāṉ Sāhab*), a deity of pneumonia, fertility, etc. The cult of the Old Gentleman has grown up around the combined spirits of two Muslim personages who lived at different times in two different districts of western Uttar Pradesh, according to Crooke's sources (1896*a*, II: 274, III: 180–81; 1896*b*, I: 217). Unlike the cult of Auspicious, who has little if any popular sacred literature in Kishan Garhi, the cult of the Old Gentleman has developed several long vernacular songs. Members of the local caste group of Weavers in Kishan Garhi sing the songs of the Old Gentleman with enthusiasm, especially when they are paid to do so for therapeutic purposes. The Old Gentleman has substantial temple-like shrines at both of his abodes in Jalesar and in Amroha. From so elaborate an indigenous cult as that of the Old Gentleman to the cult of an authenticated Sanskritic deity is but a short distance. The cult of the Old Gentleman, like the growth of a stalagmite, has nearly reached the ceiling.

The role of the material interests of Brahman priests in spreading the cults of Sanskritic deities has often been noted elsewhere. In Kishan Garhi the Weavers' interest in the cult of the Old Gentleman, like the Sweeper's interest in the cult of Happy Eyes, reminds us that the cults of local godlings may also be spread upward through the self-interested action of many other castes. One local caste group of Kishan Garhi, the Ascetics (*Jogīs*) combines the proselytizing of both a Sanskritic and a non-Sanskritic cult. These Ascetics derive a large part of their income from singing two devotional songs, one describing the wedding of *Śiva*, the other describing the miraculous history of the Saint Apparent (*Zāhir Pīr*), a merely regional deity.

In the careers of the little-traditional deities worshiped in Kishan Garhi one can also trace the elaboration, the refinement, and the systematization of the cults as such toward more universal cultic forms. One can also trace in them spatially the beginnings of a sacred geography which is continuous with the sacred geography of India's great tradition (Redfield and Singer 1954*b:* 19–20). The rudiments of Hinduism's sacred geography are perhaps evident in the Fair of the Well Godling in Kishan Garhi. This fair and its godling, villagers say, were deliberately instituted by a landlord of Kishan Garhi some thirty years ago in order to produce for himself a source of tolls and rents from concessionaires. He installed the godling in the form of a flat stone beside a well in his own garden, and announced that a fair would be held. The godling's fair has prospered, and so have the owners of the garden. But the landlord who founded the fair is now gone. People of Kishan Garhi at the present day hold mixed views as to the name and possible affiliations of this godling of the fair. Some villagers say that, since he is the "Well Godling" (*Kue kā Devatā*), he may therefore be the same as the famous "One of the Well" (*Kuāṉ-vālā*) whose abode is in a village of nearby Mainpuri District (Crooke 1896*a*, II: 364). Other villagers say that he is the "One of Agra" (*Āgrevālā*), identifying him with another Muslim deity said to be installed in or at a well in the city of Agra, fifty miles away (cf. Crooke 1896*a*, III: 81, 367). People of Kishan Garhi also hold mixed views as to whether their Well Godling is the apotheosis of a Brahman, a Muslim, a Sweeper, or several of these. Whatever their particular views, most villagers feel sure that the local Well Godling is the "branch office" of one or another greater deity. And, whatever their views, Brahmans, Weavers, Muslim Beggars, Sweepers, and Goatherds pitch into the festival as functionaries, while crowds from the nearby villages pour in to obtain the benefits thought to derive from adoring this parochial deity.

Of somewhat greater age and of greater areal sway than Kishan Garhi's own Well Godling is the "Garden Godling" (*Bāg kā Devatā*) of one village neighboring on Kishan Garhi. Sweepers of the neighborhood, who also serve as midwives for all castes, have played an important part in spreading the Garden Godling's reputation as a protector of babies. Each year at the time of the Garden Godling's festival they collect sugar and oil for his worship—and for their own use—from each of their clients in Kishan Garhi.

At still greater distances, many another local godling, goddess, mother, and cremation ground spirit (*masānī*) competes to draw worshipers from Kishan Garhi. Some of these local deities never rise to any greater refinement, but others take on more articulate and lettered forms of expression through competition. Without necessarily developing a homogeneous community of worship in any continuous region or even among the families of one village, the upward growth of such localized cults serves to connect the members of each little community with an overlapping congeries of greater communities of worship.

3. *Sanskritic identifications: effects on solidarity.*—Between the

beginnings of upward universalization among parochial deities and the downward parochialization of universal deities there remains a gap in the kinds of evidence which one village can furnish in a short time. A few months or even a few years is too short a time in which to observe the actual composition of a new literary *purāṇa* or of a new subsidiary episode in the *Mahābhārata* out of materials developed in the cult of a deity risen from some little tradition. And perhaps the modern anthropological observer is arriving on the scene a little too close to the end of the puranic age to expect to observe its phenomena in full flower.

Less conclusive than the full literary Sanskritization of a little-traditional deity, but very much alive in Kishan Garhi, is the technique of identification. By the technique of identification each local or regional apotheosis is equated with some more universal deity of the great tradition, the lesser often being interpreted as an additional form or incarnation of the greater. Identification is perhaps the premier technique of the more inclusive process which Srinivas has called "Sanskritization" (1952, chap. VII).

By identifying their local or regional deities with more widespread Sanskritic ones, Srinivas suggests, the Hindus of a region such as Coorg or the Hindus of all India come to have the same objects of worship, and therefore to have the sense of constituting a single regional or national community, respectively (p. 208).

The suggestion that solidarity arises out of Sanskritic identifications needs to be qualified for Kishan Garhi. Deities of the little tradition in Kishan Garhi are identified with deities of the great tradition in varying ways; the result is not necessarily an increased sense of community or an enlargement of cultural consciousness.

In the festival of Nine *Durgās,* for example, the mud idol is capable of the most diverse Sanskritic identifications. As noticed above, *Naurthā* is thought by many villagers to represent *Durgā, Kālī, et al.* or the goddess principle in general. But she is thought by others to represent *Śiva* and, by still others, to represent *Sītā.* While nearly all women and children in Kishan Garhi can agree that they have a common object of worship in the *Naurthā* of the little tradition, by no means all worshipers of *Naurthā* can agree on what object of the great tradition they simultaneously hold in common reverence.

The identifications of three other important little-traditional deities of Kishan Garhi demonstrate similar difficulties which would arise if villagers were to attempt to communicate with each other by triangulation through the great tradition. These three deities are the feminine godlings Stony One, Earthy, and *Cāmaṛ*. Sanskritic identifications are easily enough made for each of these feminine godlings separately; indeed, these lady godlings of the village are on the whole the most upwardly mobile of all little-traditional deities. The Stony One, for example, has for at least a generation and probably much longer been identified with a famous manifestation of the great goddess *Pārvatī* or *Satī Devī* at Nagarkot in Kangra District, Punjab. The Goddess is said to manifest herself at Nagarkot in the form of a sulphurous mountain which still glows at night with the fires in which she was herself extinguished. Members of nearly every Hindu family in Kishan Garhi worship the Stony One and identify her explicitly with the Goddess of Nagarkot (Fig. 4). Thus when pilgrims are ready to depart each year from the village to go to Nagarkot, public worship is held at the mound of the Stony One. And, while the pilgrims are away, members of their families continue to make offerings of fire and water at the Stony One (Fig. 4) (cf. Channing 1882: 35).

But this identification of the Stony One with the Goddess of Nagarkot and thence with the goddess complex of the great tradition does not go unchallenged. In the neighboring district of Agra, for example, *Patthvārī* is said by a different Sanskritic etymology to be the "Goddess of the Roadways" (Crooke 1896*a*, II: 426). Srinivas cites an instance of a similar conflict in the identification of cobras with the Sanskritic deity *Subrahmaṇya* in Coorg and Mysore, and with *Nāgās* elsewhere in India (1952: 218). Such competing and inconsistent Sanskritic identifications are not unusual but quite the rule in and around Kishan Garhi.

While Sanskritic identifications of the Stony One vary from place to place, in Kishan Garhi itself Stony One competes with *Cāmaṛ*, the mother-goddess of the village site, for identification with the Goddess of Nagarkot. Some years ago, *Cāmaṛ*'s powers were apparently believed to be very great. Refugees are said to have settled in Kishan Garhi during the Mutiny of 1857 because of the supernatural protection which she offered. *Cāmaṛ*'s credentials as local representative of the Goddess of Nagarkot were at that time also made firm. One pilgrim to Nagarkot brought back some fragments of stone sculpture from the greater goddess' temple and placed those fragments atop *Cāmaṛ*'s mound for all to see. In more recent times, however, identification with the great goddess seems to have shifted largely to the Stony One.

Like the Stony One, *Cāmaṛ*'s own identifications within the lesser

FIGURE 3. THE GODDESS *Naurthā*

In her family's courtyard in Kishan Garhi, a girl of Brahman caste (*left*), with her sisters and a friend of Goatherd caste (*right*), have built this mud idol of the goddess Ninenights for worship during the festival of Nine *Durgās* (see pp. 200–201, 215).

Figure 4. The Stony One

A Brahman trader of Kishan Garhi offers water at the local shrine of the goddess *Patthvārī*, praying for offspring, while a dog and boys of the untouchable Sweeper and Hunter castes look on (see pp. 216–17).

traditions are not without uncertainty and conflict. By general opinion in Kishan Garhi, she is certainly a goddess: many persons refer to her as "*Cāmaṛ* Mother" (cf. Crooke 1896*a*, II: 225). But in other parts of Aligarh District and in Agra District, a local deity of the same name is said to be masculine in gender (Crooke 1896*a*, I: 46; III: 81).

Earthy (*Bhūmiyā*), a third mother-goddess of Kishan Garhi's little tradition, is beset by similar Sanskritic complexities. If we join villagers of Kishan Garhi in identifying Earthy with the greater Mother (*Mātā*) and Goddess complex of Hinduism, then we will be confused in Delhi District to find Earthy identified with the masculine Sanskritic deity called "Field Protector" (*Kṣetrapāla*) (Crooke 1896*b*, I: 105). We will be further confused in another district to find that a local godling of the village site is called alternatively "*Bhūmiya*" or "*Bhairoṉ*," and is therefore identified with a manifestation of the great god *Śiva* (Crooke 1896*b*, I: 107–8). We will be still further confused in Patna District, Bihar, for Crooke reports that Earthy is there identified as a manifestation of *Viṣṇu* (p. 107). Earthy's diverse identifications indicate that villagers of Aligarh, Delhi, and Patna might more accurately sense their actual community of worship by sticking with that identical nomenclature provided by the common ground of their respective little traditions rather than by resorting to indirect, triangular communication through the discrepant *Mātā*, *Kṣetrapāla*, *Śiva*, and *Viṣṇu* of greater traditions.

The careers of these four female deities of Kishan Garhi demonstrate the facility with which identifications may bridge the gap between great and little traditions in India's indigenous civilization. They also demonstrate the confusions which resort to the medium of the great tradition can put in the way of communication between two adjacent and only slightly variant little traditions. Sanskritization may obscure as well as clarify the nearness of two little traditions: the Delhi villager who identifies his Earthy with *Kṣetrapāla* will be closer by Sanskritic idiom to the Coorg villager who worships his *Kētrappa* as *Kṣetrapāla* one thousand miles away (Srinivas 1952: 223) than he will be to the villager of Kishan Garhi one hundred miles away who also worships Earthy, but in another Sanskritic guise. Although Sanskritic identifications do not necessarily bring adjacent little communities closer to each other, they do bring the great community closer to all little communities. To each little tradition, Sanskritic identifications lend the sense of derivative participation in the great tradition which is authoritative, not only because it is indigenous, but also because it is refined, learned, and ecumenical. Sanskritization thus heightens and dignifies the sphere of communication for each little community; it does not necessarily widen that sphere.

If reference to the Sanskritic great tradition of Hinduism sometimes confounds or prevents communication within and among adjacent little traditions, it also, of course, provides a saving doctrine for some persons at a higher level. In place of disordered polytheism and endless polymorphism, the philosophic villager in Kishan Garhi is free to put pantheism—the conception that all deities everywhere, no matter how parochial or non-Sanskritic, are but manifestations of a single divine Oversoul (*Paramātma*). If all deities are one, then accurate communication about particular objects of worship becomes a matter of irrelevant detail.

C. SUMMARY AND CONCLUSION

Seen through its festivals and deities, the religion of the village of Kishan Garhi may be conceived as resulting from continuous processes of communication between a little, local tradition and greater traditions which have their places partly inside and partly outside the village. Only residual fragments of the religion of such a little community can be conceived as distinctive or separable.

Since both great and little traditions exist within the religion of little communities and there communicate, study of the religion of a little community can contribute to understanding of processes of universalization and parochialization which are generally operative in Indian civilization. Preliminary study of the contents of religion in Kishan Garhi indicates, for example, that great and little traditions may remain in equilibrium within the little community, neither tending to exclude the other: elements of the great tradition undergo parochial transformation as they spread, while the great tradition itself, where it originates as a universalization of indigenous materials, lacks authority to replace elements of the little tradition. Communication between indigenous greater and lesser traditions may proceed vertically without necessarily effecting any contiguous lateral enlargement of the community of common culture. A focus upon the small half-world of the village and a perspective upon the universe of Indian civilization thus remain mutually indispensable for whole understanding, whether of Hinduism or of the traditional forms of India's social structure.

REFERENCES CITED

BADEN-POWELL, B. H.
1892 *The Land Systems of British India*. 3 vols. Oxford, Clarendon.
1900 "The Villages of Goa in the Early Sixteenth Century," *Journal of the Royal Asiatic Society*, pp. 261–91. London.
1908 *The Origin and Growth of Village Communities in India*. London, Swan Sonnenschien.

BAILEY, F. G.
1953 "An Oriya Hill Village," *Economic Weekly* **5:**326–28. Bombay.

BEALS, ALAN ROBIN
1953 "Change in the Leadership of a Mysore Village," *Economic Weekly* **5:**487–92. Bombay.
1954 "The Government and the Indian Village," *Economic Development and Cultural Change* **2:**397–407. Chicago.

BROWN, W. NORMAN
1919 "The Pañcatantra in Modern Indian Folklore," *Journal of the American Oriental Society* **39:**1–54. Baltimore.

CARSTAIRS, G. MORRIS
1952 "A Village in Rajasthan—a Study in Rapid Social Change," *Economic Weekly* **4:**75–77. Bombay.

CHANNING, F. C.
1882 *Land Revenue Settlement of the Gurgaon District*. Lahore, Central Jail Press.

CROOKE, WILLIAM
1896*a* *The Tribes and Castes of the North-Western Provinces and Oudh*. 4 vols. Calcutta, Superintendent of Government Printing.
1896*b* *The Popular Religion and Folk-Lore of Northern India*. 2 vols. Westminster, Archibald Constable.

FOSTER, GEORGE M.
1953 "What Is Folk Culture?" *American Anthropologist* **55:**159–73. Menasha, Wisconsin.

GHOSHAL, U. N.
1929 *Contributions to the History of the Hindu Revenue System*. Calcutta, University of Calcutta.

GOUGH, E. KATHLEEN
1952 "The Social Structure of a Tanjore Village," *Economic Weekly* **4:**531–36. Bombay.

GRIERSON, GEORGE A.
1880 "Proper Names," *Indian Antiquary* **9:**141. Bombay.

GRIFFITHS, W. C.
1946 *The Kol Tribe of Central India*. Calcutta, Royal Asiatic Society of Bengal.

GROWSE, F. S.
1880 *Mathurā: A District Memoir*. 2d ed. Allahabad, North-Western Provinces and Oudh Government Press.

HANSSEN, BÖRJE
1953 "Fields of Social Activity and Their Dynamics," *Transactions of the Westermarck Society*, pp. 99–133. Copenhagen.

HEIN, NORVIN
1950 "The Ram Lila, a Pageant of the People," *The Illustrated Weekly of India* **71,** No. 43: 18–19. Bombay.

HOCART, A. M.
1950 *Caste: A Comparative Study*. London, Methuen.

HUTCHINSON, J. R.
1856 *Allygurh Statistics; Being a Report on the General Administration of That District from A.D. 1803 to the Present Time*. Roorkee, Thomason College Press.

HUTTON, J. H.
1946 "Hinduism in Its Relation to Primitive Religions in India,"in *Caste in India*, by J. H. HUTTON, pp. 195–232. Cambridge, University Press.

LALLŪ LĀL
1897 *The Prema-Sāgara, or Ocean of Love*. . . . Translated by FREDERIC PINCOTT. Westminster, Archibald Constable.

LEWIS, OSCAR
1954 "Group Dynamics in a North-Indian Village: A Study in Factions," *Economic Weekly* **6:**423–25, 445–51, 477–82, 501–6. Bombay.

MAJUMDAR, R. C. and A. D. PUSALKER, eds.
1951 *The Vedic Age*. The History and Culture of the Indian People **1.** London, George Allen & Unwin.

MANDELBAUM, DAVID G.
1952 "Technology, Credit and Culture in an Indian Village," *Economic Weekly* **4:**827–28. Bombay.

MARRIOTT, MCKIM
1952 "Social Structure and Change in a U.P. Village," *Economic Weekly* **4:** 869–74. Bombay.
1955 "Western Medicine in a Village of Northern India," in *Health, Culture and Community: A Book of Cases*, ed. BENJAMIN D. PAUL. New York, Russell Sage Foundation. (Forthcoming.)

MILLER, ERIC J.
1952 "Village Structure in North Kerala," *Economic Weekly* **4:**159–64. Bombay.

MISRA, B. R.
1942 *Land Revenue Policy in the United Provinces under British Rule*. Benares, Nand Kishore.

MORELAND, W. H.
1937 "The Revenue System of the Mughal Empire," in *The Mughal Period*, ed. SIR RICHARD BURN. The Cambridge History of India **4.** Cambridge, University Press.

MORGAN, KENNETH W.
1953 *The Religion of the Hindus*. New York, Ronald Press.

NEVILL, H. R.
1909 *Aligarh: A Gazetteer*. District Gazetteers of the United Provinces of Agra and Oudh **6.** Allahabad, Government Press.

NEWELL, WILLIAM H.
1952 "A Himalayan Village," *Economic Weekly* **4:**208–10. Bombay.

O'MALLEY, L. S. S.
1935 *Popular Hinduism*. Cambridge, University Press.

OPLER, MORRIS E. and RUDRA DATT SINGH

1948 "The Division of Labor in an Indian Village," in *A Reader in General Anthropology*, ed. C. S. COON, pp. 464–96. New York, Henry Holt.

PETER, P. C.

1952 "Theocratic Landlordism," *Journal of the University of Bombay* **20,** No. 4: 44–49. Bombay.

REDFIELD, ROBERT

1953 *The Primitive World and Its Transformations.* Ithaca, Cornell University Press.

1955 *The Little Community.* Chicago, University of Chicago Press.

REDFIELD, ROBERT and MILTON SINGER

1954*a* Comparison of Cultures: The Indian Village. Chicago, Department of Anthropology, University of Chicago. (Hectographed.)

1954*b* "The Cultural Role of Cities," *Economic Development and Cultural Change* **3:**53–73. Chicago.

RENOU, LOUIS and JEAN FILLIOZAT

1947 *L'Inde classique, manuel des études indiennes*, Vol. 1. Paris, Payot.

ROSE, H. A.

1919 *A Glossary of the Tribes and Castes of the Punjab and North-West Frontier Province.* 3 vols. Lahore, Superintendent of Government Printing.

SMITH, MARIAN W.

1953 "Social Structure in the Punjab," *Economic Weekly* **5:**1291–98. Bombay.

SRINIVAS, M. N.

1951 "The Social Structure of a Mysore Village," *Economic Weekly* **3:**1051–56. Bombay.

1952 *Religion and Society among the Coorgs of South India.* Oxford, Clarendon Press.

1954 "Village Studies," *Economic Weekly* **6:**605–9. Bombay.

STARR, BETTY W.

1954 "Levels of Communal Relations," *American Journal of Sociology* **60:** 125–35. Chicago.

STEWARD, JULIAN H.

1951 "Levels of Sociocultural Integration: An Operational Concept," *Southwestern Journal of Anthropology* **7:**374–90. Albuquerque.

STEWARD, JULIAN H. and ROBERT A. MANNERS

1953 "The Cultural Study of Contemporary Societies: Puerto Rico," *American Journal of Sociology* **54:**123–30. Chicago.

SWAMI SIVANANDA

1947 *Hindu Fasts and Festivals and Their Philosophy.* Rikhikesh, U.P., Sivananda Publication League.

TEMPLE, RICHARD C.

1883 *A Dissertation on the Proper Names of Panjābīs. . . .* Bombay, Education Society's Press.

1884–1900 *The Legends of the Panjāb.* 3 vols. Bombay, Education Society's Press.

THOMASON, JAMES

1838 "Report on the Settlement of the Ceded Portion of the District of Azimgurh . . . ," *Journal of the Asiatic Society of Bengal*, n.s., **8**:77–136. Calcutta.

1858 *Directions for Revenue Officers in the North-Western Provinces of the Bengal Presidency*. . . . New ed. Calcutta, Baptist Mission Press.

UNDERHILL, M. M.

1921 *The Hindu Religious Year*. Calcutta, Association Press.

WARNER, W. L.

1949 *Democracy in Jonesville*. New York, Harper.

1953 *American Life: Dream and Reality*. Chicago, University of Chicago Press.

WEISS, RICHARD

1946 *Volkskunde der Schweiz*. Zürich, Eugen Rentch Verlag.

WHEELER, Sir MORTIMER

1953 *The Indus Civilization*. The Cambridge History of India, Supplementary Volume. Cambridge, University Press.

WISER, WILLIAM H.

1933 "Social Institutions of a Hindu Village in Northern India." Unpublished Ph.D. dissertation, Cornell University, Ithaca.

1936 *The Hindu Jajmani System*. Lucknow, Lucknow Publishing House.

THE WORLD AND THE WORLD VIEW OF THE *KOTA*[1]

DAVID G. MANDELBAUM

I. INTRODUCTION

THE WORLD VIEW of a people is their characteristic outlook. It is the inside view, the ways in which a person of the group typically sees himself in relation to his world. It includes his mapping of that world, that is to say, the categories he uses in his perception of the familiar and of the strange. It includes the emphasis he places on what he sees, the choices he makes from among the alternatives he knows.

Few will deny that a statement of this inside view is a most desirable resource for anthropological analysis; more will wonder whether it is possible to make a valid and testable statement of this sort. Difficulties suggest themselves at once. Whose world view? Even in so numerically small a society as the *Kota*, there are many status positions, each invoking a somewhat different outlook. Thus there are different perceptions expected of a priest than those normally required of a layman. There are differences in typical outlook—at least in some respects—as between people from different villages, or as between a man and a woman. In one of the writer's published studies of the *Kota*, the difference in outlook according to age was noted, and the consequences of the varying perceptions as between young men and older men in the society were indicated (Mandelbaum 1941*a:* 237).

In the same study, personality differences in characteristic outlook were traced. Not the least of other possible variations in outlook are those which ensue from special environmental situations, such as dire physical deprivation. A people desperate for food—as the *Camārs* described by Cohn sometimes are—may be expected to view

1. Field work among the *Kota* was carried on from April, 1937, to May, 1938, under a fellowship of the National Research Council. It was continued from September, 1949, to January, 1950, with grants from the University of California and as part of a Guggenheim fellowship. The present paper was written in connection with the Indian Village Studies project of the Institute of East Asiatic Studies, University of California, Berkeley.

the world about them somewhat differently than they do when hunger pangs are not so insistent.

Yet despite all these variations, a field ethnologist—no less than an observant administrator or traveler—often gains the impression that there is a characteristic way of seeing the world among the people he is studying. It is characteristic because it may be discerned through the whole range of personalities and status positions within the society and because it is expressed in a broad variety of life-situations. Thus in Lewis' paper in this volume we read not only of certain specific differences between the villages he knows in Mexico and in India—as in cultivation, social organization, settlement pattern—but also of certain broad differences between the two in their approach to the standard human experiences and to the people about them.

The problem is to transcribe the impressions which register on the sensitized observer into clear statements which can be tested repeatedly in various contexts and which can then be compared with formulations of world view among other peoples.

It might seem that the *Kota* offer a particularly favorable field for a start toward the analysis of world view. They are a small society; their seven villages together now hold about a thousand people, hardly more than a fair-sized village in most of India. Yet they clearly have a distinct society and culture, with language, religion, ceremonies, all obviously different from those of their neighbors. They were aboriginally one of the tribes who inhabited the relatively inaccessible Nilgiri Plateau, and they still follow a good many patterns of their old tribal culture. Within the villages there are not the elaborate social stratifications found in most of the other villages described in this volume, and their culture appears to be relatively homogeneous, if for no other reason than the absence of diverse caste practices.

However, it would scarcely be proper to present *Kota* society as a simple, relatively undifferentiated social organism within which the world view shines forth in a clearer, more comprehensible fashion than among, say, the manifestly complex Brahmans of Tanjore whom Kathleen Gough describes. Far from it. The *Kota* case presents many complexities, both structural and historical. True, the *Kota* and their neighbors atop the Nilgiri Plateau were quite isolated, until a century ago, from the main currents of Hindu influence on the plains below. But in recent decades they have been moved, as we shall see, by the double impact of Sanskritization (to use Srinivas' term) and of Western-urban influences. The earlier isolation was not, in any event, a complete insulation. There is an inscription of A.D. 1117 in Mysore which refers to the *Todas* and the Nilgiris, and the earliest known report of the Nilgiri peoples, written in 1603 by a Portuguese priest, gives evidence of regular though infrequent trade contacts between the hill folk and the villagers of the plains (Francis 1908: 91–92; Rivers 1906: 719–30).

Thus the *Kota* case is neither more nor less isolable as a unit for study than are the other village groups discussed in this volume. *Kota* culture is certainly different from that of the nearest plains villages. Yet for all their differences from the usual South Indian patterns, all the Nilgiri peoples accorded, in fundamental ways, with the prevalent village tradition. The concept of pollution was and is strongly held, the economic relations among the indigenous tribes were much like the usual *jajmānī* system, and the tribes formed a kind of caste system of their own, although it was not in earlier centuries geared into the general caste system. Such fundamental resemblances to the world of the plains villagers, underlying many differences in phrasing and detail, encourage comparisons between these hill folk and village people in the matter of world view also. We may go on, then, to sketch some salient facets of *Kota* life and to delineate one aspect of the *Kota* world view. Following this, we shall compare the *Kota* with other villagers described in this volume, looking at the others, as it were, from the vantage point of the *Kota* villages. Such comparisons give us a notion of the world in which all these villagers live, especially the general Indic world. Within the world of India there are forces and processes which, in some degree, affect all. On the basis of these comparative comments concerning the world of the villager we shall, in every instance, ask questions about the relation of the elements of that world to the villagers' world view. The questions may thus be useful in directing attention to strategic avenues for further inquiry.

II. THE SETTING AND PERSPECTIVE OF *Kota* LIFE

The *Kota* villages lie on a plateau in the south of India, an area which is now the Nilgiri District of the State of Madras. The plateau, some 6,500 feet in average elevation, rises quite precipitously from the plains, so much so that the trip was a hazardous one before the British put through roads and a railroad in the mid-nineteenth century. The area at the top of the hills, some 15 by 40 miles in greatest extent, supported four groups before the coming of the English and of the lowlanders who came with them.

The pastoral *Todas* numbered some seven hundred in the first census of 1871 and now have declined in population to between five and six hundred. The *Kurumbas*, who purvey jungle produce to the other Nilgiri peoples and who are feared and employed by them as sorcerers, then numbered about six hundred and now are probably not far from that figure. The agricultural *Badagas*, who supplied the other three groups with grain, alone among the indigenes of the area have grown greatly in population. From some twenty thousand in 1871 they have increased to about sixty thousand in 1951.

The *Kota*, whose numbers have remained fairly stable in these years, were traditionally the artisans—smiths, potters, woodworkers—and musicians of the region. Their villages are interspersed among the settlements of the *Toda*, who still live in much the same places as of old, and of the *Badagas*, whose villages have greatly enlarged in size and number.

The *Kota* have always done some cultivation and have adequate lands of their own around each of their villages. In recent decades they have had to rely more and more heavily on cultivation for a livelihood, since their handicrafts and music are no longer in great demand among their neighbors. They now must devote most of their cultivation to a cash crop, potatoes (Mandelbaum 1952).

A *Kota* village usually has three main streets, each street being the residence of a single patrilineal clan. Near the center of the village is a green on which stand three temples, one to each deity of an ancient triad. In the village of Kolmel (*Kolme·l*), to which this discussion more specifically pertains, a new temple has recently been built to a trinity of Hindu-like gods. Around the introduction of these newest, Sanskritized deities there has crystallized a factional split in the village. The adherents of the more conservative ways are the "Old Rule" (*Ma·mul*) faction, who have resisted the innovations proposed by their opponents. The reform group is called "Cropped" (*Karap*), using the *Kota* version of the English word for haircut. Cutting off the traditional *Kota* chignon by the men of that party symbolizes their adoption of a strong reformist attitude. The two factions in this village have, as has happened elsewhere in village India, drawn apart, so that they stage separate ceremonies and do not interdine. The original issue of the factional split, the worship of the new gods, is no longer the divisive factor, since both factions worship the new as well as the old gods, although each side does so separately. One of the original reasons for the division is gone, the split remains.

For the traditional deities there are still two priests whose office is respected by conservatives and reformists alike. The priests must be kept segregate from the other villagers in many ways. They must dress only in the old style and, in general, conduct their lives in a ritually guarded manner, guarded also from some of the technological innovations which have been adopted in recent decades. The deities are additionally served by diviners, one for each god. Through the diviners, at appropriate occasions, the voice of the god speaks and tells the villagers the pleasure of the gods. The diviners must also lead more carefully guarded lives than do other villagers.

Two important occasions in the ceremonial cycle are the first funeral, where the bodies are cremated, and the second funeral at the end of the ceremonial year. Then all who have died during the year are finally sent off to the afterworld, and mourning for them officially ends (Mandelbaum 1954). A bone of the deceased which has been taken out of the cremation pyre at the first funeral is recremated in the second funeral. An important ritual element in both funerals is the bowing to the remains of the deceased.

It is at this point in the funeral, when the living give a parting bow of respect to the dead, that great quarrels frequently arise. All who have any claim to kinship with the deceased press forward to bow, and anyone present who is a *Kota* feels impelled to make this last bow. Not infrequently some men, usually the close relatives of the deceased, try to prevent others from bowing. Those who are thus barred strain with great argument and pushing (though rarely with blows) to accomplish the ritual gesture. Some of the men not directly involved in the quarrel try to separate the pushing melee of contenders and attempt to bring about a temporary calm which they try to transform into a workable compromise. Sometimes, not often, no suggested compromise avails, and one side or the other calls in the police, an act which brings to bear alien forces which usually must be mollified by suitable cash payment.

A. METHOD OF UNDERSTANDING WORLD VIEW

The study of *Kota* world view can well begin with an analysis of this recurrent situation. In so doing, we may be sure to begin with something which most *Kota* see as being highly important in their lives. If we should seek statements of world view by approaching only the more articulate and reflective persons, we may easily get a fluent and consistent formulation, but one which may not apply for many in the society. Or the observer may unwittingly select the outlook appropriate to a particular status or stratum and present that as the view of the whole people.

The selection of this situation as worthy of special note is made by the *Kota* themselves. Controversies about bowing to the dead have arisen at most funerals which the present writer has heard about or seen. Moreover, reference to such situations is made quite spontaneously in various contexts by men and women of differing ages and status positions.

Thus one man of the Cropped faction tells that he is letting his hair grow again because his father-in-law is growing old and he wants to be able to bow to the corpse when the old man dies. If he continues in the Cropped party, he may be debarred from doing so. A healer—part shaman, part physician—and a conservative from a conservative village tells how his Cropped relatives from another village tried to bow to the corpse at his brother's funeral. Violent protests ensued from his conservative fellow-villagers, and he persuaded his Cropped kin not to bow. If they forced the issue, he reminded them, he would be the one to suffer and perhaps could no longer live in his own village.

Deliberate abstention from bowing brings on societal concern as well as does deliberate exclusion. Several men become affronted during a funeral and express their grievance by refusing to participate in the appropriate gestures. The ritual proceedings are delayed until these men are persuaded to take part again. One of these men, incidentally, is a highly aberrant person—the one effeminate man in the society—but in this matter he shares the common outlook.

Why, then, is this occasion of bowing to the deceased so important to the *Kota?* Why is it the scene of personal victories and personal defeats? To which of the principal spheres of life do these victories and defeats pertain? These spheres, in the broadest sense, are the same for a *Kota* as for man generally—one's relation to the supernatural, to the material environment, and to other people.

Redfield has cogently discussed the use of this tripartite classification in studying world view. He has noted that the student has a double obligation: to see the world as the people see it, and to report what he has shared with them in terms which those of other cultures can understand. He must convert—perhaps "translate" is the better term—the inside view into an outside view. To do that he must assume that the one view is translatable into the other—that there is something in common between the two. Common to all world views, Redfield notes, is the division of the total field of human experience according to relations to God, to nature, and to man.

There are other constant categories, the biological universals of the life-cycle, some kind of economic and ceremonial metronome for the year, the necessity of arranging space and time in some regular fashion (Redfield 1952: 30–31). Perhaps Redfield might have added at least one other to the three prime categories, namely, the relation of man to special experience, as in his aesthetic creations and responses. But the threefold division holds true enough for the *Kota*, using it commits us to no untoward digressions, and in this brief survey it is a useful way of sorting out what is entailed, according to the *Kota* view, in bowing to the corpse.

In this brief survey the examination of one main tension point necessarily overlooks many of the more placid vistas of *Kota* world view. Yet the scene of conflict is also the setting for reward; both are in the forefront of a *Kota* man's view. The view thus sketched is the man's view. The woman's view, in so far as my relatively limited evidence on the woman's outlook goes, is not at odds with it.

B. *Kota* RELATIONS WITH SUPERNATURAL AND NATURAL

Funerals are generally ritual occasions, involving the participants in some kind of relation with their concept of the supernatural. *Kota* funerals are no exception: the supernatural is clearly and prominently entailed in these rites (Mandelbaum 1954: 89–90). But the gods are not importantly involved in the controversies which boil up around the business of bowing. This central concern does not have to do with the gods, nor are very many *Kota* life-problems and dilemmas concerned with relations to gods—this despite the fact that the great factional split has been precipitated by matters of worship, that worship still brings the men before the temples every morning, and that religious ceremonies still provide the great occasions of the year.

To the *Kota*, the gods—all gods, the traditional deities and the newer Hindu-like powers—are potent beyond anyone's doubt. They have strong attributes and great power to affect mortals. But they do not often appear in the center of *Kota* concern. The supernatural is handled like high voltage. If the gods are properly served, they do not act capriciously and do not intervene unnecessarily. There are exceptions to this, it is true. And the voice of the gods is regularly heard through their chosen diviners, appraising the villagers' behavior and telling them what and what not to do. For all this, the gods are addressed and invoked more as a way of turning their attention to the affairs at hand than by way of cajoling or persuading or even of imploring them to take charge. Some specific examples will illustrate this broad impression.

The *Kota* have no great interest in the afterworld. They know that there is such a realm to which the spirits of the dead go, but the nature of that bourne is only vaguely known; little curiosity is shown about it. Once the spirits are duly dispatched after the final funeral rites, they do not return to worry men. The rites are always successful, the spirit departs, there the matter ends. This spirit may later speak through a woman medium, counsel his descendants and foretell coming events, but neither this occasional message from a departed kinsman nor the regularly heard voices of the deities themselves seem to be taken by the *Kota* as anything more than tips for the general welfare. These tips have often to do with the proper performance of ritual. Here the emphasis lies—on the successful manipulation of the supernaturals rather than on inducing in the gods a beneficent state of mind.

This mechanical mode of dealing with the supernatural is exemplified in the legal fictions frequently used in ceremonies. Thus women during their menstrual periods are abhorrent to everything supernatural. They must be secluded and return to normal status in several stages. During menstruation a woman must take care to avoid being seen by a priest and must not approach anything which is specially sacrosanct, whether it be a temple or the hearth in her kitchen. However, every soul in the village must participate in the greatest ceremony of the year, the God Ceremony. All must then be refurbished and renewed. But some women inevitably will be menstruating during the days of this ceremony and should presumably be disqualified from participating in this occasion when all the village is one sacred precinct. The *Kota* solution is simple and is typical of their relations to the supernatural. Before the ceremony begins all the women go out of the village for a time as a token of menstrual seclusion. Hence any woman who menstruates during the days of the ceremony has already been in seclusion for that month, and therefore the subsequent physical condition need not be taken as true menstruation. She may participate with all the village in the holy rituals.

The malevolent manipulation of the supernatural does cause concern, but it is a concern which is met by dealing with people rather than with the supernatural directly. The *Kota* know of the evil eye, but one *Kota* cannot put the evil eye on another. If a villager should want to bring harm to a fellow-villager, or a *Badaga* to a *Kota*, the plotter must hire a *Kurumba* to perform the evil magic. The victim, when he learns of the cause of his misfortunes, must hire yet another *Kurumba* to end the evil. Nowadays *Kurumbas* are less resorted to, although still much feared; Hindu or Muslim exorcisers and amulet purveyors are patronized. In any event, the power to use directly supernatural means in a malevolent way is not an attribute of a *Kota*. The fear of *Kurumba* sorcery is considerable, but it can be met by using guardian *Kurumbas*. People—though not your own kind—can deal properly with this sort of supernatural power also.

In all, the supernatural must be given its great due, must be respectfully handled, but it can be handled successfully. In so far as a people's world view is focused on what troubles them, on the sources of their chief tensions as well as on the arenas of their chief victories, the sphere of the supernatural does not appear to most *Kota* to be either a prime source of tension or a major arena for reward.

As for the second great sphere of life which all world views must comprehend, that of relations to nature, we can summarize the *Kota* view briefly. There are some peoples for whom dealing with nature has magnetic interest. Some are engrossed in cultivation, think of and care for their fields with surpassing concern. Some *Badaga* groups strike me as having such an absorbing interest in their crops. Others may be heart and soul engrossed with their animals. The *Toda* are clearly so engrossed. There are artisans whose stakes in life lie in their craft. But the *Kota* share none of these absorptions. They have been and still are artisans. But they work in the smithy just to get a job done. In recent decades only one man in Kolmel village has ever been moved to lavish his skill in turning out a particularly fine and ornamented blade. Few other *Kota* have tried, as he did, to fashion an ax that would be a thing of uncommon strength and beauty. They have turned out axes in great numbers, and they have skill as smiths. But an ax for them is something to trade or use, not something which may bring special joy or prestige. It may have been different in the past; many a fine skill has in India been washed out by the flood of goods made by Western techniques. In the memory of the living Nilgiri generations, the *Kota* are professional artisans but indifferent craftsmen.

So it is with their activities in dealing with plant and animal. They keep a few cattle, goats, buffalo, but there is nothing of the

Toda zeal for their beasts. They cultivate and now must earn most of their living at it. But in comparison with the nearby *Badaga* fields, the *Kota* fields are not so well tilled. Their crop yield is usually lower, their attention to farming more indifferent.

Note that these are general and comparative statements. There are some *Kota* who are excellent cultivators and take pride and joy in their fields. But most are not as interested in farming as are most *Badagas*. The *Kota* do not lack industry; they can work hard and steadily on occasion. But the general occasions of cultivation do not evoke notably effective efforts. A *Kota*'s main interest generally lies in another sphere; not in his relations to the gods, not in his necessary dealings with plant and animal and matter, but in his relations to other men. Around these relations cluster *Kota* concern; it is here that the matter of bowing at the funeral becomes a matter for passion and pride.

C. RELATIONS AMONG MEN

Man's prime struggle is with man: this idea comes through in life-histories, in anecdotes, in folklore. In some societies, as among the Tanjore Brahmans studied by Gough, there is great concern with the self: a good part of the struggle is with the self. This is not so for the *Kota*. They have little worry about their impulses. Most men and women enjoy a vigorous sex life which starts at a quite early age. While most men are much interested in sexual activities over a large span of the life-cycle, the interest is in satisfying the impulses rather than in denying them. There is something of the widespread Indic belief that overindulgence is harmful, but this belief is expressed more as an explanation for a manifest ailment than as an immediate guide to conduct.

Nor is strong drink eschewed in principle or in practice. The aversion to this means of self-gratification, common to the higher castes and now expressed in the Madras prohibition law, is not shared by the *Kota*. They grumble about how difficult it is now to get liquor and how the welfare of the people has suffered from the governmental prohibition.

Kota men generally do not question their physical needs and gratifications, and they show little sign of worry about their roles in life. They give the impression of a vigorous self-confidence; life-histories usually display evidence of what may be called a firm sense of ego-identity.

Similarly, in relations with women, *Kota* men give few evidences, direct or indirect, of special anxieties. If the main struggle is not with the self, it is also not between the sexes. Some special points of friction develop. Not infrequently a younger brother will move out of the joint family household because he does not get along with the elder brother's wife. But frequently also this brother's wife is the lad's special friend. In ritual the link between husband and wife is very close, and the two stand as one at some crucial ritual junctures. It is not with women that a *Kota* man feels he must contend.

The struggle lies among males, particularly among peers. The close kin of the older and of the younger generations are one's allies and supporters. In tales and in small talk, a man's father, his father's brothers, his mother's brothers all appear as supportive characters. The mother's brother, having no great disciplinary responsibility for his nephew, is expected to be and frequently is a kind and benevolent figure who provides emotional refuge as well as material aid. Often enough he is, in the *Kota* system of preferred cross-cousin marriage, the father-in-law as well.

A man's relations with his father, as recounted and as observed, give little indication of any strong oedipus-like reactions, such as those noted for the Brahmans of Kumbapettai in Tanjore. Nor is there any special reason why such tensions should prevail here. Fathers do not and, indeed, cannot well dispossess or disinherit their sons. The society encourages youths to be quite independent. And sons are a man's most precious possession.

In the last matter, the *Kota* are at one with the vast concourse of Indic peoples, from Tanjore Brahmans to Madhopur *Camārs*. Without a son, or at least a child, a *Kota* feels himself scarcely a person. A childless couple does not often go many years without a child in the house. A man takes in a brother's son to feed and raise, or an orphan lad with no close kin is adopted, or a succession of wives is taken until one yields a child. In some manner a man must have someone in his house to call him father.

Children are thus tremendously important, and a man who has none does not rest easily until he does have a child, preferably a son, more preferably several. Few men remain long incapacitated on that score. If they do not become biological fathers in due course, they manage to be sociological fathers. Once children are acquired, however, their rearing seems not to be a major focus of concern. There are problems, of course, in rearing children, in getting them healed if they are sick, saved if they are bewitched, married if a bride price must be scraped together. Great anxieties may be aroused in a man's life on any or all of these scores, but he typically meets these problems as they turn up; he does not keep these possibilities in the forefront of his view.

What is central to a man's social perception is his relation with his peers. In the first instance it is his relation with his brothers, both real and classificatory. Brothers are allies. They usually work as a co-operative group in the fields, in the smithy, in providing music. If a man has no uterine brothers, he generally works with several of his classificatory brothers of the clan.

The brothers face the world together, as a single group. When one is threatened, all are supposed to rally to his support and usually do so. In one rare case in which two brothers belonged to opposing factions, there was a dramatic display of the strength of the fraternal tie. Ordinarily the two do not go into one another's house or interdine. But when one suffered a psychotic episode in which his life was endangered and there was no other man willing to care for the sick one, the well brother did drop all factional enmity, nursed and cared for his sick brother until the man was able to carry on in society. Since then the two have reverted to their separate ways and factions.

In ritual, one brother can stand as a perfect substitute for another. When a man goes on a formal mission, as when he goes to take his bride from her father's house, he must have a brother along with him. Many of the folk-tale motifs occur as happenings to a set of brothers.

For all that there is this brother bond, however, there is also a sharp awareness within the brother group of the rights and duties of each. Each brother must have an equal share in everything the group attains. Though the harvest may be pooled and the family purse and kitchen be jointly shared, no one brother may take a larger share than another. Elder brothers are given due respect by their juniors, the needs of the brothers with more mouths to feed are duly taken into account, but each one feels equal in rights to every other. There must be a fraternal equivalence in all things, and many are the quarrels among a set of brothers about such things as cultivation, sharing the work of the smithy, and the division of property. The equal sharing occurs in sex relations as well, but quarrels about these relations are not directly expressed (Mandelbaum 1938: 579–80).

Within a set of brothers, then, there is strong identification and co-operation, but there is also a strong sense of individual rights. These rights are jealously guarded so that the identification with the brother group does not wipe out a man's very lively sense of his status as an individual in the group. A *Kota*'s notion that he has not been given his proper due among the brothers not infrequently leads him to split off from them, to arrange some new alliances, perhaps with classificatory rather than uterine brothers, or to carry on economically only with his sons or affines.

Such procedure prevails also in the widening circles of a man's social relations. When the clan is involved, each clansman guards, as much for himself as for the clan group, those prerogatives which belong to his clan. When the villagers of Kolmel deal with men of another *Kota* village, they are quick to defend Kolmel's full measure of respect or gifts or whatever may be involved. Factional divisions now complicate the scene. A conservative from Kolmel attending a ceremony in another village may strive to bar a Kolmel man of the opposing faction from participating in the rite. Yet he may have some feeling that his own status as a Kolmel man suffers when his fellow-villager is roughly handled.

As against the *Badaga*, all *Kota* factions are as one. While some still provide music to those of the *Badaga* who want *Kota* music, all *Kota* steadily claim more from the *Badaga* than any *Badaga* is now willing to grant. This contention with the *Badaga* is very much in the *Kota*'s view, though most *Badaga* do not take much notice of the few and, to their minds, lowly *Kota*. The *Kota* sees himself as a kind of peer of the *Badaga*, perhaps not as pure as some or as wealthy as others, but a peer nonetheless in that the *Kota* believes he has certain rights and duties toward the *Badaga* and, more especially, that the *Badaga* should have certain obligations toward him.

Whether as brother among brothers, villager among villagers, *Kota* among Nilgiri peoples, a man's chief interest is in dealing with other men in the proper way—the proper way being that way which preserves his full rights or what he deems to be his full rights. These dealings and the contention about them are the common currency of talk and the patent focus of interest among the *Kota*.

How then are men to be dealt with? The mode of confronting one's fellows may be termed "aggressive defense." A man must ever be wary lest his rights and privileges be encroached upon: if they are, defensive response must be quick and vigorous. He must react sharply to any possible slight. He must be instantly jealous of his status.

That is why bowing to the relic of the corpse is so important. In the usual course of the ceremony, everyone present expects to bow as a last gesture of respect and alliance with the deceased. The gesture symbolizes that the one who bows belongs to the social network, that he has the status of a *Kota*. Whatever factional side a man may take, he does not want to cut loose from the whole society of his people; rather he wants to bring them all to share in his ways.

On the other side, those in charge of a funeral are zealous to keep away from their deceased kinsmen anyone who is not a complete *Kota* in their view. If such a one should bow, they would all feel demeaned, their own status undermined. Hence members of one faction try to bow, those of the other try to prevent them, and great rows are precipitated.

Such quarrels commonly delay ceremonies for hours. *Kota* men, possessing as they do a strong sense of their worth and independence, carry on the arguments with great vigor. But the arguments are almost always on the verbal level only; rarely do *Kota* come to physical aggression or even to attempts at magical manipulation. This may be because each man seeks, not to undermine the other man, or forcibly to subordinate him, but rather to protect his own rights.

The use of bezoars, concretions sometimes found in the alimentary system of ruminants, illustrates *Kota* notions of how a man should conduct himself. Bezoars are ground up and fed a child so that he may have "anger and common sense." "Anger" is a straightforward interpretation of the *Kota* word; "common sense" is a translation (suggested by an interpreter) for the quality of being able to make sound, practical judgments. Why, then, "anger and common sense"? Anger so that he may fight vigorously in defense of his rights; common sense so that he may know when his rights have been transgressed.

Important to this self-defense is the avoidance of ritual pollution. A person so defiled is also socially disabled. He loses, at least temporarily, his full previous status. And he is made specially vulnerable to such loss by contact with the biological experiences of birth, menstruation, and death. There are other sources of ritual and social disablement, but these are among the most dangerous. Thus when a *Kota* dies, his closest kin are barred from ordinary social contacts. A main emphasis of the elaborate double funeral is to reinstate the mourners to normal social status (Mandelbaum 1954: 91). So long as a person is defiled on this account or on some lesser score, he is dangerous to his fellows. The danger is only partly thought of as supernatural; it is quite vividly the danger of degrading others to a comparable state of social paralysis.

It is as though all social relations are in delicate balance, so that any one of many ritual impairments can throw them out of balance. Once dislocated, these relations must be put back in order by proper ritual purification.

In this delicate balance, withdrawal from social relations is a main procedure, both as an individual's weapon and as the group's disciplinary means. If a man feels affronted, believes his proper rights have been slighted, he will withdraw from participation in the social enterprise in which he has felt himself disparaged. Thus in the episode mentioned earlier, in which several men refused to participate in a funeral ceremony because they felt slighted, these men believed, in effect, that they had been detracted and that further participation would signal that they accepted a lowered standing. The others involved in the ceremony were eager to have them participate—and eventually arranged a compromise which brought them back in—because less than full participation would reduce the worth of the whole ceremony and so take away something from each person who did carry on with it.

Viewed from the other aspect, withdrawal by the group from the individual is the traditional way of dealing with transgressors. One who violates the group's standards of conduct thereby demeans everyone within the group. Hence social relations with him are severed until he repairs his transgression and symbolically affirms that he is at one with the group again. This is the common Indic practice of outcasting. In Kolmel village the Old Rule people have cast out every Cropped man. The Cropped have retaliated by forming a factional group which takes the stand that it is they who have thrown out the others. However, the Cropped men still adamantly strive to bow to the corpse at funerals conducted by Old Rule men and are as adamantly hindered from doing so.

There is a certain amount of physical pushing and pulling during such encounters, but generally a transgressor is not subject to physical coercion to make him behave properly. The important note is not one of forcing the wrongdoer to conform but rather of enforcing the break of social relations until such time as the miscreant makes amends.

Positive achievements also contribute to the defense of one's status. Every man has a lively sense of his rights as a *Kota,* as an equal among equals. If an individual commands personal esteem, it is more likely that his own appraisal of his rights will be accepted by the group. There are various means of achieving personal respect.

One of the qualities necessary for becoming headman is a talent for mediating quarrels, for maintaining the societal equilibrium. Other avenues to personal prestige are attaining wealth, excelling in debate, performing ritual and social obligations meticulously. We have noted above that a man without children feels himself something less than equal. But having sons does not alone guarantee the assured preservation of one's rights. Other accomplishments bolster a man's claims.

Not that there is a dead level of equality in all things. There is a very strict order of precedence, for example, in ceremonies. All men precede all women, elders precede juniors in age, secular officers go ahead of ordinary villagers, sacred officers lead all with the senior priest in front. But two men may differ as to their respective positions within this rank order. One may feel that his should be the prior place in the funeral feast because he is of closer kin than another man who may be the elder of the two. In such disputes, the one who commands greater respect is apt to have his demand supported by most people and to win his claimed precedence.

There are personality differences in claims made and in personal sensitivity to perceived slights. But even the less sensitive man, even one who gets scant regard from his fellows, nonetheless rises in sharp protest if he detects that he has not been given his just deserts.

What a *Kota* considers the world to owe him has changed in recent decades. Claims on the *Badagas* are still voiced but with not much hope of having these demands met. Claims on the government are beginning to be more prominent, but government is still too remote and awesome to be grappled directly. Meanwhile intramural struggles rage between those more ready to accept innovation and those less ready to do so. These struggles are fought out over such matters as bowing to the corpse. In these struggles *Kota* attention is not riveted on change as much as it is on the societal consequences of adopting new ways. The *Kota*'s interest is in preventing any personal derogation either in the course of change or—from the viewpoint of the Cropped faction—in not changing some of the older *Kota* ways. Change can easily be accepted so long as man is assured that personal loss of status will not thereby be suffered.

This formulation of one aspect of *Kota* world view has not touched upon other aspects which could properly be included in a more lengthy discussion. It has presented what seems typically to be in the forefront of a *Kota*'s perception—that man must struggle with man in defense of his social self. Like all condensed formulations, this characterization is subject to modification according to particular circumstances and personalities. But it is generally valid for *Kota* life, as are the other general views abstracted from *Kota* testimony. One such view is that the gods are potent but not capricious: they can be dealt with effectively. Nature can be recalcitrant to man's efforts, but is not the center of interest. The best man is one who does not allow himself to be deprived, one who responds vigorously to any threat of deprivation in social relations.

III. THE WORLD OF THE INDIAN VILLAGER: COMPARISONS

The *Kota* are not a typical Nilgiri society or culture. The numerically predominant *Badaga* have a differing cultural orientation—much more like the main Hindu tradition of village Mysore—and the distinctive *Toda* have yet another cultural set. So the *Kota* are not even typical of their small district, much less of the plains villagers in the linguistic regions adjacent to the Nilgiri Hills: Tamil, Malayalam, or Kannada. And yet a good part of the *Kota* world view as here described does not seem totally alien to views held widely in India. It may be instructive to compare the *Kota* with some of the other villagers discussed in this volume. As noted above, such comparisons will afford a view of the world in which the *Kota* live as well as provide a comparative background for understanding their particular world view. Their world includes forces of which they are not aware—forces which are apparent to an observer who has access to information and ideas not available to *Kota* villagers. Comparisons of Indian villages in various areas and circumstances may bring out some of the common forces playing on them.

A. RAMPURA: A VILLAGE MORE UNIFIED THAN KOLMEL

Closest to the *Kota* in space, only some seventy air-miles north of them, are the villagers of Rampura in Mysore, described by Srinivas. Rampura is noted to be a relatively conservative village, in which traditional social relations have not been violently disturbed, and it does resemble the more conservative *Kota* villages rather than the more volatile ones. Yet there are many parallels between changing Kolmel in the Nilgiris and Rampura in Mysore.

In both, for example, there is concern with maintaining permanent and stable relations among different groups. In Kolmel the stable relations of the past have been irretrievably unsettled, but there still is the notion, as in Rampura, that payments in grain for services make for more stable relations than do payments in money. This for two reasons which apply widely in village India. One is that monetary inflation in the war and postwar period has prejudiced any scale of payment previously set. Moreover, the money could buy only what was available in the ration shops established by the government in the Nilgiri District. As often as not, the grain sold in the ration shop is not the choice of the villager either in kind or in quality.

An older and more general reason why the *Kota*, the Rampura villagers, and many other Indian countrymen prefer grain payment to money payment is that it makes the transaction a direct and intimate one. When a *Badaga* gives cash payment to a *Kota* for repairing his tools, there are many disadvantages to the *Kota*. He must then buy his grain from a shopkeeper, and even the official ration shop must take some share for its profit and expenses. Once in a market, he finds his small change frittering away with less food to show for it and more hunger later. And money is generally felt to be the solvent of the old, traditional relations between *Badagas* and *Kotas*. Even the more radical *Kotas* would like to retain something of their old independence as craftsmen on whom the *Badaga* had to depend. Many *Badaga* nowadays want to throw off this more intimate relationship with the *Kota* and try to make payments in money when they can.

Land is as pressing a problem in Rampura as in most of village India; it is highly valued as prestige payment and as the means of establishing durable bonds among people. It is a less pressing problem among the *Kota*. As indigenes they had ample lands legally assigned to them in the nineteenth century. Since their population has remained stable, land has been something which could be sold from time to time to the *Badagas* who craved it. Kolmel villagers still are not very pressed for cultivable land, although certain other *Kota* villages are less well off. While they have land, this alone has not been sufficient to raise their position in the social hierarchy of the area. Only as they come increasingly within the orbit of the main Hindu tradition, give up more of their traditional practices and adopt more Sanskritic customs, will their ownership of land come to count as a force in their social favor. By then, they well may have sold off a good part of the lands which they now have. Even though Kolmel is different in the strategic matter of land hunger, it still resembles Rampura in fundamental ways.

Thus the *Kota* repeatedly united, as do particular Rampura castes, to protect the interests of the whole caste group against the other peoples. This consolidating factor has faded as *Kota* monopolies have yielded to bazaar competition and imported musicians. In disputes between *Kotas, Badaga* elders might arbitrate just as the elders of the dominant Rampura caste administer justice to all villagers. This *Badaga* function also has become less common with the passing of the traditional relations.

The concept of pollution governs with the *Kota* as it does in Rampura and was reported from the Nilgiri peoples long before they were exposed to the full influence of the main Hindu tradition. With this exposure, the reformist faction in Kolmel village has accepted the standard Hindu concept of the hierarchy of diet and occupation. Hence their efforts to induce all *Kota* to give over carrion eating and music. Not only is Sanskritization thus affecting *Kota* culture from within, but it is also, and to none of their liking, impinging from without in the matter of the Madras law, noted above, against alcohol. While some *Kota* take willingly to Sanskritization by diffusion, all object to this Sanskritization by legislation.

The maneuvering for heightened social standing described for Rampura is replicated in the Nilgiris. In the Nilgiris also the ranking of villagers in day-to-day relationships will vary by situation and according to the specific combination of evaluative factors. It would be, in a sense, false to set up a rigid rank order of castes in many villages of modern India. For some ritual purposes, such a listing may prevail. But individuals and even groups may be given one rank order in a particular context and a different ranking in another context. The case of the wealthy Rampura Toddyman is an example. Srinivas notes that for purposes of contribution to common village festivals he is put in a division along with some members of higher castes. What is quite constant is a set of criteria for ranking; what varies is the interpretation given in a specific instance to a particular combination of characteristics. Thus one *Kota* who is relatively wealthy, who has had some advanced education and has been a schoolteacher, who has worked with Europeans and who sometimes even wears full Western dress, is usually treated quite differently by the *Badaga* who know him than is the ordinary long-haired *Kota* villager. This man, like the patrons in Rampura, has built up his own following and invests in people so that he may be able to use his followers for political or economic advantage. His social experiences, wider and more varied than those of the other *Kota,* have given him a special notion of what the proper status of a *Kota* should be (Mandelbaum 1941*b:* 25–26). Hence he strives to fulfil and defend this status with means similar to those used by Rampura patrons.

The description of Rampura gives us a picture of a village in which there are generally effective mechanisms for maintaining the social hierarchy. Hence the unifying links which weld the disparate groups into a functioning community can clearly be discerned in Rampura. These unifying links are not absent in Kolmel, but they are less effective than they were before external disruption came to bear. Can it be, then, that the central concern of the *Kota* villager with self-defense is a concern which has been magnified because of the weakening of some main props of the traditional social structure? Comparisons of world views in a village like Rampura with those in similar but more perturbed villages should indicate how forces thrusting from the external world may affect the internal world view.

B. NAMHALLI: AN URBAN-INFLUENCED VILLAGE

The external world has been very much with the villagers of Namhalli, as described here by Alan Beals. Namhalli is a village which has had to choose progress. Its people could hardly have escaped, even if they had wanted to, from the effects of the progressive measures fostered by the Mysore government: irrigation, health procedures, transport, schooling. In geographic distance, Namhalli is some one hundred and forty air-miles northeast of the Nilgiris; Rampura is thus about midway between Kolmel and Namhalli. But in social change, Kolmel seems midway between the other two. Rampura has been less affected, Namhalli has been more altered, than has Kolmel. The picture of Namhalli is that of a village which has been strongly buffeted by exterior forces. It has been specially vulnerable to such vagaries as those of fluctuating prices just because it has become so closely meshed into a national and world economic system. The net results in Namhalli have many parallels in Kolmel. In both places the village-wide ceremonies have been reduced in scope and significance. Occupational specialties have declined; those who continue to provide artisan services find it more difficult to collect what they believe to be their proper share. The increasing use of money has helped to enfeeble the traditional reciprocal relations among castes, and there has been a general reduction of co-operative effort. Similar processes have been reported widely from village India; accounts for over a century have depicted, usually with some dismay, these developments. There has been considerable variation in the pace of happenings. The rate of change appears somewhat less swift in Kolmel than it has been in Namhalli.

The question is whether the greater atomization of the social order in Namhalli makes for an even greater sensitivity to status defense than prevails in Kolmel. Factionalism is rife, and it is capricious in Namhalli—conditions which seem to indicate that a villager there is ever ready to rise in wrath to a point of personal status. Many things are seen as impinging on personal status, and the defensive alignments vary a good deal from issue to issue (Beals 1954: 224–30).

The example of Namhalli then raises other questions pertinent to the study of world view. To what extent have the villagers there resisted some potential changes and accelerated others in accord with their general views? Beals properly emphasizes those forces over which the villagers had little or no power of decision. Yet there are many junctures at which they can and do make decisions. Some villagers, for example, quickly make use of educational opportunities; others—for whom education is equally accessible—remain long indifferent to it. Given a heavy preoccupation in Namhalli with defending one's position in society, it would be useful to know how those villagers who have attained special status, say, schoolteachers and government employees, view the internal struggle. Perhaps in their view it is now more important to establish some new social framework than to fight increasingly for relative status in the old structure.

C. KASANDRA, ITS *Rajpūts*, AND THEIR CODE

A traditional social structure in which a man had constantly to be vigilant to vindicate his status is that of the *Vāghelā Rajpūts* of Kasandra described by Gitel Steed. Their formal code of manly conduct enshrined moral sensitivity to personal slight. No derogation of status was permissible. "A *Rajpūt* who bears an insult commits a thousand sins." For all that the *Vāghelā Rajpūts* and others in North Indian *Kṣatriya* tradition are far removed from the *Kota* in space, in social rank, in temporal power, in many details, yet the focus of their respective world views seems similar.

The differences must not be minimized. The *Vāghelā Rajpūt*'s hand slips easily to the sword hilt or its modern equivalent; the *Kota*'s hand only fans the air more violently to give added impetus to his verbal barrage. The *Rajpūt* must maintain his status lest he sink—the very notion may nauseate him—to lowly rank; the *Kota* scarcely has a lower stratum into which to fall. Both personal and caste pride are bound in the *Rajpūt*'s defensive posture; the *Kota*'s defense is more often personal than it is societal. Yet there are underlying similarities also, related to status sensitivity. Pollution is important; ritual vulnerability brings on social disability to both. The means of defending and manipulating status in both areas now includes the use of litigation—a use and overuse which developed in some places soon after courts of the Western type were established. But while the *Vāghelā Rajpūt* seems fully as much concerned with status defense as is the *Kota*, and while some of the gauges of that defense, such as pollution, are similar, there are yet clear and wide differences in the respective world views. In further comparative work between such diverse peoples, it would be worth considering how the world view of one may coincide with that of another in certain respects and differ widely in others.

D. MADHOPUR *Camārs:* THE PERSPECTIVE FROM BELOW

Less difference obtains, in hierarchical ranking at least, between the low-caste *Camār* of Madhopur in North India and the *Kota*. Both these low-ranking groups use social techniques common to most Indic ranks and areas. Just as the members of one faction in Kolmel try to maintain their status by withdrawal from social relations with the other, so does one subcaste among the *Camārs* refrain from marriage into or eating with another subcaste. As both factions in Kolmel have adopted Sanskritic traits in ritual and have displaced some practices disparaged in the classic tradition, so have the Madhopur *Camārs* taken on more and more practices of the literate corpus. Both are now imbued with an urge toward upward mobility, the *Camārs* perhaps more urgently than the *Kota*, but both peoples are convinced that they deserve a higher ranking (and concomitant perquisites) than they get. Both have a rationale for their current and presumably temporary low state, and both—as is common in the lower echelons of the social order—refer to a tale which tells of a fall from higher grace through no fault of their own.

The Madhopur example well illustrates the common process whereby a trait is pre-empted by one socially mobile group while it is being forsaken in the higher rank. As the *Camārs* take practices followed by the *Ṭhākurs*, the *Ṭhākurs* tend to drop some of these same customs for patterns more in the Western manner. The process has been noted on a broad scale for family relations and especially in the matter of purdah (Mandelbaum 1948: 137–39). It occurs also in the Nilgiris. Thus the *Kota* have taken to staging street shows for themselves of a kind formerly performed in *Badaga* villages. The *Badagas* have generally given over these more rowdy street performances, partly because low-caste Tamilians also put them on, and they now present stage plays in the more restrained and literate Kannada manner.

Another widespread trend pointed out in Cohn's description of Madhopur *Camārs* is the augmented unity of a have-not group as against those better endowed. So long as lower-caste families had mutually supportive relations with higher-caste patrons, they would, in time of need, rally to their local patrons rather than join forces with caste fellows. As former bonds and rewards have lessened, bonds of caste and class have strengthened. On the Nilgiri scene also, the *Kota* now tend to be more unified against the *Badaga* than they were even a decade or two ago, even though the crucial factor of land hunger does not play the part in Kolmel that it does in Madhopur.

In Madhopur the introduction of elections seems to have released forces or accelerated antagonisms that had been latent. The effects of village elections, in addition to their primary political consequences, merit similar examination elsewhere in India. Also apparent from the Madhopur example, as it is in Kolmel, is the importance of the schoolteacher as a vector of social change. This is a strategic social status in many villages: the influence of the incumbent in the villages and of the status on the incumbent would repay close study.

The *Camārs,* then, illustrate a number of features and trends which are widespread among the people of the land and, in particular, among low-ranking castes. *Camārs* too are sensitive about status and about status loss through pollution. They too use the familiar techniques of withdrawal as a social weapon. How, then, does their perspective differ from that of people at the top of the social scale?

E. KUMBAPETTAI BRAHMANS: THE PERSPECTIVE FROM ABOVE

The account of Kumbapettai, a village of the Tanjore District in South India, given by Gough, provides a number of useful clues toward an answer. In this Brahman-dominated village, Gough's sketch reveals familiar processes, similar to those taking place in Madhopur and, indeed, in almost every village described in this volume. In Kumbapettai there was in earlier decades a degree of village autonomy, both economic and political, which has lessened rapidly in recent years. Under the suzerainty of the resident Brahmans, all castes maintained a village solidarity strong enough to exclude the intrusions of alien authority in internal matters. Here, as was not uncommon, the police were manipulated so as to keep them out, even in cases of murder. Here, too, economic changes together with expanding social contacts have weakened the former bonds of unity and have undermined the traditional authority of Brahmans. The traditional village ceremonies, which once vivified village unity and reinforced the social order, are declining here as in Kolmel and elsewhere; this is a result of socioeconomic changes and is a factor contributing to accelerated changes (Mandelbaum 1954: 87). As in Madhopur, the low castes are coming together in a new-found unity against their traditional superiors. And in Tanjore there is the added factor of the Communist party which tries to provide these restive villagers with new authority and leadership, new legend and world view, new ceremonies and social tasks, all designed to appeal as a furthering of their demands for proper rights.

The relation among Brahman peers in this village is characterized as an uneasy one. Aggression against peers, while strongly inhibited from mounting to physical violence, is manifested in quarrels and in the leaderlessness of the village Brahmans. Among both *Kota* and Kumbapettai Brahmans, peer relations appear to be the source of a good deal of tension. *Kota* generally seem fully as alert to the protection of their status rights.

As self-protection is a concern common to *Kota* and to these Brahmans, so do pollution and pollution avoidance enter prominently into the protective posture of both. Brahman avoidance is enormously more catholic than is *Kota*, and Brahman pollution rules help cope with a more electric fear of freely exercising bodily functions. But in both groups pollution and purity have prominently to do with bodily functions (as well as life-crises), and in both there is no neutral state of being; so delicate is the balance that one is mildly pure and therefore fit for social relations, or impure and unfit.

No matter how aggravated interpersonal relations may become, there is no physical aggression among peers in both groups. The Brahman of Kumbapettai shows extreme concern with wealth and with minute details of status. With the average *Kota*, both conservative and nonconservative, there may not be quite the same steady vision for wealth, but there is a similar concern for details of status.

While there is this common ground among *Kota* and Tanjore Brahmans, the two deviate markedly in other aspects relevant to world view. The difference in degree of sensitivity to pollution is very great, albeit the cultural grounds for this sensitivity are common. Quite different, too, is the locus of a man's major concern. With the *Kota* it seems to lie in peer relations. With these Brahmans peer relations give concern but probably not as much as do lineal relations, especially between a man and his elders in the family.

To hold tight rein, check rein, over one's sensual impulses, is to be a proper Brahman and a fit, pure social being. To give way to impulse is to desocialize one's self. That may be why shamanistic possession and the liking for liquor, so common to lower castes in South India, including the *Kota,* are discountenanced among Brahmans. The reality of Brahman behavior is more flexible than is the ideal. Yet the ideal concepts govern enough in daily life to provide an outlook quite different from that of the *Kota* in the stress on subordination-submission, in the view of women, and in the depreciation of the pleasures of the flesh.

A broad question suggested by Gough's presentation has to do with the relation of a people's institutions to their world view. Peer relations can be devalued among Kumbapettai Brahmans, age-mates need not join in co-operative action, because neither in economic, social, nor religious relations do peers have to depend crucially on joint strength. Brahman landowners in Tanjore have not had to band together—in recent centuries at least—for mutual benefit. The *Kota* do not devaluate peer relations to the same degree perhaps because brothers and age-mates still must aid each other in getting a living. Could atomistic peer relations prevail among people where economic techniques enjoined peer co-operation? As these Brahmans leave their traditional economic base, or as it becomes necessary to maintain this base by joint action, will there be a greater prizing of peer relations? Formerly, Kumbapettai Brahmans who quarreled were usually brought together again in the context of ceremonies. Now that the traditional ceremonies are becoming flaccid affairs, will some new view of quarrels (perhaps more intolerant of them) and new methods of conciliation arise?

F. KISHAN GARHI: THE INDIC TRADITIONS AND THEIR STUDY

The relation of the world to the village is a main theme of McKim Marriott's discussion of Kishan Garhi in Uttar Pradesh. Some fundamental questions are asked in this paper concerning the concepts used by the analyst in studying that world of Indic village life. Hence Marriott asks whether Kishan Garhi has been isolated enough from the world outside its bounds to form an isolable unit for study. And he shows that in many ways it has not been isolated at all. Various spheres of outside interests have affected the village, and the villagers have long participated in distant circles of relationships. Not the least of the trespassing influences has been that of the British government, whose nineteenth-century land-revenue policy has profoundly affected such characteristic features of village life as the lineage system, the settlement pattern, and the recurrent factional conflicts.

Long before the advent of the British Raj, most villages could hardly have been strongly isolated. The very existence of the Mohenjo Daro–Harappa cities of the third millennium B.C. indicates that their influence, for the procurement of food and fuel if nothing else, must have been felt over a wide swath of the countryside. It would indeed be difficult to find truly isolated peoples on the Indic subcontinent—their number in the world at large is small. However, as Marriott indicates, the Indian village is nonetheless a real entity, has firm bounds both in the view of the villager and to the eye of the observer. While the isolated little community may not exist in its ideal form in India, the village is a surely useful isolate for study and will continue as such at least so long as the first inquiry made of a stranger is, as Marriott reports, "What is your village, sir?" The study of the village as an isolable entity does not preclude, rather commits, the student to give proper notice to external forces to the degree warranted by the purpose of his research and the availability of evidence.

The *Kota* case illustrates some aspects of the problem of cultural isolation and analytic isolability. They were far more isolated, at the beginning of the nineteenth century, than were any other of the villagers described in this volume. Yet, as was indicated above, we know that a military expedition had penetrated the Nilgiris in the twelfth century, also that the *Badagas* very probably came as refugees from wars and persecutions in Mysore, that the Nilgiri peoples made periodic trips to the plains to get cloth and other goods. These contacts presumably had effect on the *Kota* and their hill neighbors, though just what effect we can now but little deduce. It is clear, however, that the force of any state did not regularly reach to the villages atop the plateau. Nevertheless, the Nilgiri peoples did maintain a kind of caste system without regulation from a state power or constant example from an urban center. States and cities certainly had great influence on the classic system of caste; the Nilgiri example implies that they were not absolutely essential for the maintenance of a caste social order.

As we have seen, the *Kota* are now subject to the full force of the main tradition of India, and Marriott's paper points out some of the general attributes of this force. While for purposes of analysis the terms "great tradition" and "little tradition" may be of some use, the data indicate to me that the "great tradition" is essentially a convenient abstraction. It is not followed in its pure literary form in the village or for that matter among city folk either. There is, of course, the vast corpus of scripture and literature, a reservoir from which elements may be selected for prominent notice during a particular period or among a special group.

The main tradition, as it is in fact empirically manifest in village behavior, is always in localized form, part of it derivable from scripture, part of it parochial practice. Thus the local goddess *Naurthā*, as Marriott tells us, is thought of by most villagers in Kishan Garhi as an aspect of the Big Goddess, and part of a complex of goddesses in both scriptural and popular Hinduism. And localized cults develop into parts of regional or all-India sacred geography. Because the villager is aware that other localities have other phrasings of the same tradition, there is no strong urge to make one parochial version entirely consistent with another or to have the scripture itself meticulously consistent in internal details.

Hence the *Kota* can take on the Sanskritic elements in the main tradition at their own pace and can feel free to adapt elements of their more purely parochial tribal culture to attractive features of the main tradition. Within a *Kota* village there may well be hot dispute as to which elements should be adopted and how rapid the pace of adoption should be, but there is no notion that they must either abandon their local culture or try to imitate everything they know of non-*Kota* culture. Full participation in the main tradition thus is gained gradually, by internal decision more than by external insistence. This attribute of gradualness of the main tradition has been described among the Coorgs by Srinivas (Srinivas 1952: 226–27).

But we must note also that in addition to the main tradition villagers generally now utilize some of the newer, world-shared, patterns of science, industry, commerce, and political movements. Scarcely a village in India has been unaffected by this newer complex and its agents; in the papers of this volume these influences have been shown in many instances. The various aspects of the new complex have not been as closely fused and as continuous with the older tradition as are the Sanskritic literate and the local patterns with each other. One reason among others for this discontinuity is that the specialist carriers of the new tradition to the village, who themselves were not of the village, such as medical men, agricultural experts, civil servants, have not been integral elements of village society (Mandelbaum 1953: 4–7). Still, the ways of the new tradition have penetrated deeply into village culture, and there has been only sporadic revulsive reaction against them. Few Namhalli villagers, for example, want to abolish buses and shun electric lights.

In some ways an easy adjustment is coming about of old belief and new technique. One example, cited from Namhalli in Mysore, is the use of a radio broadcast time signal at the astrologically propitious moment for tying on charms: with the time signal, there are broadcast the proper Sanskrit verses. This is a small, if vivid, instance. Radio and other devices of the new complex enter at other levels, as when some villagers in Bombay are said to follow the broadcast price quotations as a guide to the economically propitious moment for selling their crop.

These new artifacts, techniques, and ideas are now more effectively disseminated to the villagers because certain of them are being brought in by people who are part of village society—schoolteachers, leaders of local economic or caste associations, villagers returned from work in the city. These agents of cultural diffusion can adapt the innovations to accord with the villagers' view, as the specialist carrier who is alien to village society has not often done. It is noteworthy that many of the same agents are now the carriers to Kishan Garhi of the scriptural Sanskritic tradition. Marriott observes that those few persons and groups who have taken on Sanskritic forms in recent times have done so, not from the local higher castes, but from itinerant teachers, from urban-centered associations, from schools or the market place.

Therefore, a worthy question for an understanding of world view and its change relates to the views of schoolteachers and other villagers who are carriers of innovating ideas, either Sanskritic or Western or both. To what degree do they find conflict between the two complexes? In what degree are they impelled toward innovation by reason of their achieved status?

Whatever techniques may be used for ascertaining world view, there is one strategic area of investigation which is almost untapped. It is humor. Marriott's paper happily makes use of one illustrative example, the joke about how villagers kowtow to those of the son-in-law's village. Such anecdotes provide insights to the villager's view of himself and of his world and can well be used in formulating world view.

G. RANI KHERA AND TEPOZTLAN: VILLAGES IN DIFFERING CIVILIZATIONS

Two differing worlds are compared in Lewis' paper on Rani Khera in Delhi District. While the comparison is in the first instance between Rani Khera and the Mexican village of Tepoztlan, it also carries wider implications. Rani Khera is Indic in many salient features, similar to all the other Indian villages herein described, while Tepoztlan differs in these characteristics from all of them.

The *Kota* village Kolmel is as far apart from Rani Khera in geography and in cultural detail as is any other Indian village here discussed. It is a hill village, and Lewis notes that this geographic factor may make for a more localized outlook than prevails on a vast plain such as that on which Rani Khera is sited. Another factor mentioned by Lewis as one which may well influence the villagers' outlook is village exogamy. Among the *Kota* there is not the stress on village exogamy which is found in Rani Khera and widely in North India. Rather the preference is for closer marriages, preferably with cross-cousins, although there is also a good deal of marrying out of one's own village.

Despite such differences between the two, the *Kota* world view does not seem more markedly circumscribed. Culture and society in both appear similarly based. The ranked groupings, some of the same concern with pollution, the wide contractual and informal relations with other villagers and other groups which we have noted for *Kota* are found also in Rani Khera. We read that in Rani Khera there is, as compared with Tepoztlan, a reluctance to delegate authority to leaders, a jealous guarding of traditional functions by each village, a wide social interdependence—in all of which Kolmel no less than Rani Khera stands in contrast to Tepoztlan. Neither Nilgiri topography nor difference in village exogamy obliterates the common Indic outlook of the two villages. Presumably other Mexican villages, quite different in detail from Tepoztlan, would nevertheless be classed with it in contrast to the Indic villages.

Most interesting for a comparative understanding of world view are Lewis' impressions of character differences—which entail differences of world view also—as between Tepoztlan and Rani Khera. He notes that in Tepoztlan the world is conceived as hostile, the people are reserved and psychologically restricted. In an atmosphere of tension and fearfulness, each person, each family, stands alone. The women are drab, bemeaned, and feel martyred. In contrast, Rani Khera women are proud, feel independent, wear brilliant colors and are bold. The Indian village is described as a much more convivial place, without privacy, but evidently without the air of tension. "In Tepoztlan, outside the home, faces are generally unsmiling, unrevealing masks. In Rani Khera faces seem more secure. Children are more open-faced and laughing, old men are bland and peaceful, young men restless but unrebellious, women straight and proud." This despite the bitter factionalism which Lewis observes in Rani Khera. Can it be that the quarrels, the status competition, the defensive machinations, add up to a world view and a world which is generally more rewarding than another which may be as well endowed physically but not as well provided with societal extensions of the self? In Rani Khera and in Kolmel the individual sees himself as always identified with a large range of people, as part of a main. In Tepoztlan the individual evidently more often sees himself as an island, or perhaps as part of an archipelago.

IV. INTERRELATION OF INDIAN WORLD AND VILLAGERS' WORLD VIEW

In Marriott's discussion of Kishan Garhi we have seen how, as he puts it, the outside world has long reached from far away into the core of village society. In the present day, a decision reached in an international conference room to make a loan for a fertilizer plant in India can, in a relatively few years, enable a *Kota* villager to use more of the vitally needed fertilizer and to harvest a more abundant crop of potatoes.

Yet the basis on which such high-level decisions must be made rests in the villages. The success of development programs in technology or education depends on how the people take to them. Here the perspective of the villager becomes a vital factor. His motivations, his acceptance of the product, his interpretation of innovations—these and similar responses determine what effect the new factory will have. The decision at the center is relatively easy to study. The decisions in hundreds of thousands of villages are more difficult to observe but no less important in the general outcome. We know that they merge into a grand decisive force, but the process of village decision-making is not as yet well understood.

The study of villagers' world view is one avenue toward such understanding. The concept needs more refining: related concepts are used under various labels—"ethos," "value orientation," "national character," "motivational system." World view also entails both ideal and reality—how the people like to see themselves, how they in reality chart their action. But both the ideal and the reality of a world view limit certain potentials of behavior and encourage others.

Kota world view is clearly focused on relations among men, particularly among peers. In this aspect they are at once most interested and most sensitive. We have suggested that a useful approach to understanding a people's world view is the close examination of a situation which is recurrent in their lives and is of high importance to them. This area of importance does not include all which falls within their view. Other areas come within their habitual notice, and their focus of interest may well shift in time from one cognitive area to another. But the influences from the non-*Kota* world which now impinge on them are perceived through the lens of their current outlook.

Some of those influences have been discussed above comparatively. Certain of them, as the Sanskritic phrasing of pollution, are influences old in India and not completely new to *Kota* culture. Others are of more recent advent, as the status and influence of the schoolteacher. Still other important forces in the modern world of India, such as the pressure of population, have not come into the principal comparative discussions here.

The comparisons do sketch something of the Indic world. We have asked some questions about the relation of this world to the world views held among Indian villagers. As we looked at such villages as Rampura and Namhalli, we were directed to inquiries about the effects of social change on world view and of world view on social change. It appeared that, as between two peoples, *Kota* and *Vāghelā Rajpūt,* there can be congruence in some aspects of world view and wide differences in others. We would like to know more about such possible concomitants and variations. We have questioned—stimulated by the *Camār* and Kumbapettai Brahman data—whether world view typically differed by social level and economic circumstance. We were even emboldened, by the Rani Khera–Tepoztlan contrast, to ask about the ultimate human rewards attainable via differing world view. In the course of our comparisons and inquiries there appeared to emerge some views common to the diversity of villages represented in this volume. It may be that future inquiry will be able to draw more clearly the outline of an Indic world view.

REFERENCES CITED

BEALS, ALAN ROBIN

1954 "Culture Change and Social Conflict in a South Indian Village." Unpublished Ph.D. dissertation, University of California, Berkeley.

FRANCIS, W.

1908 *The Nilgiris*. Madras District Gazeteers **1.** Madras, Government Press.

MANDELBAUM, DAVID G.

1938 "Polyandry in Kota Society," *American Anthropologist* **40**:574–83. Menasha, Wisconsin.

1941*a* "Social Trends and Personal Pressures," in *Language, Culture and Personality*, ed. LESLIE SPIER *et al.* Menasha, Wisconsin.

1941*b* "Culture Change among the Nilgiri Tribes," *American Anthropologist* **43**:19–26. Menasha, Wisconsin.

1948 "The Family in India," *Southwestern Journal of Anthropology* **4**:123–29. Albuquerque.

1952 "Technology, Credit and Culture in an Indian Village," *Economic Weekly* **4**:827–28. Bombay.

1953 "Planning and Social Change in India," *Human Organization* **12**:4–12. New York.

1954 "Form, Variation, and Meaning of a Ceremony," in *Method and Perspective in Anthropology*, ed. ROBERT F. SPENCER, pp. 60–102. Minneapolis, University of Minnesota Press.

REDFIELD, ROBERT

1952 "The Primitive World View," *Proceedings of the American Philosophical Society* **96**:30–36. Philadelphia.

RIVERS, W. H. R.

1906 *The Todas*. London, Macmillan.

SRINIVAS, M. N.

1952 *Religion and Society among the Coorgs of South India*. Oxford, Clarendon Press.

CONTRIBUTORS

ALAN R. BEALS is professor of anthropology and chairman at the University of California, Riverside. He has done anthropological field work among California farmers and townsmen, among flying crews of the U.S. Air Force, and particularly among villagers of Mysore and Madras in southern India. He is the author of *Gopalpur: A South Indian Village.*

BERNARD S. COHN is professor of history and anthropology at the University of Chicago. He has published elsewhere on the results of his extensive studies of the social and political history of eastern Uttar Pradesh in the eighteenth and nineteenth centuries. He has since published numerous articles on Indian society and social history.

E. KATHLEEN GOUGH (KATHLEEN GOUGH ABERLE), professor of anthropology at Simon Fraser University, took her Ph.D. in anthropology at Cambridge University after field work in three villages of Kerala State in southwestern India. She has published extensively on the kinship systems, religion, and politics of that area, as well as on her comparable, subsequent studies in two villages of Tanjore district, Madras State. She is co-author with David M. Schneider of *Matrilineal Kinship.*

OSCAR LEWIS, who is professor of anthropology at the University of Illinois, received his doctorate from Columbia University. He has done field work in the Blackfoot tribe and among farmers of Texas and Washington in North America, as well as among peasants of Mexico, Cuba, and Spain, and citizens of Harlem, New York. He is the author of *Life in a Mexican Village: Tepoztlan Revisited, The Children of Sanchez, Five Families, Tepoztlan Restudied, Life in a North Indian Village,* and many papers in the field of cultural anthropology. More recently, he has made studies of the "culture of poverty" in Mexico City, New York City, and San Juan, Puerto Rico.

DAVID G. MANDELBAUM is professor of anthropology at the University of California, Berkeley. A graduate of Yale University, he has done ethnographic field work among the Apache and the Plains Cree of North America and in several parts of southern India. He is the author of many articles on South Indian tribal peoples, on funeral ceremonies, on Indian village life, and on problems of personality and culture relations. His books include *The Plains Cree* and *Soldier Groups and Negro Soldiers.* He has edited *Selected Writings on Language, Culture and Personality by Edward Sapir* and is preparing a comprehensive study of Indian society.

MCKIM MARRIOTT is professor of anthropology at the University of Chicago. He has conducted anthropological field studies in villages of western Uttar Pradesh in northern India and in towns of Maharashtra in peninsular India. He is the author of *Caste Ranking and Community Structure in Five Regions of India and Pakistan* and a co-author with Albert Mayer and Richard L. Park of *Pilot Project, India: The*

Story of Rural Development at Etawah, Uttar Pradesh. He has written elsewhere on caste, communications, medical sociology, religion, and technological change in India.

MYSORE NARASIMHACHAR SRINIVAS is professor and head of the Department of Sociology at the University of Delhi. He holds the Ph.D. degree of Bombay University and also the D.Phil. of Oxford University. He lectured at Oxford in Indian sociology until 1951 and then inaugurated the study of social anthropology at the M. S. University of Baroda. He is the author of *Marriage and the Family in Mysore, Religion and Society among the Coorgs of South India, India's Villages, Caste in Modern India,* and *Social Change in Modern India.*

GITEL P. STEED teaches at Hofstra University in New York. A former research fellow in anthropology at Columbia University, she has also taught at Fisk University and Hunter College and, under Fisk University auspices, has edited a national magazine on race relations. She has also served as editor on a cross-cultural survey project at Yale University, as an analyst of Chinese culture with the Columbia University Research in Contemporary Cultures, and as director of the Columbia University Research in Contemporary India Field Project.

INDEX